DUQUESNE STUDIES

Theological Series

1

FAITH AND THE WORLD

by

ALBERT DONDEYNE, PH.D., S.T.L.

DUQUESNE STUDIES

Theological Series

1

FAITH AND THE WORLD

by

ALBERT DONDEYNE, PH.D., S.T.L.

DUQUESNE UNIVERSITY PRESS, Pittsburgh, Pa.
EDITIONS E. NAUWELAERTS, LOUVAIN
1963

DUQUESNE STUDIES

THEOLOGICAL SERIES

Henry J. Koren, C.S.Sp., S.T.D., Leonard A. Bushinski, C.S.Sp., M.A., S.T.L., S.S.L., Leonard J. Swidler, Ph.D., S.T.L., editors.

Volume One—*Albert Dondeyne,* FAITH AND THE WORLD. XI and 324 pages. Price: $5.00 cloth.

In preparation

Volume Two—*William A. Luijpen,* PHENOMENOLOGY AND ATHEISM.

DUQUESNE STUDIES are published in the following series:

Annuale Mediaevale

Philological Series

Philosophical Series

Psychological Series

Spiritan Series

Theological Series

Catalog upon request.

A discount of twenty percent is given on continuation orders for any of these series, except the *Annuale.*

Imprimatur

H. van Waeyenbergh
episc. Gilben., rector magn. univers.
Lovanii, die 19 septembris 1962

Library of Congress Catalog Card Number 63—8795

Original title: *Geloof en Wereld* © by Uitgeverij Patmos, Antwerpen.

Printed in the U.S.A. by
The Ad Press, Ltd.

CONTENTS

PART TWO

TODAY'S WORLD

PART THREE

FAITH AND POLITICS

CONCLUSION

IS CHRISTIANITY STILL OF TIMELY INTEREST?

PREFACE

Our title FAITH AND THE WORLD points to a dialogue or conversation of the Christian believer with the present middle twentieth-century world. The importance of such a dialogue is immediately evident.

We note first that the Christian believer appears in the world as the bearer of "glad tidings," of the announcement of good news. This means that he is a witness, that he must speak, that he must hold conversation.

Besides this, the Christian believer is a man among other men, with other human beings. To be a man means both for believer and unbeliever to be a fellow-man, to be drawn into constant conversation with his fellow-men. For man is by nature the builder of a world (*Weltbildend*), that is, one whose task it is to transform raw and crude nature into a world of civilization and culture; in other words, he must make of it a social dwelling in which all feel at home and where prosperity, living space and freedom are destined for all. The fact that the Christian believer has a special well-defined vision regarding the meaning of life, and that he has organizations for his special purposes, should never lead him to "apartheid," to setting himself apart from the world.

Thirdly, he ought to realize that mankind is at a turning-point in its history. The world is becoming one from the geographical, social and international standpoint. This great event of our time, this becoming "one world" suddenly gives to the conversation and dialogue of men and their cultures a new content and importance.

Keeping all this in mind, we must ask ourselves whether the Christian believer exercises on today's world an influence that is sufficiently effective. We should ask more particularly whether his presence in the world has the necessary openness to produce a fruitful dialogue; in other words, whether he is as willing to listen as he is to speak, as ready to receive as to give. It is immediately evident that this sort of dialogue gives rise to problems. Hence the purpose of this book is to examine these problems with honesty and objectivity.

This work is, in fact, the fruit of conversations conducted over a number of years with students and alumni, with fellow-Christians, and those who do not share the faith. Hence this is not the first time that the author speaks or writes about the subjects treated in this book. Until now he had expressed his thoughts in short articles, in lectures and discourses on special occasions. A few friends formed the plan of gathering all these scattered papers, some of which lay buried under the dust of oblivion, and publishing them in book-form. Father N. Wildiers, Ph.D., the expert paleontologist, undertook the task of disinterment. However, when everything was restored to the light of day, it was clear that there was too much repetition in those documents; that some belonged to a period that itself lay buried; that too many questions had not received sufficient treatment; hence it was found impossible to construct an orderly and meaningful whole out of those remains, a whole that could be presented as the work of a *homo sapiens.* The only thing to do was to return to our desk, and rewrite most of the articles and then to fill in and complete the work now offered under the title *Faith and the World.* We make no claim, of course, that this book treats the topics exhaustively.

In it we have paid attention mainly to the speculative questions that arise when the Christian faith is brought face to face with what we call the "world." Another, but shorter, book called *Priest and Layman* deals with the more practical problems that are involved. These latter concern the building of the Church in our time, a construction that requires the labor of the entire community of the faithful, both priests and lay people.

We wish to express our thanks to Father N. Wildiers, to Mr. Paul Leemans and Mr. Guido Vanhoof, the editor, Mr. A. J. M. Pelckmans, and, last but not least, to the many who have participated in the conversations from which this book was born. We owe much to those conversations. They have taught us that nothing is more dangerous for a theologian than to believe that he possesses the monopoly of the truth, that no one can teach him anything and that those who disagree with him are not truly "thinking" men.

The University of Louvain — ALBERT DONDEYNE

Apart from slight adaptations in some examples, the American edition of this book faithfully follows the original Dutch text. The translation was made by Father Walter van de Putte, C.S.Sp., and carefully checked by the undersigned. Our thanks are due to Fathers Charles J. Fenner, C.S.Sp., and J. Gerald Walsh, C.S.Sp., for reading the manuscript and suggesting corrections of language and style.

The third part of this work contains numerous references to specifically European situations. Although the author's penetrating remarks, therefore, do not apply directly to the English-speaking world, we have not hesitated to retain them in this edition. For, as Professor Dondeyne points out, our world is rapidly becoming more and more unified; hence it is important that the English-speaking reader also learns to see the European situation in the light of the principles propounded in this study.

The original edition of this book was received so well that it had to be reprinted three times within a few months. It is our hope that the work will be equally welcomed wherever English is spoken throughout the world.

Duquesne University
Pittsburgh, Pa. — HENRY J. KOREN, C.S.Sp.

PART ONE

PROBLEMS OF FAITH

CHAPTER ONE

CONTEMPORARY PROBLEMS CONCERNING FAITH

In our own day one particular problem about faith overrules all other problems. It is this: that faith itself has become a problem, to a greater or lesser extent, for a considerable number of men.

Something becomes a problem for the human mind when it ceases to be something about which we say, "It goes without saying" or "it stands to reason."

The moment when something becomes a *problem,* when something is questioned, is important in the development of the life of the human spirit. It is a crisis through which the naïve, the impersonal, the unreflecting consciousness must pass in order to attain to personal reflection and personal insight. Nearly all our thoughts, views and convictions are at first received from the milieu in which we begin our existence in a sort of anonymous way. It is only later that we begin to question things. That Santa Claus with reindeer-drawn sleighs brings Christmas presents from the North Pole is part of the natural milieu of the child. It offers no particular problem to his mind; it is no more a problem to him than that daily intervention of good and bad spirits is a problem to the minds of primitive people. What is supernatural and preternatural is "obvious" and "natural" to them, as natural as the sun, the moon, and anything else pertaining to nature.

The fact that, when we open our eyes, our gaze encounters things themselves raises no problem for those who have never come in contact with philosophy. And it is not unlikely that if such persons were to attend a philosophical convention, and hear those learned men who call themselves philosophers, discoursing endlessly about the problem of the immediate perception of objects and declaring the question to be a thorny one, they would come to think of the convention as an asylum for the insane or weakminded. They would no doubt remark: "Is anything more 'natural,' more 'evident,' more 'obvious' than that our eyes perceive objects themselves?" "Were our eyes not made by 'nature' precisely for such a purpose?"

The same thing applies to most of the views and convictions that have found a home in human minds. They blossom forth into problems from the moment when they lose their characteristic of "everydayness," of being "unquestionable," and as Gabriel Marcel would express it, of being "quite natural." Thus, the "questioning of the unquestionable" manifests itself in the form of a crisis which may turn out well or unfavorably according to the care that is given it. It is in fact a sort of crisis of growth and maturation that opens the way to a fuller personality and insight, to a more living possession of the truth and a truer freedom.

1. *Contemporary Crisis Regarding Faith*

It is undoubtedly true that many today are passing through such a crisis with regard to their convictions in the matter of faith. The medieval man without much education had no problem with his faith; it was for him the most natural thing in the world. On the contrary unbelief appeared to him as something unthinkable, as an impossible attitude of mind. Until recent times this was still so for the vast majority of people who from childhood had grown up in the faith; but today we are evidently in the midst of a change.

Anyone who is in frequent contact with youth has the opportunity to notice how many modern teenagers are troubled with religious problems which the older generation discovered only at a later time. They are questions regarding God and Providence, revelation and inspiration, original sin and salvation, Purgatory, Heaven and Hell. When I became professor at the University of Louvain in 1933, at the time Flemish nationalism was at its high tide, the one religious problem that was predominant at student gatherings was that of the authority of the Church in political affairs. Today the principal topics for discussion are those that concern articles of faith. Basing myself once more on personal experience, I recall that I have given quite a number of lectures in my life and yet when I compare the subjects that I was formerly asked to treat, with those that today appear principally on the program, I must conclude that the interest of the public has undergone a rather profound change. Less than twenty years ago, faith and politics, religion and culture, the nature of the Catholic action of the laity were the favorite topics. Today we are asked: "Can modern man still believe while preserving his freedom?" "Is Christianity still something that is *actual,* up-to-date?" "What is the significance of Christianity in the present world whose problems encompass the whole of mankind?"

We must confess that a certain uneasiness lies behind such questions. In fact, when we place Christianity face to face with today's world, there wells up in us a feeling of helplessness, of impatience and anxiety. There rises up in our minds such questions as, "What importance does Christianity still have in our present world?" "Does it still mean anything for our world?" "Who still wants to listen to Christianity?" "What will happen to Christianity in a world that is striving for oneness, a world that aims at building a common dwelling for all men, where all peoples and races, cultures and religious forms of belief and worship will want to live peacefully together under one roof?"

I know, of course that every period of time has had its own problems regarding the faith. The first Christian centuries were marked by Trinitarian controversies; the fourth and fifth by Christological questions. In the Middle Ages the question was of how the philosophy of Aristotle could be reconciled with the faith. In the sixteenth century, the period of the Reformation, the structure itself of the Church, her hierarchical organization came under scrutiny. The nineteenth century was troubled with the problem of faith versus science. But, in contrast with these centuries, our time is marked by a two-fold characteristic. First of all, in our century the problems raised by faith have become much more general because the discussion encompasses not merely an elite but ever-widening circles of average people; secondly, the questioning is much more radical in the sense that it tends to go more to the roots of Christian belief and to scrutinize the very meaning of faith.

Now it is indeed a question of "to be or not to be." The thing questioned by modern man is not so much this or that article of the faith, but the very meaning of belief itself, the supernatural, the divine character of Christianity; in a word, the nature of our religion. Do Christianity and the Church of Christ truly have their origin in an actual entrance of God into the history of mankind, or is Christianity simply a cultural phenomenon? Is it a product of the human psyche, like the mythologies of the Greeks, the ethics of Confucius or the prayer-asceticism of Buddha?

Is Christ only a wise man, a religious genius alongside the many other founders of religions? Or is He actually the Emmanuel, the God-with-us, God's Word who came to dwell amongst us and must be accepted as the One and Only Savior?

These are the question which affect the minds of modern believers. But we cannot be satisfied with recording the shift of the center of gravity, the radical change of the "problematic of faith." It is more important to investigate what are its *causes*.

2. *Two Unsatisfactory Explanations*

First of all, let us not maintain that it is a question of *knowledge* or *intelligence*. The trouble does not come from a diminution of learning or of mental acumen. The fact that men now appear to be generally less religious and that the faithful have more religious difficulties than formerly is not a sign that modern man is less intelligent or less capable of following a theological argument. It is rather because he is more demanding in this field, as he is in many others. But this does not mean either that the man of today has attained a higher level of intelligence. Modern man undoubtedly "knows" more than his ancestors, but whether he has also progressed farther in "intelligent thinking" is quite a different matter. The possession of information and intelligence are two different things. There have been geniuses in every age. Thinkers like Aristotle and Plato, Ambrose and Augustine, Anselm and Thomas Aquinas are certainly not inferior, in mental depth and sharpness, to the great minds of modern times, such as Descartes and Kant, Hegel and Marx, Husserl and Heidegger.

One often hears it said that contemporary problems about the faith and especially modern incredulity are connected with a *weakening of moral resistance*. The faith, it is claimed, has lost its unquestionable acceptance, because our world has sunk to a lower ethical level. In other words, modern man feels it more difficult than his forebears to recognize God's voice in Christianity because he prefers to follow his own ideas, because he follows his lower instincts rather than listening to the voice of his conscience, and *a fortiori* that of God. According to that view, everything, in the last analysis, could be reduced to a question of ill will or bad faith. But this too, is not an adequate explanation. Far be it from us to maintain that there is no connection at all between religious belief and morality; in reality, belief in God is to the advantage of good morals and, in their turn, moral shortcomings are obstacles to the developing of an intense religious life. It is perfectly clear that modern unfaithfulness to church practices and religious doubt are to be attributed to the fact that the moral life of many of the Christian faithful is not in harmony with the laws of the Church. But this does not give us a complete explanation, for we might say to ourselves: many sins were committed also in the Middle Ages and yet this did not affect man's faith as such.

It is important to note that religious belief and morality are not so closely connected that they are always marching with equal steps. Genuine expression of good morality is found also among those who walk outside the field of faith; and, in reverse, faith does not *of itself* produce good morality. The Scandinavians are famous for their warm hospitality and their steadfast spirit of justice although they certainly cannot boast about a flourishing religious and church-affiliated life. On the other hand, some inhabitants of the countries of Southern Europe where faith (and also superstition) have, as it were, been incorporated in their nature, can hardly be proposed as examples of strict self-control in matters of honesty and sexual morality. The Middle Ages are often extolled as the high tide of Christian faith, but we may ask ourselves whether morality stood at an equally high level. Sunday preachers in these highly praised times harped on the hitherto unheard-of deterioration of morals just as much as our modern pulpit moralists, but with this difference: many of the lower and the higher clergymen themselves were then involved in that moral deterioration and set a bad example in many ways, a thing which is certainly not true today.

Our present culture, no doubt, has its dark sides, but this should not make us blind to its bright aspects. Our times are not wanting in moral greatness and heroism. At no time in the past has as much care been bestowed on children, adolescents, the sick, older people, and the weak; even criminals are not forgotten. I know that the hardy "praisers of time past," will object that such works of mercy are unrelated to morality since it is the anonymous and even amoral State that has taken over the tasks formerly performed by the private initiative of the virtuous. A reply to this objection is not difficult. We merely ask, "Is it the 'anonymous' State that watches at the bedside of the sick, that sustains parents, that labors for the moral re-education of the criminal, and thus tries to restore him to normal social life?" The modern State merely collects the necessary funds in order that our fellow-men may receive more extensive help. The funds, however, do not drop from the skies nor do they come from the anonymous State, but they come from the purse of citizens; they come from the intellectuals as well as from the mass of workers who through payment of taxes deliver part of their hard-earned wages to the community, in order that there may be a little less suffiering and a little more joy in the world. Unfortunately, there are still many faithful who are so full of a "bourgeois mentality" that they see no moral value whatsoever in helping their fellow-men by paying their share of the taxes. Their moral feeling is satisfied with the giving of some small alms after evading the payment of taxes.

And when we analyze the "social progress" which characterizes our time, we discover that here also there is much more involved than a mere increase of wealth and a rise in economic welfare. Social progress signifies also a moral advance, for it testifies to a greater appreciation of truth and justice, of equality and fraternity, of solidarity and collective responsibility. Moreover, this social progress did not come about spontaneously, but was the result of much suffering and great sacrifices, of long years of struggle, even of heroism.

Charity, likewise, has not vanished from our world. Whenever a small group of fellow-men is struck by one calamity or another—be it in the mines, through floods and snowstorms or earthquakes—immediately an influx of help springs up from all sides. Many even will do the impossible to save the lives of a few fellow-men. The fact that the present practice of charity is no longer the monopoly of religious institutions does not take away its great ethical significance. On the contrary, it is a proof of the extent to which the Christian idea of the "neighbor" has conquered the world.

In any case, our time also has its own moral greatness. It would be wrong to see in the present crisis of the faith nothing more than a deterioration and a lowering of the moral level of mankind. There is more to it than this. As we shall see, the fact that many Catholics have no consideration for the evidence of moral greatness of our time is, it seems to me, one of the causes leading to the present decadence of the faith. For this form of blindness is the reason why frequently Catholic preaching of the faith is out of touch with our present world, there often is no longer any dialogue so that the proclamation of the faith fails to affect the moral sensibility which is alive in every human being and which is often the first step toward the recognition of the all Holy and Good God.

3. *The Image of Our Time and Today's Religious Crisis*

Certainly much will be written in the future about the causes of the religious crisis through which the human community is presently passing and it offers, no doubt, a wide field for research to modern sociologists. In the meantime one fact is clearly established; namely, that this religious situation is connected with the general situation of man in our contemporary world or, as some would express it, it is connected with the "image of our time." More correctly stated, it is connected with modern man's being-in-the-world, with the way he experiences and lives his existence *as bound to the world.*

By "being-bound-to-the-world" we mean here the following. Man has a fourfold connection and relation that make him human; namely, first, with himself, his past and his future; secondly, with surrounding nature; thirdly, with his fellow-men; and lastly, with the mystery of being in which he is rooted. Now we use the terms "being-bound-to-the-world" to express the way man feels, lives and interprets those connections, the way he works them out in various forms of behavior and in all sorts of cultural creations such as science, technique and philosophy, literature and works of art, in his juridical and political legislation, in his ethical conduct and religious rites. All these together constitute man's "world."

The term "world," as used here, does not signify the world of crude forces but the world as humanized by man, the world insofar as it bears the stamp of the human spirit. It is in this sense that we speak of the medieval world, the world of the Renaissance, the world of modern man, the Eastern and Western worlds, or also the world of the child, the world of the adult. The thing that characterizes each one of these worlds is not solely a number of geographic, technological and economic conditions, but rather and mostly in connection with those conditions, a proper spiritual *ethos,* that is, a certain atmosphere of thought and feeling. The principal component element of this *ethos* must be sought in a sensibility to some particular value. It prompts a man who belongs to a particular culture or period to be specially attracted to this value, to be attuned to it, to fight for its realization.

Let us now examine how our present world, with its proper sensibility to some values, influences the religious life of our time.

Sense of Exactness and Sober Historical Reality

When we analyze the being-in-the-world of modern man we find in it a first element which has great significance for his faith; namely, *a critical sense of exactness and sober realism.* The exact *exploration of nature* together with the *historical sciences* have taught man to be critical and autonomous. They have sharpened his appreciation of the real. Hence contemporary man is less naïve, more exacting in the field of truth and knowledge, especially in regard to supernatural realities.

Primitive mentality, and this applies to a certain extent to prescientific ways of life, is characterized by a spontaneous, a *quasi-natural* familiarity with things *preternatural* and *supernatural.* We use these terms here in a broad and vague sense to designate not only the mysterious and sacral dimension of the world which surrounds and supports us but also the powers that are truly "above nature." Primitive man feels more at home in the invisible and mysterious world of the supernatural than in the clear laws which exact science discovers in the order of nature. The intervention of supernatural powers, such as angels, devils and God, in the play of natural phenomena and in the course of history, present no problem to him. All the major events that are beyond the power of man, such as thunder and lightning, rain and sunshine, birth, sickness and death, he spontaneously attributes to supernatural powers. This is why the God of archaic cultures always has the features of a nature-god: thunder and lightning are instruments of God's anger; rain and sunshine are signs of His good pleasure, the rainbow is the symbol of man's reconciliation.

Life and death especially are events over which man has no control; whence, the primitive considers them direct interventions of God. God gives the breath of life and God takes it back again, says Scripture. Modern man, on the contrary, first looks for the natural explanation provided by the forces present within the physical world. Through the progress of the sciences, man had discovered that nature is a closed system, that all natural phenomena, great and small—and this applies also to man's biological life—are subject to the laws of nature. Hence man today first demands an explanation within the framework of natural laws.

It goes without saying that the world has thus become, as it were, "de-sacralized," divested of its sacred character. There is grave danger affecting the preservation of the "sense of the supernatural." We continue, of course, to speak about "the weather God gives us," but even this expression has lost much of its religious meaning; after all, do we not listen daily to weather broadcasts and do we not expect that man will eventually be able to make his own sunny and rainy days? Does this mean that our forefathers were wrong in seeing God's presence in the great natural phenomena and in the events of history? Certainly not, since nothing can escape from His almighty power. We merely wish to point out that there still remains in us a remnant of the mentality of primitive man. When everything is running smoothly and normally, we seem quite able to "do without God." Shocking events affecting life and the physical world, phenomena that are beyond our powers, such as wars, catastrophes, sickness and death, seem necessary to remind us that God and His Providence have not ceased to exist. We forget, however, that in this way we considerably desecrate and weaken our idea of God. God becomes a sort of *"deus ex machina,"* an artifice, for which there will be less room in the world according as man himself acquires more control over the world.

Not only modern physical science but also the study of history have sharpened our sense of exactness and have strongly influenced our attitude toward the supernatural.

Faith and the World

The thirst of modern man for truth is characterized by an unsurpassed respect for sober facts. The most lowly fact or event of the past, if established with historical certainty, means more to us than the most sublime heroic epic insofar as the latter is only poetic fiction. What moves us in the Iliad is not the plot of the story and the intrigues in which the Homeric heroes are caught, but the true world of Greek culture which we see mirrored in Homer's work; namely, how the ancient Greeks of Homer's time experienced their being-in-the-world, how they wrestled with the eternal human problems, the problems of suffering and death, of liberty and fate, of guilt and evil. The heroes of Christianity are the saints, and the Christian epos is known as "hagiography," that is, the story of their heroic deeds. The early lives of the saints were principally intent on making them constantly miracles of God; a saint was a marvelous creature destined from birth to be different from the ordinary mortal. Modern hagiography, on the contrary, strives above all for historical accuracy. For the thing that impresses us in the saint is that he is a man like ourselves, who has to struggle just as we have to, with this difference, however, that we usually fail, whereas the saint remains faithful and allows no rest nor restriction in respect to the demands of God's voice and the promptings of His Spirit.

Now this desire for historical accuracy has also entered religious sciences and has occasioned a profound renewal, especially in the realm of biblical scholarship, the study of the origin of Christianity, and the development of dogma, Church history, and Apologetics. The interweaving of sacred and profane history has thus appeared in a totally new light. As a result of this, the role of historically-situated man in the supernatural history of salvation has received far greater attention.

A few examples may serve to bring out our meaning. It had been known for a long time that Sacred Scripture, which contains the word of God, did not drop down from heaven. But now we realize much better that these books are authentically human literature, the product of a definite culture, and belonging to one or the other literary genre. Thus we realize that we must investigate their exact meaning and bearing by using the same scientific methods as for any other literary text which we desire to study. A better knowledge of Old Testament literature has thus given us a more correct insight into the history of Israel. For modern theologians the miracle of Israel is no longer to be found in the fantastic events of its national and political history, as if this history consisted of an unbroken chain of miraculous happenings: God personally walking with Adam in the Paradise, God coming to speak with Abraham in his tent, or handing the Tables of the Law to Moses, God in a luminous cloud leading the Jews during their pilgrimage in the desert, fighting on the side of Joshua for the capture of Chanaan, or ordering Saul, through the mouth of the Prophet Samuel, to "slay Amalec and utterly destroy all that he has, both man and woman, child and suckling, ox and sheep, camel and ass" (I Samuel, 15, 1-3).

On the contrary, the things that the modern theologians find exceptional in Israel is the history of its religious way of thinking and feeling, how his people under the influence of a few men of God lived close to the Lord; how through numerous trials that are man's lot on earth, it rose to an unheard-of degree of purity of life; and how Israel became historically God's instrument in His work of salvation.

We also have a better knowledge of the historical personality of Jesus. The critical study of the New Testament literature has taught us that the presence of the Word of God in Our Lord did not diminish His being also a man.

We thus better understand the fact that the Word of God assumed a human nature; that is, that He came to dwell amongst us as a concrete man within the framework of a definite historical culture.

In fact, the historical method has rendered inestimable service to theology. It has freed man from a too anthropomorphic concept of the faith and from a craving for the exceptional, a craving for things that are more apt to excite the imagination than to bring us closer to God and to the reality of daily life. In other words, that method has put the religious dimension and the historical character of the Christian mystery of salvation in a brighter light. Christianity is not first of all a doctrine telling us about the origin of the earth and of life here below; it is not an explanation of the world's history. It is not even a philosophical system alongside many others. It is, on the contrary, God's *message of salvation;* or more precisely, it is the *work of salvation* of God, who through His Word and His Spirit manifests and communicates Himself to mankind in the course of history and hence through the ministry of men who are situated in history.

We shall repeatedly turn to this historical character of the Christian faith regarding salvation, particularly in the next chapter, for it is very significant and constitutes the central theme of contemporary theology. For the present we merely want to point out that the renewal of theology under the influence of the historical method has not come about without battle or struggle. That renewal was preceded by numerous tensions and crises of the faith, the most painful of which was Modernism.

The crisis undergone several years ago by theology on the scientific level—and it might be asked whether it has ended yet—is now being repeated on a larger scale on the level of the faith of the laity. It is not a secret to anyone that thousands of our laborers and intellectuals, whose catechetical formation was often very elementary, have long since ceased to "believe," as they say, in the creation of the world in six days, the origin of the woman from Adam's rib, the paradaisic life of the first human couple, the deluge covering the entire earth, the fact that the sun stood still at the command of Joshua, Jona's dwelling in the belly of the whale, etc. This in itself is not a serious matter. What is much worse is that they find in it a pretext for "throwing out the baby with the bathwater," i.e., that they are led to question the most essential articles of faith and consider Christianity as a view of life and of the world which science has left behind.

I know, of course, that these difficulties concerning the faith are unsubstantial and that they have long since been overcome by modern theology. Even in grade school the children are now taught, for instance, that the books of Holy Scripture are not scientific treatises but religious writings come from ancient times, and that they were written in the style and language of the people. Nevertheless, we must deal seriously with these difficulties, and this for two reasons. First of all, we must not forget that many difficulties which we now so lightly pass over, were not so simple fifty years ago even for men of learning and caused many students of theology to waver in their faith. Secondly, those difficulties, however trivial they may seem, have their origin in something that lies much deeper and is of overwhelming importance for the religious life of today; namely, a sense of, and craving for contact with reality and historical truth.

An idea of faith in which the fantastic, the marvelous, and the "unbelievable" predominate no longer appeals to modern man, but makes him more inclined to be skeptical than to believe. The fact that Christianity attunes man to the "supernatural" must not give the impression that it leads him into an unreal and fantastic world. "Supernaturalness" is not synonymous with "unnaturalness," in the sense of being against nature. Moreover, when theology declares that the supernatural does not disturb the natural, it thereby implies also that the supernatural does not upset the natural course of history. The grace of faith which brings man close to God does not remove him from the world, from an historical existence in this world, but it places upon him a new responsibility for his everyday life and the history of mankind. The great task of contemporary catechetics is the formulation of a presentation of the faith that brings us *closer to God* and, at the same time, closer to the *historical reality of life.*

The Unification of the World

The unification of our world, together with the immediate resultant *broadening of the horizon of our life* constitute the second component of our being-in-the-world. It is not less important for our religious situation than the first.

Medieval man lived in a world that was spiritually homogenous. He was in his religious thinking and acting a child of his milieu. If he wished to adhere to another view than that held by his neighbors, he had to become a revolutionary and was treated accordingly.

Technology, however, has wiped out the frontiers that formerly separated men, countries and peoples. Man has become a citizen of the world. Thus, modern man finds himself in an environment without spiritual unity or religious homogeneity. Every day puts him in contact with the most diverse concepts of life and civilizations, with believers and unbelievers. He learns about those who think differently not only by means of stories or books but through daily contact. He meets everywhere honest and dishonest men, those who are convinced and those who doubt. Understanding, broadmindedness, and tolerance have become indispensable virtues of contemporary man, and much personal insight and conviction are demanded of him if he does not wish to fall into skepticism and relativism. The fact that he is much less supported by his surroundings in respect to his moral and religious life makes the faith of his childhood seem less self-evident and unassailable. He asks himself where precisely lies the difference between the Christian and the non-Christian concept of life; how Christianity can claim an absolutely superior value; and on what foundation rests its contention that it alone offers the message and the means of salvation?

Moreover, together with the need to justify the claim: "there is no salvation outside the Church," the question comes up concerning the exact scope and meaning of that ancient theological theme. He knows that Christianity represents only a minority of the world's population; besides, he learns that the population growth is much greater in the non-Christian world than in the Christian. What, in the eyes of God, is the meaning of those vast multitudes of non-baptized? Our love for equality and fraternity no longer lets us consider ourselves as the chosen ones among a "multitude of the lost." In other words, we shiver at St. Augustine's thought about the *"massa damnata"* (the vast mass of the damned), and it hurts our democratic sensibility.

This danger of falling into religious indifferentism and relativism is so much the greater because modern man discovers at the same time that Christianity, as seen in the framework of the world's history, constitutes quite a recent phenomenon. The world-view of medieval man had come from the Bible and naturally found its key in the figure of Christ. To the mind of medieval man there were only two chapters in the history of the world—namely, the Old and the New Testaments. Only two peoples really "counted" in history, the ancient and the new People of God, for the world of the pagans was after all but a world of second rank. Christocentrism was for medieval man not only a truth of the faith but it was, as it were, the very structure of his being-in-the-world.

The world view of modern man is wholly different, it has such totally different dimensions that he no longer sees Christocentrism as so "self-evident." The earthly globe has become for us an insignificant spot in boundless space, a lost planet which seems to have but little importance or significance in the frame of the geophysical cosmos. Mankind appeared on this earth around five hundred thousand years ago or more, while Christianity is not even two thousand years old. I realize, of course, that such facts do not affect Christ's place in the mystery of the faith, but they do once more raise the question of the meaning of the Christian faith in the totality of the world's history, i.e., the question of the universality of Christianity as the good tidings for the *entire* human race.

The Complexity of Contemporary Civilization

There is still a third aspect of our being-in-the-world which has a great repercussion on the religious life of modern man—namely, the *complexity of modern civilization* and the present task of civilization.

It is a fact that we have come to a turning point in the history of civilization. We are at the entrance of a new era. Modern science and technology have opened prospects for new and gigantic possibilities and projects of mankind. Man is thus confronted with a new destiny and charged with new tasks of cultural development.

This puts heavy burdens and great responsibilities on modern man. We have, as it were, become the slaves of our own creations. The technology, which generated them for our liberation, overwhelms us and carries us along in a process of development over which we have no longer full control.[1] All problems become more and more involved, the struggle for life becomes even harder, the task of the State becomes daily more burdensome and demands such an extensive administration and organization that the life of the State is threatened to be choked to death. And in respect to the international community, here especially problems are so complicated and the situations so hopelessly entangled that man feels incapable of mastering them.

But, we may ask, what has all this to do with the religious life of man? First of all, it means that man's center of interest has shifted. There is danger that his religious life will give increasingly way to the absorbing, profane tasks of civilization. Medieval society was, when looked at from the spiritual standpoint, not only homogenous but intrinsically one. The view of Christian faith constituted both its foundation and its soul. The profane and the religious intermingled and permeated one another in all realms and phases of individual and social life. Modern society, on the contrary, maintains a clear and sharp distinction between the profane and the religious. In itself this is a good thing, for a growing differentiation of the various functions and values belongs to the very nature of cultural development.[2] However, because of the growing complexity of modern civilization, there is the danger that it will demand man's total commitment to that labor of development, thus leaving scarcely any room for religious life. In today's noisy world, so full of stress and strain, there is but little time left over for thought and recollection.

Secondly, when we observe the course of modern development of the world, we receive the impression that Christianity

---

[1]Concerning this point, see Andrew G. van Melsen, *Science and Technology,* Pittsburgh, 1961. Tr.

[2]In a primitive society the ruler is simultaneously king, judge, and priest.

has little influence upon it, that it lives withdrawn within itself, far removed from profane history and the processes of civilization. It would be hard to maintain that the Christian himself is not to be blamed for that situation.

Professor Rogier, of the University of Nijmegen, in one of his lectures, used a striking figure to make us realize that absence of the Christian community from what is taking place in today's world: "The Church," he said, "has become a sort of reservation amidst a de-Christianized community; whereas it is her task to impart God's blessing to a world in its journey to eternity." If we want to realize how true that is we have only to recall the three great events that are at the origin of our time and that still continue to determine its specific character. These events are 1) the formation of modern science through Descartes and Galileo, and later through Darwin in the field of biology; 2) the dissolution of the Old Regime and the birth of the democratic regimes of freedom; 3) the social breakthrough in the latter half of the last century. When we consider these great unheavals, we must confess to our shame that the Catholic community reacted very slowly to them, that it showed hesitancy and fear, and that it had its eyes riveted more on the past than directed to the future.

It is quite evident that this hesitancy of the faithful to take part in those changes has affected the prestige of Christianity; especially, because, as we have pointed out, these movements, which still dominate our times, contain authentic moral values. For a long time, the Catholic community seems to have had little appreciation of those great moral values. When we were still students and in our course of Apologetics heard about the case of Galileo and that of Vesalius, our teachers did the impossible in trying to excuse the theologians of the Holy Office; but hardly a word was said about the courage of those who laid the foundations of modern science and, contrary to the spirit of the times, remained faithful to their scientific ideal.

We could say almost the same thing regarding the way our teachers spoke about the rise of democracy and the first breakthrough of the social revolution. In some Catholic circles the French Revolution is still considered the starting point of every misfortune. The first labor strikes and First-of-May labor celebrations are still considered signs of rebellion and disobedience. Many seem blind to the fact that on those occasions men suffered hunger and risked their lives in order to insure a better future for their children and grandchildren and to create a little more truth and justice on earth.

This blindness on the part of many Catholics has caused great harm to Christianity. Every era has its own sensitivity to values in the realms of art and literature as well as ethics. When, however, Christians reveal no openness to the values pursued by their contemporaries, a dialogue between Christianity and the world becomes impossible. We are then somewhat in the position of the parents who fail to realize that their boy is no longer a child, that he has become a young man, and that he now aims at other values and ideals. There is then an estrangement, a growing apart of parents and child. The young man loses confidence in his parents, for he gets the impression that they do not understand him. Whatever he does is misinterpreted by them.

4. *Conclusion*

What should we conclude from all this? At least, that the connection between the religious situation of modern man and his relations with the world, is very important for the future of Christianity. If we were merely in the presence of ill will and bad faith, our judgment about our own time would be quite pessimistic. Let us, however, take account of modern circumstances of life and modern appreciation of values which make adherence to the faith less obvious to twentieth century man who must pass through a questioning stage in order to remain himself. Considered in this way, what we are witnessing is not so much a falling away from the faith but rather a crisis of growth which may lead to a purer, more personal, and more authentic life of faith, characterized by a broader spiritual élan. This also is a characteristic of man's being-in-the-world; man never undergoes his world with total passivity but has to do something with his world. As we shall often repeat, the world for man is not only a total of situations but it is one of tasks also, it is not merely a dwelling but also a realm in which his freedom goes to work.

Karl Jaspers rightly says that our world "has lost its naiveté." No doubt, there is no longer any place in it for a faith that is naïve, anonymous and formalistic, a faith that is merely passively undergone, that does not speak to man's profound freedom because it excludes all questioning. But this is not bad at all. Faith, even in the beginning of Christianity, was not an "unquestionable" affair. But, in spite of that, the ancient faith, because it was pure and authentic, conquered a world: "This is the victory which overcomes the world, our faith." (I, John, 5, 4). Only true faith, a faith that is open and evangelical bears within itself the guarantee of victory.

Hence the first and most necessary task of the Christian community today, the practical problem of faith of our time is that of *rediscovering our faith.* This re-discovery or, to use a word of Péguy, this *"ressourcement,"* this going back to the source, must be accomplished in a threefold dimension. First and above all, we must return to the *essence* of faith as we find it in the first Christian community. We must re-discover what "to believe" truly means, what Our Lord and the apostles meant by it. Secondly, we need a justification of the faith that is adjusted to the needs of our time. Modern man does not merely desire to know what are the things he ought to believe but he wants to know the reasons why he should believe. Being thrown in a world of unbelief, he must be able to justify it personally. Thirdly, we need to re-discover the *humanistic and historical value* of our faith, its meaning for the present development of civilization. It is true, of course, that Christianity is not primarily a type of humanism or a factor of cultural development. Christianity directs man Godward and heavenward, but it would be wrong to conclude that Christianity has no role to play regarding profane life and that it can henceforth withdraw within its own shell. The problem of the relationship of Christianity to culture is a perennial one and belongs to the very nature of the Christian message. For, if the Gospel proclamation is not in tune with the world to which it addresses itself, if it does not take into account the variable appreciation of values which causes time to change and makes it necessary to divide it historically into different "times," including our own, then the impression is created that Christianity "belongs to another time," that it is "a thing of the past."

CHAPTER TWO

CHRISTIANITY: A MESSAGE OF JOY

Our conclusion in the preceding chapter was to the effect that the most urgent task of today's Christian believer is to reflect upon the *essence* and the *meaning* of his faith, i.e., to ponder the Christian *Creed.*

Now this one fact predominates in a most evident way: Christianity was experienced by the first Christians and appeared to the world as an *evangelium,* as *"glad tidings" of salvation;* that is, it brought a message of freedom and liberation. As St. Paul expresses it, "The Spirit yields love, peace and joy." (Gal. 5,22).

We believers of this Twentieth Century must dare ask ourselves whether we still clearly understand that our faith means a "message to the world," and especially whether we actually live our faith as "glad tidings," whether we bear witness to it and broadcast that message as a "light to the revelation of the Gentiles" (Luke 2, 32), a light that enlightens and gives courage to men and peoples of our time, both in their daily battle against life's difficulties and their toilsome search for peace and joy, for truth and justice.

Nietzsche reproached the Christians of his time for giving the impression of being tired, sad, withdrawn and for showing no evidence of being "risen" (with Christ) on their countenance. Could not the same reproach be levelled at us? Have we not largely forgotten that Christianity is first of all a message of salvation? Suppose that someone from China or Japan who knows nothing about Christianity were to open our traditional catechism to study the meaning and significance of our faith. Would such a man be struck first and above all by the joyful character of the message?

To the question, "what is the nature and meaning of faith?" many catechisms reply: "Faith is the divine virtue by which we accept the truths which God has revealed and which the Church believes and teaches." This is no doubt a correct answer, yet it could give a wrong and poor idea of Christianity for the two following reasons.

First, it puts the accent almost exclusively on knowledge. However important the cognitive aspect may be in faith, to believe is much more for the Christian than to acquire knowledge; it is more than "accepting as true" what Church authority "teaches." "*Credere in,*" "to believe in" also means "to have confidence in," to "place one's trust in someone who lives and is present," in our case, in God Himself who is present in the world by His Word and His Spirit and who works out our salvation. It is clear, therefore, that the relation to God arising from faith goes much deeper than mere knowledge.

Secondly, the definition of faith we have quoted suffers from another deficiency. Using philosophical language we should say that it is almost purely "formal," i.e., it does not even mention what constitutes the *content* of "the truths which God has revealed and which the Church believes and teaches." Yet this point is of fundamental importance if we wish to determine the *meaning* of faith. For the expression that the Christian believer "accepts as true all that God has revealed and the Church teaches" could be wrongly understood and might give the impression that believers have access to other channels of information than the ordinary mortal about astronomy, physics, and biology, economics and politics. If this were true, there could be no fruitful cooperation with the Christian in many departments of civilization and culture. The Christian would then appear in the history of civilization of mankind as the disturber, a sort of magician who claims to possess extraordinary esoteric knowledge and ability in many fields. Christianity would lose its significance as a message of salvation. Must we conclude, therefore, that Christianity has no role to play in respect to man's earthly existence? If so, Christian faith becomes a kind of *alibi* and the Christian is a man who flees from the world. The question comes up once more: How can there still be question of a message of salvation, of a power and a spirit that will yield "love, joy and peace"?

If, therefore, we wish to determine the nature and the meaning of our faith, we must not be satisfied with a definition that is too "formal"; we should give our attention principally to the *content* of the message of faith, to *what* has been announced, and also to the *person* who brought the message, to the one who issued the message. For if the messenger offers no guarantees, even the most beautiful and sublime message might be nothing more than an erroneous swindle and illusion.

Now what characterizes the Christian message is the fact that here *message* and *herald* coincide and are, as it were, one and the same: the herald is God and that which is announced is also God: *that* He is, *Who* He is and what His *intentions* are regarding men—namely, *to be God for man,* He Himself thus being our Savior and our salvation.

This self-revelation of God did not come about all at once, but in the course of a long history of salvation, of which Christ is the keystone. Through the instrumentality of the men of God of the Old Testament and especially through Jesus, the Word of God, who inaugurates the New, God has shown us, or rather has made us feel, that He still exists, that He is a God who mercifully stoops down to us in spite of our sloth, our hardness of heart and sinfulness, and becomes God-with-us-and-for-us, our "Emmanuel," as He is called in Scripture. In this sense we are allowed to say that the whole of Christianity was already potentially contained in the words which God spoke to Moses: "I am with you" (Ex. 3, 12). Thanks to the Incarnation of the Word of God and the communication of His Spirit, Christianity is the eschatological fulfillment, the definitive and highest possible realization of those mysterious words which are so full of promise: "I am with you."

We could express all this also in another way. The saying that the Christian faith rests on a *divine* revelation has a very special meaning and points to a revelation that is, as it were, *doubly* divine; doubly in that not only does it come from God but also has God and God's work of salvation for its object. This is why the Christian message is not a profane news proclamation but one that is religious. It is a message of God regarding the religious salvation of man, it is God's answer to man's questions about, and his expectation of salvation.

These remarks indicate the way for our further discussions. It is our aim to reflect upon the meaning of the Christian message of faith. That is, we want to know exactly what is meant when we proclaim to our world, in our Creed, that we believe in God, the Father, the Son, and the Holy Ghost, and in the Church of God. However, before we deal explicitly with this question in the *third section* of this chapter, we shall first have to determine what is meant here by the world "salvation" *(first section)*. Otherwise we would not be able to reflect fruitfully on the mystery of salvation which we profess in our Creed. And it is also necessary to examine first the nature of the Jewish expectation of salvation in the Old Testament, for the Christian message of salvation is a fulfillment that transcends all expectations *(second section)*.

1. *The Pre-Christian Concept of Salvation*

Evidently, Christianity could never appeal to us as a joyful and liberating message of salvation if we did not feel the least need for salvation, for liberation and conversion. This is the reason for entitling this section "The Pre-Christian Concept of Salvation." It is not so much that we want to unfold a concept but rather that we want to awaken our awareness to a cry of alarm that has perhaps been repressed; that we want to make vocal a cry for salvation; a cry springing from the lowest depths of our being, a cry for liberation and freedom, for openness and space, a cry of astonishment and admiration, a cry of innocence and pardon: *"De profundis clamavi,"* (out of the depths I have cried).

In religious literature, "salvation" is almost synonymous with liberation. It signifies an ideal situation of fullness of existence, of freedom and liberation from the many kinds of serfdom, loneliness, consciousness of guilt and helplessness, from the many kinds of estrangements, as our contemporaries say, which weigh down upon man and are so many obstacles to his restless striving for openness, for self-realization and creativity, for joy and peace, for truth and justice. In contrast to inanimate things which have no desires, and to the non-free animal which is contended with its existence, "restlessness" belongs to the very being of man, "Our heart is restless . . ." (St. Augustine).

A modern philosopher has said that "man is a sick animal," man is an animal that is always unhappy, that cannot be satisfied. He cannot nor does he want to be satisfied like an animal with what he received at birth or with what he receives day by day from his surroundings. The reason is that he is a questioning being, for to ask questions is already a first way of "taking a stand" in regard to what *surrounds* us, with respect to what presses us from without. Instead of accepting immediately and going along with what we see and hear and what is declared by others, we first ask, "Is that so?" "Why this?", and "What is the purpose of that?" etc.

Neither inanimate things nor the animal are plagued with questions nor do they experience astonishment and admiration. Questioning, astonishment and admiration, reflecting upon the past, all these break our bonds with the immediate surroundings and situation; they thus open for us so many roads, they give us room for expansion, widen the horizon of our spirit, announce freedom and independence. From the power of questioning is born the possibility of reflection, of rational judgment, the ability to say "Yes" or "No" with conscious choice. He who is not able to say "Yes" or "No" is like a ball in the hands of a child.

Now all human questions, as Kant correctly states, can be reduced to one or three fundamental types, which shows that there are in man three dimensions of questioning that liberates and makes us free.

First, there are the numerous questions concerning what man *can do,* questions regarding man's power over the world. What can we do to be less slaves and victims of the brutal powers of nature, to dominate the world and make it a fit dwelling place, to transform the raw materials of nature into a world of culture and civilization? It is from this question that technology and civilization were born.

Secondly, man asks himself a question that comes from a deeper dimension of his spiritual being. It is the moral question: What *must I* do, what *ought I* to do to act in a manner that suits man, that is worthy of a human person, so that what I *can* do may always be in the service of humanity? For I am able also to make a wrong use of my power over nature; I can use it to enslave others whereas I ought to foster their freedom; but if I listen to the interior voice of my conscience, which makes me responsible for the way I recognize human dignity in the world, I *may not* do that. It is from this question: "How *ought* I to act that my action may be worthy of a human being?", that ethics, as well as positive law which fosters justice in the world, are born.

Thirdly, even the ethical question is not yet the most profound question in man, for man knows that neither technology nor ethics and the creation of legal order of justice are able to satisfy man's craving for peace and happiness, for truth and justice. In spite of prodigious efforts, man, in the last analysis, sees earthly life as a miserable failure for which he, to a certain extent, bears both individual and collective responsibility, even though, paradoxically, the failure seems unavoidable.

There is as it were a threefold power that dooms mankind to helplessness in its ascent to freedom and liberation. There dwells in man himself a "power to sin" that paralyzes his will and his endeavor to live a morally good life, so that he repeats: "I do not do the good that I wish, but the evil that I do not wish, that I perform" (Rom. 7, 19).

Secondly, there is the tyranny of "Blind Fate" which does not seem to take account of morality in the distribution of joys and sorrows, which knows no distinction between good and bad men, and, as it were, maintains a state of radical injustice in the world.

Finally, there is Death, that mightiest among the tyrants, which mercilessly levels everyone and everything by annihilating them, thus establishing, as it were, absolute absurdity and meaninglessness as ruler over the world: "And I said in my heart," wrote the Preacher, "if the death of the fool and mine shall be one, what does it avail me to have applied myself more to the study of wisdom? And speaking with my own mind I perceived that this also was vanity . . . Vanity of vanities, and all is vanity. What has a man more of all his labor that he does under the sun?" (Eccl., 2, 15; 1, 2 and 3).

And so besides the question, "What is the extent of what I *can* do?", and after the question, "How ought I to use my powers to be a *good* man?", there comes a third question that sounds like a cry of hope and expectation of salvation: "What *ultimately may I hope for?*" It is hope which in man is the ultimate power of life that gives meaning to everything. "To hope" is to project a future before us, for whose realization we do not count solely on our own powers and efforts but also on the willing cooperation of the others. When I take a train to Brussels, it is my *hope* that I will get there on time. I realize that my arrival on time does not depend on me alone, for example, on my boarding the train on time, but depends equally well on the care of engineers and conductors. Since everything that man does is related to, or dependent on others, all his enterprises are fed by a secret hope. Now this is especially true about the great and all-embracing enterprise which constitutes his very existence, his *being-in-the-world,* with respect to which he hopes that "all his labor under the sun" will not have been in vain, and that Death has not the last say about man. "There is but one truly serious philosophical problem," wrote Albert Camus in his meditation on *The Myth of Sisyphus,* "namely, suicide. To judge that life is or is not worth living is to reply to the fundamental question of philosophy."

This question, whether or not life is, after all, worth living, is the supremely human question. It is in fact a question about *salvation,* that is, a confession of radical impotence, an agonizing cry for help, for understanding and protection "from above," since no enterprise "here below" is capable of giving a satisfactory answer to this ultimate question. Faced with death, man can only *hope* that his *being-in-the-world* is not the last word regarding his life; that behind this present life there is a hidden Power of goodness and forgiveness, of wisdom, truth, justice, which is Lord and Master over life and death and is able, beyond death, to make all things end well.

When Socrates learned that he had been sentenced to death, he rejected the suggestion of his friends that he take flight. He said: "I do not mind it too much that I have to die; on the contrary, a firm hope lives in me that another life exists beyond death, a life which, according to our ancient tradition of faith, is much better for the good than for evil doers." It is precisely this hidden Power of goodness and wisdom, of truth and justice which mankind has always designated and invoked under the name of "God." The ultimate and radical expectation of salvation in man is fundamentally a religious one. This is why man is not only a being which creates a civilization and builds a world, but is also a religious being in which the religious cry is a spontaneous expression of his attitude. And precisely because there is in man a sort of pre-Christian hope of salvation and expectation of salvation, Christianity was able to announce itself as a *message of salvation,* as an answer to a question about salvation.

Moreover, Christianity is not the only message of salvation that the world has known. All great religions announce themselves as bringing a message of salvation. The Christian believer must not take offense at the fact that there are other religions besides Christianity and that some are even older than Christianity. For they are expressions of that pre-Christian religious longing which Christianity needs in order that its message might find a resonant echo in the soul.

Hence Christians should approach all religions with reverence and respect, as was done by St. Paul in the Areopagus of Athens: "Men of Athens, I see that you are extremely religious in every way. For as I was going about and observing objects of your worship, I found also an altar with this inscription: 'To the Unknown God.' What, therefore, you worship in ignorance, that I proclaim to you." St. Paul here tries to reveal the religious Athenians to themselves. He insists that the religious differences that separate us, at the same time bind us and that they ought to arouse in us a feeling of kinship: "God is not far from any one of us. For in Him we live, we move, and have our being as indeed some of your own poets have said, 'For we are also His offspring' " (Acts, 17, 22-28).

This awareness of spiritual kinship should remain the background of the Christian message of faith, the atmosphere in which it is proclaimed. It must always preserve the character of a conversation that is animated by understanding, of a living witnessing, without violence and social pressure. This is of very great importance in our time when the freedom of "thought, conscience and religion" has been inscribed in the Declaration of Man's Universal Rights. After all, a message, a "good tidings" that is imposed by force hardly deserves its name, but is more a command which generates fear instead of joy. Hence fanaticism and religious wars are not at all expressions of true religiousness.

2. *The Old Testament Expectation of Salvation*

Among the many religions that have presented an answer to the question of salvation in the course of human history, Christianity stands out by the fact that, through Christ, it is connected with Israel's faith in salvation: "Do not think that I am come to destroy the Law and the Prophets; I have not come to destroy but to fulfill" (Matt. 5, 17). Likewise, it is one of St. Paul's main doctrines that the Christians are "true sons and heirs of Abraham."[1] For, according to God's designs regarding mankind, what unified Israel historically, with Abraham as common ancestor, was not their biological descent from him nor even the rite of circumcision, but belief in Yahweh and Yahweh's work of salvation which was to reach its completion in Christ. It is for this reason that Israel could consider itself to be "God's chosen people"; that the Christians constitute the new Israel of God, and that they are the true descendants of Abraham, the "father of the faith."

[1] Cf. especially his Letters to the Galatians and the Romans.

The Church has never foresworn the Jewish origin of her faith. She continues to borrow gratefully from Israelitic piety in order to nourish her own religious life. Even when she gathers her faithful around the "Table of the Lord," when in accord with the Lord's command, "Do this in memory of me," she recalls His life, death and ressurection, when she breaks the Bread that He brought from heaven—"I am the bread that came down from heaven"—and drinks the Cup of benediction which He won for us with His Blood—"This is the Chalice of the New Testament in my Blood"—she weaves around it a rich liturgical ornament of readings, prayers and hymns taken from the Old Testament.

Strange to say, this does not disturb the Christian faithful. On the contrary, those texts are so rich in authentic human expression and so full of religious meaning that they continue to appeal to modern man and to feed him with new ideas. They have some of the freshness of pure spring water; and this is not to be wondered at since our faith by way of a long tradition is traceable to the same source. "The Old Testament," writes an eminent catechetical author, "is the youth of Christianity. It is the imperfect and gradually unfolding revelation of God to men and it is man's first experience of that work of God in him. These primitive experiences contain the essential elements of every relation with God, which Christ would later bring to complete unity and harmonious fullness. But precisely because those ancient expressions of religious insight and feeling go back to the religious youth of mankind, they continue to grip us and serve to express our personal piety.[2]

Since the faith in God of the Old Testament still constitutes the basis of our Christian Creed, it is, as it were, by way of the Old Testament that we must seek to understand and live

---

[2]J. de Vooght, "Katechese Nu," *Het woord van God brengen in onze gemengde wereld,* p. 66. Discourse at the Catechetical Convention of Brussels, 20-21 Sept., 1959.

our Creed. This assertion, however, should not be misunderstood. The Old Testament faith of Israel found its fulfillment and confirmation in Christianity. It was in Christianity that its essential truth attained its full maturity and purity, and it is in Christianity that, freed from unclean elements, it preserves its original meaning. Following the example of St. Paul, we must make, in the faith of Israel, a distinction between what is essential and what is not, between what comes from God and what is merely a cultural-historical dress and embodiment. Or to put it even more clearly, we must try to find out what God actually said and intended, by distinguishing it from what was added, often unconsciously and with the best of intentions, by the Jewish community, in the form of ideas, purposes and embellishments.

The faith of the Old Testament essentially goes back to an extraordinarily lofty experience of what we could call the *Nearness of God.* It is a nearness in which God introduces Himself, as it were, to the religious-minded soul; a nearness in which He makes Himself *present* not only as "God-for-us," as our Sovereign Lord and Master, but also as our Savior and our Salvation, as our Liberator who gives us our most profound freedom and the security of our existence: "Yahweh is my light and my salvation: Whom shall I fear?" (Ps. 26, 1). In *Exodus* we find the most powerful expression of the meeting of the time-bound human mortal with the all-time-embracing eternal God, a meeting that is both terrifying and pacifying. This meeting is recorded by Moses, perhaps the greatest among all the men of God: "I am with you," Yahweh said to Moses (Ex. 3, 12) and again, "I am who am" (Ex. 3, 14).

For Moses, God is no longer a mere concept; He is a presence that reveals itself "in the first person": *"I am with you";* God here is the First. Moses is drawn into God's designs concerning Israel and, through Israel, he becomes involved in God's designs regarding the entire human race.

He has become the "servant" of God; he has entered the service of God's will and work of salvation. In other words, the expression: "I am with you" is a *promise* that opens a mysterious future for all mankind. Moses and all men of God after him, and the whole of Israel with them, are the bearers of that promise.[3]

In this way we understand that the words, "I am with you" which God spoke to Moses, dominate the entire history of Israel. Israel as a group—just, after all, as every individual man—was to learn only gradually the full content of these words. They were to learn it in the course of *a long and painful time of instruction and trial,* just as a child, says St. Paul, is under guardians for a long time before it is given full adult liberty (cf. Gal. 3, 24; 4, 1). God is not something obvious; He is a hidden and holy God ("Verily thou art a hidden God, the God of Israel, the Savior") (Is. 45, 15); He is an "awe-inspiring and fascinating mystery"; and "His ways are not the ways of men."

God is God, the totally Other, who surpasses and transcends all human concepts, considerations and expectations. That is why God will always be a "scandal" to man, a "terrible and jealous God," who tolerates no competitors. Just as man, on the other hand, will always be inclined to win God for his own earthly designs and, as it were, to take God in his service for working out man's economic, national and political programs, rather than to serve God and enter into His plans. The expression, "I am with you," which originally was a word which God addressed to man and which pointed to an initiative, a sanctifying grace of the thrice holy God, is thus twisted around and profaned. It thus becomes a vulgar "God

---

[3]We may note here that every experience of the presence of one who reveals himself "in the first person" as benefactor, protector or lover, has the meaning of a *promise,* for it opens up a *new future.* This, *a fortiori,* is true when it is God Himself who is present, for God is inexhaustible.

is with us," the ever-repeated battle cry, invented by man in every period of time to endow his greed and ambition with a sort of divine power.

Israel also did not rise in one day to a pure confidence in God. It often stained its faith in the protecting closeness of God with all sorts of by-designs. That is why Yahweh was a great source of offense and disappointment for Israel: "Arise, why sleepest thou, O Lord? Arise and cast us not off to the end. Why turnest thou thy face away and forgettest our want and our trouble?" (Ps. 43, 24-25). It was precisely through this seeming absence of God—of which the Babylonian captivity and the occupation of the Fatherland and the holy city of Jerusalem by foreign powers were the most grievous experiences—that Israel learned to discover the true face of God. Purified by many trials, it would gradually understand what God originally meant by "I am with you." It would thus prepare the world for the definitive revelation of God, the Theophany *par excellence,* which was to take place in the person of Jesus of Nazareth, in His Crucifixion and Resurrection.

As we have said in the previous chapter, the unsurpassed greatness and providential significance of Israel do not lie on the secular level, as if the earthly, national and political history of Israel could be reduced to an unbroken series of miraculous, quasi-magical interventions of God. They consist rather in the purity and solidity of its religious attunement, by virtue of which Israel was the instrument of God's salvific work in the world and the first stage of a history of salvation, the second stage of which was to be inaugurated by the coming of Christ.

In that faith of salvation of Israel we find *three chief ideas* which raised it at once high above all other religions of salvation and still are the substructure of the New Testament creed. They are the ideas of creation, mediatorship, and covenant.

The Idea of Creation. First and before all, there is the idea of creation, by which Judaism differs from all other religions whether they be mythological or any kind of Eastern Yoga mysticism. For this idea of creation makes it possible to do full justice both to God's sovereignty and man's independence and historicity, thus showing the value of earthly life.

The God of Israel is not a vague abyss of being, an abstract principle of being, or a blind life force, but a living, personal God. Everything that exists is in the product of His Word, so that He is the Sovereign Lord and Master over life and death, over nature and history. His omnipresence permeates, knows and animates everything.

God, however, created man according to His image and likeness. He entrusted the earth to men, established them as lords and masters over all the things that grow and live: "God blessed them saying: 'Increase and multiply, and fill the earth and subdue it. And rule over the fishes of the sea and the fowls of the air and all the living creatures that move upon the earth' " (Gen. 1, 28). Whence the pious Jews would chant the praise of life with gratitude and confidence as a blessing from above: "I will behold thy heavens, the work of thy fingers; the moon and the stars which thou has founded. What is man that thou art mindful of him? Or the son of man that thou hast made him a little less than angels; thou hast crowned him with glory and honor; and hast set him over the works of thy hands; thou hast subjugated all things under his feet" (Ps. 8, 4-8).

Man's sovereignty over the world does not mean, however, that God abandoned man to himself and that He is no longer concerned with man's lot. Once again we note that the God of Israel is a living God who like a devoted Father stoops down to His children and has pity on them. He listens to their prayers and forgives their sins. Moreover, He is a God who, especially through trusted servants, the great "men of God," enters into intimate communion with mankind and makes them feel His protective and sanctifying presence: "I am with you." This leads to a second fundamental idea.

The Idea of Mediatorship. This idea is closely related to the idea of God's transcendence and sovereignty. God, as creator of heaven and earth, is a transcendent God, the totally Other, the Invisible who is beyond all human conception and representation. Hence it is not permitted to make an image of Him, for He cannot be represented. It is impossible to picture Him or to make Him present in some created object of nature, such as the sun, the moon, and living animals, or in any human artifact.

How, then, is God present on earth and how does He cause us to feel His presence? By means of the men of God, His trusted servants to whom He directs His Word and whom He fills with His Spirit. The Jews, in contrast with the Greeks, did not consider "sight" the highest spiritual power of the human soul. For them the supreme power was to hear and listen to God's mighty voice, and liberation came from the command of Him "whom to serve is to rule." Obedient service of God in the spirit of faith makes man free, for it delivers him from the chains of passion and darkness. It allows him to walk in the light of God's truth and introduces him into God's salvific will which encompasses all time.

This is why Israel greeted the appearance of a man of God as a grace, whether he was a pious leader, a judge or a king, a prophet, an inspired poet or a holy priest. It saw in him a symbol and an instrument of God's liberating presence in the midst of His people, just as a Saint in our midst is still considered to be a grace of God. When there were no longer any prophets, Israel got the impression that God Himself had abandoned His people; it had no longer anyone to whom it could cling. Hence when Jesus of Nazareth appeared as the Holy One of God, a shout of joy went up from the people and they sang, "God has once more visited His people!"

There is one important conclusion we can draw from the theme of mediatorship; namely, that the Old Testament faith in salvation, though directed to God Himself—for Yahweh is the Savior and Salvation, the only One upon whom it is possible to build—has also at the same time the character of salvation that forms part of human history. It is impossible to divorce it from a *history of salvation,* a *"sacred history,"* for God manifested His liberating presence by a series of meaningful events in which the men of God were the principal bearers of the message and agents. These are the wonder-works of God, the great deeds of salvation of God, the outstanding expressions and proofs of Gods fidelity to the promises which were hidden in His words, "I am with you."

We are now ready for the third fundamental idea which is, as it were, the synthesis of the other two—namely, the idea of the covenant.

The Idea of the Covenant. God, by means of His chosen and trusted servants, made a covenant with Israel. Israel is thus permitted to consider itself the beloved people of God, a collective and historical unity which, by the grace of God's special presence, is charged with a religious mission.

In this idea of the Covenant the prominent element is a kind of mutual agreement, a mutual commitment, contracted between God and Israel through the mediatorship of the men of God. This involves on the part of God His promise of a protective presence, fidelity to His "I am with you." On the side of Israel this agreement implies the right and duty to place its trust in Yahweh to the exclusion of all other gods, to take refuge with Him in the most oppressive circumstances, to honor God's name, to keep His commandments, and especially to exercise justice without ever becoming guilty of sin by oppressing the poor, the widows and the orphans.[4] For

---

[4]Regarding the importance of the virtue of justice in the religion of Israel, cf. Cl. Tresmontant: *La doctrine morale des prophètes d'Israel,* Paris, 1958.

the God of Israel is a "holy" God, He is not merely the "totally Other," but also a God of truth and justice.

The "Kingdom of God," the ideal and final dominion of God over the world, was the dream of the devout Israelite and the object of his faith in, and expectation of salvation. Whatever the way it was conceived, the essential element of this kingdom was that it would inaugurate a time of truth and justice.[5] Let us recall how Isaias, for instance, describes this penetration of God into history by the work of His Anointed, His Messiah:

"He shall not judge according to the sight of the eyes, nor reprove according to the hearing of the ears. But He shall judge the poor with justice and shall reprove with equity for the meek of the earth. And He shall strike the earth with the rod of his mouth, and with the breath of his lips he shall slay the wicked. And justice will be the girdle of His loins and faith the girdle of His reins" (Is. 11, 3-5).

One of the most remarkable characteristics of Israel's piety is the fact that it does not permit the separation of religion, the service of God, and *morality*. Religion is not first of all a ritual, but it is a holy fear of God, incarnate in a morality of religious inspiration. "Thou shalt love the Lord, thy God, with thy whole heart and thy whole soul, and thy whole mind, and thy neighbor as thyself." Jesus would be able to say that "in this is the whole Law and the Prophets."

Those three fundamental ideas of Israel's religion still constitute the fundamental fabric of the Christian faith in salvation.

3. *The Glad Tidings of the Christian Creed*

The Christian faith, which rests on the Old Testament belief in salvation, appeared to the world as "glad tidings," a

[5]In Israel especially at the time of Christ, there existed actually several views regarding the coming of the Kingdom of God.

message of joy, precisely because it announced the fulfillment of the Old Testament's expectation of salvation or, to use scriptural language, the *eschatological,* the *definitive* realization of God's promise to Israel, "I am with you." "God, who at sundry times, and in divers manners spoke in times past to the fathers by the prophets, last of all in these days has spoken to us by His Son" (Hebr. 1, 1).

We know that the fulfillment of the promises was not accomplished without much pain and grief. Jesus, before being recognized as "God's Anointed" *par excellence,* that is, as the Messiah, as the "Emmanuel" or "God-with-us," was for many, and not least for His own apostles, a bitter disappointment and a scandal. Paul had even persecuted the Lord before he became His disciple. In fact, Jesus had not delivered Israel from the power of its enemies which oppressed it; He had not restored David's dynasty to the throne; He had not even restored Solomon's Temple to its former luster, and He had certainly not transformed the earth into an earthly paradise where henceforth "the wolf would dwell with the lamb, and the leopard would lie down with the goat" (Is. 11, 6). In fact, He had done much more than all that, precisely because He had done nothing else than fulfill what God had meant by His "I am with you"—namely, that He would be God-with-and-for-us, thanks to the incarnation of His Word and the outpouring of His Spirit. Jesus truly inaugurated the *"eschata,"* the "end of the times." But this did not mean that with His coming the world had come to its end, as many Jews had expected; for this surely is *too human an interpretation* of God's promises of salvation, an interpretation which would make the end of the human race and of history be a grace of God, a favor, for mankind! Jesus ushers in the true *"eschata"* because He installs amidst mankind the definitive, the *highest possible,* liberating presence of God in virtue of His death on the cross, His Resurrection, and the outpouring of the Holy Spirit.

It is precisely this liberating Presence of God which the Christian professes in His Creed and proclaims to the world as an *"evangelium,"* "good tidings": "Go and teach all nations, baptizing them in the name of the Father, and of the Son, and of the Holy Spirit." Let us then proceed, taking the Creed for our guide.

I BELIEVE IN GOD, THE FATHER

God is the beginning and the end of our Creed, as He was the beginning and the end of Israel's faith in salvation. Beginning and End, Alpha and Omega, for there is question here of God's manifestation of Himself to man and the fulfillment of *"I* am with you." Pascal has expressed this in a manner that has not been excelled:

> God of Abraham, God of Isaac, God of Jacob,
> Not of philosophers and savants. . . .
> God of Jesus Christ; *Deum meum et Deum vestrum;*
> Your God will be my God . . .
> He is found only through the ways taught by the Gospel.

What God was for Abraham, Isaac and Jacob, and still more, what he was for Jesus Christ, this He wants to be for us also: a "Father" who dwells in heaven. Hence, just as Abraham, Isaac and Jacob put their confidence in God and, still more, just as Jesus surrendered entirely to the will of His Father, so we also can, in and above all, trust in God; and in all that *we* will, we must give preference to God's holy Will regarding the world: "Thy will be done. Thy kingdom come." In this does God's will concerning man consist: "to be conformed to the image of His Son, that He should be the firstborn among many brethren" (Rom. 8, 29). Briefly, by faith we are introduced into the providential relations that existed between Jesus and His Father, we become

"God's Children," not only in name but in reality (Gal. 3, 26; Rom. 8, 15; I John, 3, 1-2).

For this reason the New Testament describes the nature of God less as a mystery of omnipotence, omniscience and terrifying concealment than as an unfathomable mystery of grace and love: "God is love. In this has God's love been shown in our case, that God has sent his only begotten Son into the world that we may live through Him" (I John, 4, 8-9). This new life points to a communion with the Eternal God, by way of communion with Jesus the Son of God, in unity with the Spirit. It is an "everlasting life"; it begins already on earth by faith, hope and charity: "This is everlasting life, that they may know thee and him whom thou hast sent, Jesus Christ" (John 17, 3). Of course, only later, when, after this earthly existence we are united with Christ, shall we fully understand what possibilities of peace, joy and freedom are contained in those words. But the "peace that surpasses all understanding" is already a foretaste of it here on earth (Phil. 4, 7).

If the Christian Creed is first of all a song of praise of God and a proclamation of trust in Him, it is also a *hymn of life,* for not death but life will have the last word about man's destiny: "I believe in God . . . I believe in life everlasting." This "everlasting life" is God. God is named at the beginning and at the end of the Creed because He is the Alpha and Omega of everything. The Christian believes in life because it is everlasting, eternal since it is directed to the eternal God. Hence, for the Christian there are only two irreparable calamities, since all things, even those that are most painful, "work together unto good for those who love God" (Rom. 8, 28). No doubt, God's ways do not always coincide with the ways of men, but if we put our trust in God, a situation that first seemed hopeless is often the way in which God accomplishes His liberating work in us, a work that makes us free for Himself. This is the great lesson given us by Christ who through his suffering and the Cross reached the Resurrection.

I believe in Jesus Christ, the Word Become man

As is evident from what we have seen, this second article of faith is already contained in the first: In the idea of God's fatherhood ("I believe in God, the Father") there lies an inner hidden reference to the *Sonship* of the Lord Jesus, whose "co-heirs" we are, which entitles us to be called in our turn "children of God" (Rom. 8, 17).

Christ, in other words, is the central event of salvation, the definitive Theophany of God's Revelation by which He, after speaking in divers manners through the prophets, definitively and in a perfect way enters history, reveals Himself to mankind in the twofold biblical sense of the term, viz., He makes Himself *known* and makes Himself *present.* This is why the gospel calls Jesus the "Emmanuel," the "God-with-us." For Christ is, as St. John tells us, God's Incarnate Word, the *Logos* of God, who from all eternity was with God, who became man, took up His abode among us and, as it were, put up His tent on earth.

This suggests the question which must be our main concern: What is meant when it is said that Jesus is the Word of God, and that God makes us free and saves us through His Word? It means at least this much: Jesus, in the mystery of God and of His work of Salvation, by the fact that He is the Word become man, plays more or less the same role—with due changes, we may even simply say, plays the same role—as the human word, the *logos* of the Greeks, in our *being-man* and in the manifestation of this being-man in history.

"Logos" in Greek does not merely mean the power of *speech,* of expressing one's thoughts or feelings by external signs. It also means *reason, understanding,* that is, the power to learn, to understand, to be spoken to by reality. The fact that both powers are designated by the one term "logos" is very instructive. It indicates that they should not be separated but should be considered as two sides of one identical fundamental faculty, namely, the power that makes us human, intelligent beings, who *understand* things and *understand one another* by means of things.

In fact, what is it that distinguishes us from the "mute," "dumb," "irrational," and "non-free" animal? Why do we make those four terms, "mute," "dumb," "irrational," "non-free" synonymous? Do not also animals produce sounds? They do, of course, but the animal does not *speak,* because it has *nothing to say,* and it has nothing to say because it is not "spoken to" by its surroundings. The dog which by mistake gets into a museum and escapes by the door as soon as he sees a chance, has nothing *to say* because he has not seen anything: the things that hang on its walls and arouse emotions in us, *say* nothing to him, they do not *speak* to him. The world with its truth, goodness, and beauty remains *closed* to the animal; hence it is incapable of leading others in the world to this truth, goodness, and beauty, and of making them free for this world through meaningful speech.

Man's attitude to the world is totally different. "When the soul listens," as the priest-poet Guido Gezelle has said, "everything becomes a language for us," and what we have learned from the language of things we in turn can express in language and say to others. The tree and the flowers, the smile of a child and the worried look of a mother speak and have something to say to us.

The bottomless world of sentiments and emotions within us and the limitless space around us "speak to us." As Pascal wrote, "The eternal silence of these infinite spaces frightens me." That is why we are able to communicate *"understandingly"* and *"meaningfully"* with everything around us.

We can move others to have similar meaningful contact with them; we can carry on intelligent conversation with each other; not the conversation of a deaf man with a mute but one that permits us to understand one another, to enter into each other's thoughts and feelings, to meet each other because we have had a meaningful meeting with reality itself.

Consider, for instance, the word of an artist, a scientist or a philosopher. Art is a word, speech, and through this speech new worlds *open* before us; the curtain that hid them is raised and they stand *revealed*. An authentic word is a power that *brings revelation*. The same is true of science and philosophy. It is in this that ultimately lies the wonderful power of the word. Hence the *logos* in man is not simply the power to dish out words and utter sounds, for this is often but a way of saying *nothing*. But the *logos* is also "reason" and "speech," that is, the capacity of learning and of communicating knowledge, of listening and speaking. It is thanks to the word that there is light, life of the spirit and freedom in mankind; that history is made, and that the history of mankind never stands still.

Now, what the word of man does for the benefit of secular history, God's Word accomplishes in sacred history for the benefit of our salvation. For also in God there is a Word. God is not a blind life-force, no vague abyss of being, no abstract principle of existence, but a living personal God. He is Word, Love, Freedom. The Word of God is He whose nature and role it is to reveal God.

In the revelation of the mystery of God and of His Will of salvation through God's Word, we can, according to the Prologue of St. John's Gospel, distinguish, as it were, three movements, three stages.

Firstly, there is the revelation of creation that is the work of God's Word: "All things were made through him, and without him was made nothing that has been made" (John

1, 3). The created world, for the Christian believer, is a book that speaks of God: "The heaven shows forth the glory of God, and the firmament declares the work of his hands" (Ps. 18, 1). The visible world manifests somewhat "his invisible attributes and his everlasting power" (Rom. 1, 19).

Secondly, there is the work of revelation performed by God's Word in Israel: to whom "God spoke at sundry times and in divers manners by the prophets" (Hebr. 1, 1). Israel in fact, owed its existence to faith in the word which God spoke through His servants. It became an historical unity only through fidelity to this word; it became a people which could call itself the people of God because it was in the service of the Word of God and was, as it were, the dwelling place of God's Word on earth: "The Word came unto His own, and his own received him not" (John 1, 11).

Finally, there is the definitive revelation of God, the supreme Theophany, of which all earlier revelations were but the prelude and the foreshadowings: "The Word was made flesh and dwelt among us, and we saw his glory, a glory as of the only-begotten of the Father" (John 1, 14). He is the "Emmanuel," the "God-with-us," in the full sense of that term. God's liberating presence has now become a reality, for "to be present" means to show the others what one is in one's hidden self; it means becoming for others what one is in oneself: "No one has at any time seen God. The only-begotten Son, who is in the bosom of the Father, he has revealed him" (John 1, 18).

Like any other revelation, God's revelation through the Incarnation of the Word, saves and liberates. He who listens to the Word, to Jesus, is introduced into the world where the Word lives, namely, "in the bosom of the Father." He is liberated, made free, for the mystery of the living God, for God's love and glory, His will and work of salvation. He is taken into a communion of life and love with God, He is re-born of God for a new life, the free life of the children of God: "To as many as received him he gave the power of becoming sons of God" (John 1, 12). By that fact man is also revealed to himself. In the light of God's truth he walks out of the semidarkness in which he so readily remains in order to hide his own wretchedness from himself and from others; and he thus comes to realize clearly and to confess sincerely what he in reality is, a creature and a sinner.

To be man, however, does not merely mean leaving the mother's womb as a human being. It means to dwell as man among men, to take up one's manhood and bring it to completion until death. If the Incarnation of God's Word is, as is principally emphasized by the Greek Fathers, *the* outstanding liberating and revealing event of salvation, this does not take away the fact that the redeeming death and resurrection of Christ and the outpouring of the Holy Ghost by which we become sharers in His Resurrection, also occupy an outstanding and essential place in that salvific event. It is only on the Cross and in the glory of the Resurrection that God's liberating love stands fully revealed to us and achieves its highest and most complete effectiveness (John 4, 10). Christ's death on the Cross and His resurrection are not accidental events in His life. They are, as it were, the crowning features and completion of the mystery of God's-Word-made-man, viewed as the mystery of the reconciling and unifying meeting of God and man in the person of Jesus Christ. Every meeting with God, and especially the hypostatic union,[5] which is rightly called a *grace of union,* is a living *dialogue* with God; otherwise we should have to look upon it as no more than a lifeless juxtaposition of things.

---

[5]The "hypostatic union" is the union of the divine and human natures in the one concrete person of Jesus.

Every dialogue with God comprises *three* moments in which God speaks the first and also the last word. On the Cross it is God's love that takes the initiative: "who through the Holy Spirit offered Himself unblemished unto God" (Hebr. 9, 14). Here everything takes place under the impulse of the Holy Spirit and the prompting of God's love; this is the first moment. Then comes Christ's answer, which is the second moment: on the Cross Jesus delivers Himself entirely to the will of the Father for the salvation of mankind, "becoming obedient to death, even to the death of the cross" (Phil. 2, 8). And finally, in a third moment, there is God's reply: This is why "God also has exalted him and bestowed upon him the name that is above every name" (Phil. 2, 9). By the Resurrection Christ's humanity becomes completely involved in the power and glory of God. Christ is made *Kyrios,* the Lord to whom all things are made subject (Phil. 2, 11). Or, to express it somewhat differently, Jesus is established *"Son of God in power"* (Rom. 1, 4), He is clothed with power to sanctify us and make us sharers in the glory of His Resurrection. The risen Christ thus becomes for us a sanctifying principle of life: "The last Adam became a life-giving spirit" (1 Cor. 15, 45; cf. II Cor. 3, 17). He is the *new Adam,* the progenitor of those who, through baptism and belief in God's Word are reborn of God and united into one new "people of God," the true "posterity of Abraham" (Rom. 4, 13-19), the new Israel, or "the Israel according to the spirit."

I Believe in the Holy Ghost

We have now reached what may be called the central point of our analysis of the Creed as Tidings of Joy. To believe in the Holy Ghost means that we believe that the Spirit of God is still present in the Church in this twentieth century, and that He is at work in it as He was in the first Christian community. In other words, we believe that the Spirit of God is even now present wherever God's word is preached in the Lord's Name and is listened to with faith, and that He insures complete fruitfulness to that word, so that it produces within man an *effective* salvation, liberation, and resurrection. It is in the last analysis this concurrence of the proclamation of God's word and the resurrectional presence of the Spirit of God that constitutes the significance of Christianity as God's message and work of salvation.

To appreciate this, we must keep in mind that the Lord's Resurrection and the coming of the Spirit soon thereafter were, for the first Christians, an indivisible whole. They were the high point of the entire history of salvation, the long postponed moment of the grace which ended the expectation of redemption and replaced it by the eschatological or definitive realization of salvation. Thus the Resurrection and the coming of the Holy Ghost constituted the frontier between the Old and the New Testament. For, indeed, the first Christian community had experienced the outpouring and operation of God's Spirit, which had begun shortly after Christ's glorious Ascension, as a *participation in the Resurrection of the Lord.* This took place in the form of an effective liberation from the paralyzing and crushing power of sin (Rom. 6 and 7). It constituted a rebirth from God to a fresh, untrammeled and confident life as children of God (Rom. 8, 9-17), and a radical transformation of interrelations among men under the impulse of a love that made everything new, that inspired a new mode of life, a mode of living proper to those who are liberated, who have risen. "You have been called to liberty, brethren," St. Paul wrote to the Galatians (Gal. 5, 13-25); "only do not use liberty as an occasion for sensuality [that is, for unruly and sinful passion] but by charity serve one another. . . . But I say: 'Walk in the Spirit and you will not fulfill the lusts of the flesh.'. . . The fruit of the Spirit is charity, joy, peace; patience, kindness, goodness; faith, modesty, continency."[6] This, indeed, is the way of life of the free children of God.

Thus was fulfilled the spiritual renewal foretold by Ezechiel: "I will give you a new heart and put a new spirit within you" (Ez. 36, 26). Everything seemed so new that there was no hesitation to speak about a new creation of mankind, a creation having as first progenitor and model no longer the first earthly Adam, but the new, heavenly Adam, the glorified risen Christ (I Cor. 15, 35-50). Christ's Resurrection, through the outpouring of the Spirit, was not so much a private event affecting Christ but rather *the* outstanding event of salvation involving each individual believer and the whole of mankind.

However, the Spirit of God is not a magic force which befalls man from the outside. What the Holy Ghost operates in us, says St. Paul, is rather something like an inner disposition, a longing for the things of the spirit ("The spirit lusts against the flesh" Gal. 5, 17). He prompts us to "seek the things that are above, where Christ is seated" (Col. 3, 1). And in fact, the gift of the Spirit of God is nothing less than the presence of God's love in man (Rom. 4, 5), which enables him to love the things of God, that is, the things about which Jesus, as Word Incarnate, speaks and for which He has to free us. "Only through love," says St. Augustine, "does one enter into truth." In order to *"enter into,"* to understand, a particular truth so that we live by it and are interiorly liberated by it, we must possess within ourselves a certain sensibility, an openness, a disposition favorable to what is said by truth. This is precisely what love operates in us.

One who visits a museum without having a "feeling for," a "liking for" the things that are exhibited, will not under-

[6]Cf. also 1 Cor. 13: Hymn to charity.

stand anything. The *openness* that is required in order that the word of the poet, the artist, the philosopher may *speak to us interiorly,* and that we may be *introduced* into the world from which that word is sent, is not so much a matter of understanding, but rather of a spiritual sensibility which causes us "to feel for," "to like something."

This is particularly true in respect to God's Word. The Holy Ghost, because He is the Charity of God, develops in man the sensibility that is necessary for him to enter into the world from which God's Word speaks to us. That is why the Gospel of St. John calls the Holy Ghost the "Paraclete" of Christ, the "one called to help us"; also the "Spirit of Truth whom the world knows not. . . . He will teach you all things and bring to your mind whatever I have said to you" (John 14, 17-26). The Spirit really works in the Church as "Paraclete of the Word." It was only with the coming of the Spirit that the apostles actually *understood* what Christ meant (Acts, 1, 6-7). He who listens to Christ sooner or later will find God. But to find God, he must well-intentionedly, by way of the Word which Jesus is, seek God and not something else. This well-intentioned search is the work of the Spirit of God, or, as we commonly say, of God's grace in man. Only then does the Word effectively make us free.

"The truth shall make you free," Jesus said to His disciples (John 8, 32). These words contain the entire meaning of Christianity. The first Christians recognized Christianity as a liberating truth, as glad tiding of liberation or, as St. Paul says, "a power of God unto salvation to everyone who believes" (Rom. 1, 16). Where God's word was proclaimed with faith and received in the Spirit of God, a liberating resurrection was accomplished through a threefold yet inseparable process of reconciliation: *a reconciliation with God, with oneself, and with others.* It was, as it were, a passage from a disorderly and diminished life to the blooming of an existence characterized by reconciliation and openness, an existence marked by "love, joy and peace" (Gal. 5, 26). This risen life itself was in reality the work and the sign of God's liberating love, a love which had thus been revealed to the world in the person of Jesus Christ and in the brotherly love of the believers gathered together in a living unity in Christ. "No one has ever seen God," St. John wrote, but "if we love *one another, God* abides in us and his love is perfected in us" (I John 4, 12).

When, therefore, we say that Christianity is "glad tidings of salvation," this must be understood properly. It is not merely a doctrine of salvation or a theory of salvation of which Christians are the messengers; but it means *a work of salvation, which God through His Word and His Spirit brings about by means of Christians acting as living witnesses for the faith.* In other words, this salvation is brought about because Christians appear in the world as liberated and as risen, as the people of God's new Covenant, as Israel "according to the Spirit." This new Israel St. Paul designates by the word "Church." This brings us to the fourth great article of faith which is inseparably connected with the three previous ones, our faith in Holy Church.

I Believe in Holy Church

The Church is the new Israel; hence she is not something accidental in the economy of salvation. She represents the second stage of the history of salvation and in fact the last or definitive stage, the "last times." This means that the realities of salvation, especially the risen Christ with His sanctifying power, are already present in the world. The presence of course is still under sacred signs *(in sacramento),* while we are waiting for His return, for the final revelation of the Lord to every one of us individually and to the world as a whole.

It might, at first, seem paradoxical that we are expected to *believe* in the Church. Faith is a theological virtue, a trustful and obedient surrender to God himself, to His Word and His Spirit. How then can it also have for its object the Church, the visible, historically situated group of the faithful? In other words, how can the belief "in *God* . . . in His only begotten Son . . . in the Holy Ghost," also comprise: "I believe in Holy Church"? For we are still concerned with one and the same attitude of faith, through which we live attuned to the *mystery of God* and His liberating work of salvation. How can the Church, as an historically situated community of the faithful, form a part of that *divine* mystery of faith?

The answer to this question is contained in the foregoing. The Church (called *"Ecclesia,"* which means the group of those who are called) is not merely the visible community of the faithful who have accepted Christ's message, just as the Buddhist community is the assembly of all those who have grouped themselves around the word of Buddha. The Church as the historical community of the faithful, is part of the mystery of faith itself, for she is the Sacrament of God's presence on earth, that is, the "holy place" where God through the risen Christ and His sanctifying Spirit dwells in our midst and constantly accomplishes His work of salvation. And this work of salvation is, in fact, addressed to all mankind and has even, according to St. Paul, a cosmic significance: "that God may be all in all" things (1 Cor. 15, 28). However, the exact scope of this all-encompassing work of salvation will be hidden from us until the end of the world. But, in any case, the Church is the instrument of the work of salvation. She has the mission and the function of appearing in the world as the "Sign of God among the nations," the sign and instrument of God's saving presence among the nations.

Holy Scripture, in its description of the mission and function of the Church in God's plan of salvation, uses a series of concepts and images taken from the Old Testament. These excellently express the meaning of the Church in the history of salvation. There is, first of all, the very term, the "gathering of God" (*Ecclesia Dei*). It means the group of those who are called; this term is used in the Greek translation of the Old Testament to designate the gathering of the Jewish people in the desert around the Ark of the Covenant, which the Jews considered the preferred dwelling place of God amidst His people.[7] There is, secondly, the idea of *"People of God."* The Church is indeed God's people, the new Israel according to the spirit, (e.g., 1 Peter, 1, 9). There is also the figure of *"Spouse of God,"* "Spouse of Christ," "Spouse of the Lord." It also is taken from the Old Testament and points to the intimate bond of love and life that exists between God and His people. The Church is the beloved of God, associated with God's Word in view of the work of that Word (Eph. 5, 25; 2 Cor. 11, 1-2). Finally there is the very beautiful figure of *"Temple of God, tent of God among men,"* God's dwelling place among men (1 Peter 2, 4-5; Apoc. 21, 3).[8]

A dwelling is the place where someone lives and works; where others can come to him, where his presence is manifested to others, where what he is and is able to do is put within the reach and at the service of others. The Church is that holy place on earth where God dwells and lives and works, where He manifests Himself and gives Himself to

---

[7]Cf. Cerfaux, *La théologie de l'Eglise suivant Saint Paul,* Paris 1942.

[8]We may note here that all those figures are intermingled in the well-known passage of the Apocalypse, 11, 2-5, which is used in the Epistle of the Feast of the Dedication of a church: "I saw the Holy City, New Jerusalem, coming down out of heaven from God, made ready as a bride, adorned for her husband. And I heard a loud voice from the throne saying, 'Behold the dwelling of God with men, and He will dwell with them, and they will be his people, and God himself will be with them as their God.' "

the world, where He liberates the world by His Word and His Spirit.

However, let us not forget that the Church is that holy dwelling of God upon earth as *historically situated,* and as *a community of the believers which makes history,* in other words, as a living community of faith, worship and charity. Again, there is no room in the mystery of God's work of salvation for anything that smacks of magic. That God, through His Word and His Spirit, works out our salvation does not mean that God attacks us with magic powers and addresses Himself to the world through magic signs. To put it more plainly, God's grace does not exclude man's historical cooperation, but gives to this cooperation a special form, which Scripture designates by the words "election," "ministry," and "faith." Man's cooperation is indispensable even, so that one may say in this sense that "God needs men." Otherwise we would land in the realm of magic and could no longer speak of a genuine *history* of salvation.

This history of salvation, we have said, is nothing other than the history of God's "I-am-with-you," the history of God's saving presence through His Word and His Spirit. This presence is brought about through the mediation of real, historical human beings. In the Old Covenant it came about through Israel and its men of God, especially its leaders, inspired poets and prophets. When the fullness of the times had come, that presence was brought about through Jesus Christ, the Word made flesh. After the Lord's Resurrection, it is obtained through the Church, the new Israel of God, born from the belief in the proclamation of God's Word by the apostles, which is gathered into a unity through this faith.

Without Christian holiness and without saints among the Christians, the Church could hardly appear in the world as the "Bride of the Word," as His faithful and loving associate, or the "holy dwelling place of God among men." The Church then could not appear as the place where God is worshipped "in spirit and in truth," where the many who seek God feel naturally at home. The "marks of the Church" as the characteristics of God's Church are called, its unity, holiness, catholicity and apostolicity, are not merely signs of the presence of God's Word and His Spirit, but are also a program for the faithful. This program and project must constantly be undertaken anew, taking account of the historical situations and especially of human weakness and sinfulness. That is why faith implies both belief and fidelity.

4. *Conclusion*

By way of conclusion we distill a few thoughts from what we have considered in the previous pages concerning the nature and the meaning of our faith. These, in turn, will more than once serve as our guides in the remainder of this work.

First, in general, regarding the nature and meaning of our faith, the Christian religion is not a metaphysical theory, not a philosophical doctrine concerned with the ultimate causes and ultimate structures of everything that is. Nonetheless, a certain metaphysics, for instance, the idea of creation, is contained in the Christian view of the world and of life. Again, our faith is not an ideology, after the manner of Marxism, it is not a rigid and closed system of theoretical concepts regarding the course of history and the imperatives that flow from them in regard to social and political practices. Finally, Christianity, unlike the many forms of Eastern Yoga, is still less a technique, a method of meditation and purification that enables man to free himself from the slavery of his passions and desires.

Christianity is a religious message of salvation in the service of the work done by God, through His Word and His Spirit and by the instrumentality of historically situated men, for the sanctification of sinful man. When we say that the

Christian message is in the service of God's work of salvation, we mean that it makes that work known, proclaims and announces it, but above all, that it, as it were, makes that work *present* through that proclamation. This is possible because "to believe" means to say "Amen" to God, to enter into, and cooperate with God's saving will and work. In other words, God's work of salvation is made present in the Christian message because Christianity is a "word" and a love in which God's Word and God's Spirit are present. Hence Christianity forms a part of a sacred history, of a meaningful whole of salvific events that finds its keystone and source of meaning in Christ.

Secondly, since Christianity is a message, great care must be taken to prevent it from ever losing its character of being a message. A message is something in the order of words, of testimony and dialogue. Violence, social pressure, and appeal to power are out of place in a message, for it is only in a free and sincere dialogue, in reverence for the other party, that testimony has its value; only then does it *speak,* i.e., reveal and make free.

This is of great importance in our present world, for today freedom of conscience and of religion are honored as fundamental rights of man. To combat irreligion by alms and social threats, to make primitive peoples embrace Christianity through colonization and the use of force are things of the past. The only means now available for the preaching of the faith are the living, unselfish testimony to the faith by those who believe, by both priest and layfolk.

Hence, one of the most pressing needs for the preaching of the faith in our time is that the word of God be given its former freedom to appear as a religious message of salvation, an answer to man's great question about salvation. This freedom can be obstructed in two ways. On the one hand, men can close their ears to the message, on the other, the heralds of the message can make their religious proclamation of the message too dependent on a number of economic, social, political or other conditions that have nothing or little to do with God's Word.

Thirdly, Christianity is "Glad Tidings," a message which even on earth brings liberation and freedom, peace and joy, truth and justice. For Christianity is a power of reconciliation with God, which is at one and the same time a reconciliation also of man with himself and with his neighbor. We are going back to an ancient tradition that reaches St. Paul and St. John and finally, the Lord Himself, when we declare that love of our brethren and love of God are one and the same love. Although the Christian faith is directed to God Himself, it is not an *alibi* removing us from the world, but a caring for others establishing us in this world.

Lastly, we return to the question with which we began: How does Christianity appear to the world of today? Differently expressed, what *impression* do the Christians make on the world? Do they appear to the world as bearers of joyful tidings? As bearers of a *power* which, flowing from fidelity to God's Word and God's Spirit, brings reconciliation, and produces peace, joy and brotherly love?

Our time also is a time of sinfulness, of heartlessness, of contrasts, but at the same time it is a period of great expectation and painful search for truth and justice, freedom and liberation, reconciliation and union. Do we, Christians, stand in the midst of the world as a power for liberation, and do we live the life of men who have been freed, who have risen? Do we not rather give the impression of living at the edge of the world's events?

Pope Pius XI said once that all of us share in the guilt for the loss of the numerous laborers who left the Church in the nineteenth and twentieth centuries. He uses the term "scandal," to imply that the Christians themselves bear a certain amount of responsibility for that loss of faith. And it was in fact a scandal that it took so many Christians almost half a century or more to come to understand the true meaning of the social struggle, to realize that it was not merely a question of introducing new economic structures but of bringing more truth and justice into the world, a matter of attaining to a more genuine recognition of the human dignity of the laborer as a fellow-man in our world.

We may ask ourselves how much time shall we need again to understand what is happening in today's world? If, in spite of the many lessons of the past, we often react so slowly to what is happening in the world, is it not because we too frequently forget that Christianity is essentially "glad tidings," a *power* for reconciliation with God, which at the same time brings about the reconciliation of man with his fellow-man? "If we love one another, God abides in us," says St. John (1 John 4, 12). Where there is charity and love, there God is present.

Love, however, is more than a dreamy feeling; it is more than stooping down with compassion and giving charitable assistance to the needy. Love is in the first place a caring and creative concern for others whoever they may be; it means to desire effectively for them what we desire for ourselves, bringing them civilization and culture. And we thus come to a new problem: the encounter of Christianity and civilization, the meeting of sacred and secular history.

CHAPTER THREE

CHRISTIANITY AND CIVILIZATION

"Christianity and Civilization" is a modern expression for an ancient problem, the problem of the relations between faith and reason, between religion and life, between grace and nature. No matter how it is expressed, the problem comes down ultimately to an encounter between what is given by Christ, as God's Word, and what is contributed by man's own powers, to the development of man's human existence.

If the problem is as old as Christianity itself, the way in which it presents itself, as a theoretical question and especially as a practical task, differs from age to age and depends on the concrete situation of the believer as man-in-the-world. By faith man is directed to the Transcendent, to God and the hereafter, to what Nietzsche called the *"Jenseits,"* the Beyond. It is over there, as it were, that he has his habitation, his "citizenship is in heaven" (Phil. 3, 20). But this does not mean that the Christian is not, like any other human being, a man who remains established in the world of the *"Diesseits,"* of "here below." Here also he has a work to accomplish in solidarity with all mankind and here also he builds up a human existence.

Hence it is not surprising that a tension may arise between man's religious life and his secular life, nor will anybody be astonished when he sees the many forms which that tension assumes according to the task and the situation of man as man-in-this-world. That is why the question concerning the relation between faith and reason, between the supernatural and the natural, arose mostly on the occasion of some practical task, and since tasks undergo development and changes, there likewise exists evolution in the very ways in which the problem is raised.

1. *A Brief Survey of the Problem's History*

The First Centuries. "The kingdom of heaven," Our Lord said, "is like a treasure hidden in a field; a man who finds it hides it, and in his joy goes and sells all that he has and buys that field" (Matt. 13, 44). For the very first Christians the problem of reconciling heaven and earth was practically non-existent. They were no longer earthly-minded. They lived in small, separate communities, "looking for the blessed hope and glorious coming of our great God and Savior, Jesus Christ" (Tit. 2, 13).

That situation could not last. Life had to go on and as Christianity grew in prestige and drew more and more followers from the ranks of the higher world of Greek culture, the question arose: What is the position of the faith in regard to pagan wisdom? Is it necessary to condemn everything pagan or does paganism possess some elements which can be considered to presage the Christian view of the world and of life? It was the great merit of the second century "Apologists" to have dared not only to ask this question, but to answer it in the affirmative. The "Father of Christian Humanism" we can justly call St. Justin. To use the expression of Professor Cornelia J. de Vogel, we should note, however, that during the first centuries of the Christian era, the relationship between revelation and reason presented no great difficulties. It simply amounted to a question of confronting two views of life, two "philosophies," of which only one could pride itself on absolute certainty and was considered a criterion of the other.

The Middle Ages. The problem became more complicated in the Middle Ages because of the fact that to the opposition between sin and grace, on which the Fathers of the Church based their view of man, there was added another; that of nature and the supernatural. Thus the term "philosophy," as used in the Middle Ages, no longer had the same meaning as in the dialogues of St. Justin. For the latter, "philosophy" was almost synonymous with wisdom and designated the workings of the *Logos,* of God's Word in us. In the Middle Ages, on the contrary, philosophical insight, as such, was considered a distinct achievement of natural reason; hence a distinction was made between natural insight and the truth that had come directly from heaven and was imparted to us in faith. Thus, the question was no longer one of distinguishing and comparing two "philosophies," two expressions of the *Logos,* but a distinction was made between "wisdom from above" and philosophy, viewed as the work of natural reason. Of this reason Aristotle was held to be the principal representative.

It was therefore a matter of bringing Christianity into harmony with the philosophy of Aristotle. Even this, considered theoretically, did not present great difficulties, except for the fact that a role was played by a psychological factor, namely, a boundless admiration for the Greek philosopher. Medieval man found it difficult to imagine that "the Philosopher" could have made errors. Respect for his authority even went so far that some commentators, following the example of Avicenna, spoke about a twofold truth. In this connection we frequently meet the name of Siger of Brabant. However, according to recent historical research, this Belgian philosopher never defended the theory of a "double truth." For him, too, there existed but one truth, namely, that which was revealed. But then what was to be done when the teaching of Aristotle was in conflict with the faith? Siger replied that this was not a sufficient reason for philosophy to revise its teaching since it merely repeated and commented upon the teachings of the philosophers.[1] Siger's extreme careful-

[1]Cf. Etienne Gilson: *History of Christian Philosophy in the Middle Ages,* New York, 1955, p. 398, where is found a passage from a sermon of St. Thomas which refers to the position of Siger of

ness and subtlety, however, did not prevent him from getting into trouble with the Church.

It was principally against Siger of Brabant that St. Thomas constructed his well-known and classical doctrine that faith and reason are of necessity capable of being harmonized. By its very nature, truth is one, for it is rooted in God, but there are two ways that lead to the truth. One is that of supernatural revelation and of faith, and the other that of natural discovery through creatures considered by reason. Both ways come from God and lead to God, the "First Truth." The problem was thus theoretically solved in this way, and there were but few practical difficulties since at that time the achievements of natural reason coincided more or less with the philosophy of Aristotle. The exact methods of the natural sciences had not yet been developed. Thus it was not difficult to make the necessary corrections in philosophy and bring it into harmony with revelation. Moreover, a philosophy which confines itself to its own field, will hardly enter into serious conflict with the faith, since it is keenly aware of how impenetrable the mystery of human existence is.

Modern Times. In the seventeenth century the problem concerning the relationship between faith and reason took a totally different turn and began to be acute for the first time in history. The reason was that the two terms were no longer considered so much from the standpoint of God as from that of man. Faith and reason are now two expressions of the human *Cogito,* two attitudes of man's mind and both can claim to rest on their own grounds. In other words, the harmony of faith and reason was now studied less from the

---

Brabant. This sermon was delivered at the University of Paris: "Among those who labor in philosophy some say things that are not true according to faith; and when told that what they say goes against faith, they answer that it is the Philosopher who says so; as to themselves, they do not affirm it, they are only repeating the Philosopher's words."

theological standpoint than from the viewpoint of epistemology. Galileo and Descartes contributed greatly to that changed formulation of the problem.

The new physics of Galileo was constructed independently of the Bible, the Church or any ancient philosopher. Descartes, on his part, introducing his methodic doubt, and his utterly rationalistic dialectics ("after the manner of geometry"), sharpened the concept of reason's autonomy. Science and philosophy stood now on their own legs and went their own way. They became conscious of their own methods and the proper foundation of their certainty. The ground of certitude appeared to be so unshakeable in the realm of experimental science and the results seemed so undeniable that for the first time in history, faith, or rather what was generally considered to belong to faith, had to bow before reason. "E pur si muove" (nevertheless, the earth *does* move) were, according to a legend, the last words spoken by the dying Galileo.[2] In any case, these words give a good idea of the situation at that time. Experimental science had been born. Galileo had the facts on his side, and one cannot argue against facts, even if the argument seems to rest on Revelation.

If the Galileo case was a great victory for reason, its ultimate result was advantageous to faith and theology. The theologians saw themselves obliged to re-examine their doctrinal synthesis. All this led to a much clearer and more refined concept of faith. After all, the question whether the earth moves around the sun or the sun around the earth, has no importance whatsoever for man's eternal salvation.

[2]As is commonly known, not only Catholic theologians thought that the ideas of Galileo were not in harmony with Revelation. In Germany, Luther and Melanchton opposed the system of Copernicus, and in Holland, it was condemned by the Calvinists, who considered it to be contrary to the divine truth revealed in Scripture. (Cf. G. Kernkamp: *De Utrechtse Academie,* Utrecht, 1936, Vol. 1, p. 248.)

The storm whipped up by the Galileo case was soon forgotten, at least in Christian circles. The conflict between incipient science and faith had been merely a passing crisis, from which theology itself was the first to draw benefit. It was only toward the end of the nineteenth century that the conflict threatened to flare up once more. Darwin launched his theory of the evolution of species, and, moreover, around the same time, history renewed its methods, thereby rising to the rank of a strictly scientific branch of knowledge.

In regard to the doctrine of evolution, sound reason quickly took the upper hand among both scientists and theologians. A distinction was made between evolution as a scientific theory and the philosophical evolutionism which proposes evolution as the *ultimate* explanation of man and other beings.

In regard to history, there is no doubt that the application of the new historical and literary methods to the study of sacred scripture brought to light many and difficult problems, and it was only slowly that theologians succeeded in determining the relations between revelation and history. The scientific honesty of Catholic historians and exegetes contributed much to that solution, so that once more theology derived great profits from its contact with a mature historical science.

The Present Situation. Without exaggeration, we may say that the tension between faith and science is now rather a thing that belongs to the past. Who would still dare to maintain that a Catholic cannot be a good man of science? In recent times, however, the problem concerning the relationship of faith and reason has taken a new turn. It is now concentrated on the meeting of faith and civilization. Since Marx and Nietzsche, the idea has spread in many milieus of unbelievers that Christianity blunts the believers' sensitivity to the *Diesseits* (the "here below"), that it makes them insensible to the historicity of all that belongs to this world-here-below, and that it thus constitutes an obstacle to civilization. "Religion is the opium of the people," according to Marx. Christian morality appeared to Nietzsche as being the ethics of tired men, who busy themselves more with the past rather than with dreaming about a better future. And Georges Bataille, his French disciple, has the following comment: "This ethics is less an answer to our ardent desires for reaching a summit than a bolt that shuts us off from those desires."[3]

Nietzsche's criticism of Christianity re-echoes in modern existential atheism. Christianity, it is claimed, is in conflict with the demand of a humanism worthy of our era. Faith in God, so runs the criticism, kills our sensitivity to the historicity of human existence; it often leads to fixism, dogmatism, and intolerance both in the search for truth and the determination of values.

"Recourse to the absolute," to God as the absolute foundation of truth and value, says Merleau-Ponty, not only solves no problems, but it undermines all true humanism. One who imagines that he is able to attain reality from the standpoint of the last source of being and thus to have an absolute standard at his disposal by which he can measure all truth and all value, no longer needs to search. Knowledge for such a man has reached its utmost frontier and the world of values is definitively closed. Anyone who does not agree with him, he considers to be a danger to mankind and at the first opportunity he will deny him the freedom to express his opinion. "When recourse to an absolute foundation is not useless, it at least destroys the very thing which it was supposed to establish. For if I imagine that I am able to reach, with evidence, the absolute principle of all thought and all evaluation—provided, of course, I have a conscience of my own—I have the right of withdrawing my judgments from the control of

[3]G. Bataille, *Sur Nietzsche,* Paris, Gallimard, 1945, p. 73.

others; these judgments then are endowed with a character of sacredness . . . . and I piously kill my enemies.[4]

We find the same predominant theme in Sartre's *L'existentialisme est un humanisme* and Simone de Beauvoir's *Pyrrhus et Cinéas.* Sartre maintains that he who believes in God and considers Him the ultimate foundation of truth and goodness, thereby clings to a world of eternal and unchangeable norms and thus destroys the creative function of freedom. "Man invents man," writes Sartre, that is, he invents the way in which man realizes himself in a free creation of man. "Life has no *a priori* meaning . . . . , it belongs to you to give it a meaning, and value is nothing else than the meaning which you choose to impart."[5]

Briefly, the Christian is by nature conservative and reactionary. His faith makes him long for a heavenly fatherland and imposes a revealed and unchangeable ethics on him; therefore, the Christian is not fit to fulfill his role in history with full freedom and independence. A Christian, so they claim, is less free than others, is less well equipped to tackle the problems of modern life; he is in a certain sense one who is doomed to "come always too late."

This accusation is widespread at present, and it is made not only by those who openly combat the faith but also by many who are well-disposed toward it. Moreover, it is not entirely groundless. We have already pointed out in our first chapter that Western Catholics have been slow in waking up to what was happening in our modern world, especially since the French Revolution. Whether faith in God and a divine revelation does not sometimes dull the sensitivity of the believer, to man's earthly existence and to secular history is a very important question. There are many people nowadays, especi-

---

[4]M. Merleau-Ponty, *Sens et Non-sens,* Paris, Nagel, 1948, p. 190. Cf. also p. 191, "Metaphysical and moral consciousness dies when brought in contact with the absolute."

[5]J. P. Sartre, *L'existentialisme est un humanisme,* Paris, 1946, p. 89.

ally among the intellectuals, who are truly concerned about this question. It undoubtedly deserves, therefore, a thorough and honest examination.

2. *Incomplete Answers*

We said purposely that the examination should be *thorough* and *honest.* We should, above all, be on our guard against being satisfied with "cheap" answers. These are answers which, because of their vague generality, are so undeniably true that it is not possible to say anything against them, except that they neatly sidestep the difficulty and, therefore, fail to satisfy anyone who is seriously troubled by the problem.

Moreover, such answers are dangerous precisely because we might foolishly imagine that everything has been done to eliminate the difficulty and remove the danger. We then resemble students who after their examination nourish the holy conviction that they did excellently because they spoke with such ease. When, after, they hear that they have failed, they know of course who is to be blamed—surely not the student but the professor. In other words, *we* are not responsible, but the others are! Cheap, glib answers are legion. We can reduce them to three categories.

God is the Source of All Truth. First, there is the abovementioned theological dictum of St. Thomas, which states that faith and reason must, in principle, be in harmony, since both proceed from God, the fountainhead of all truth and all value. This remains undeniably true and gives the ultimate basis on which faith and reason can be reconciled. However, it fails to tackle the practical difficulty, and it is with this that we are principally concerned. We are not trying to discover here how all the kinds of truth and goodness are unified in God, but how *we* here on earth can resolve the actual tensions between faith and reason, and what criterion we can use for that purpose.

One could reply: "We have the infallible word of God." True, but that God has spoken does not mean we have a telephonic connection with heaven. We find God's word in Scripture and Tradition, but it is interwoven with secular, historical and cultural concepts and expressions so that it is not always easy to determine which elements come from God and which come from man. In fact, we are faced here with the most difficult and also the most fundamental problem of the whole of theology: What do we mean when we say that God has "spoken" in the course of history and what criterion have we to distinguish God's Word from the word of man?

Grace Ennobles Nature. Secondly, there is another well-known answer: Grace does not destroy nature but perfects it, heals it, and elevates it. Grace is not a disturber of nature. On the contrary, it raises man to the supernatural order and even heals and perfects him on the level of his natural ability and endeavors. This also is true, but we should determine its exact meaning, for otherwise one might conclude that the faithful must necessarily lead in many fields of human knowledge and achievement since their nature attains to a higher degree of perfection. History shows, of course, that this is not so. A Christian physician is not by that fact more competent than a non-Christian. The world-champion in sports, the artists, the masters of philosophy, the Nobel-prize winners are proportionately not more numerous among believers than among non-believers. The believer has to work and study like anybody else if he wishes to be successful. Hence we ought to distinguish various dimensions in human existence and determine more precisely the frontiers where nature and supernature meet.

Childlike Obedience in Matters of Faith. Finally, there is an answer that is eagerly invoked especially in times of tension. The harmony, so they say, that exists between faith on the one hand, and science, civilization and social progress on the other, lies so deep in the very nature of all these things, that no conflicts are to be feared, as long at least as scientists, pioneers of civilization and social thinkers do not transgress the limits of their respective fields and at the same time are ready with a childlike faith to submit to the teaching authority of the Church. This again is true, but it gives only half an answer. When Galileo, the founder of modern natural science got into difficulties with the Holy Office, when Vesalius, the founder of modern anatomy, had to give up his research and sought protection at the Spanish Court against the Inquisition, the fault was not on the side of the scientists. Numerous theses that are now commonly held, in the realm of, e.g. the theory of evolution, the exegesis of the Old and the New Testament, democratic freedoms, the ethics of property, fifty years ago were suspected propositions, and this is putting it mildly; they could not be taught publicly because it was not known how they could be reconciled with the traditional teachings concerning faith and morality.

What follows from all this? That faith, or more exactly the way faith is proposed, the way we actually conceive the truths of faith, shows a structure that is subject to development and perfection. As long as the divine and the human mingle too much in the way faith is conceived, there is danger that secular truths will be drawn into revelation and that theology itself will transgress its frontiers, thereby making a conflict inevitable.

All this shows where our attention has to be focused. If we wish to arrive at an honest confrontation of Christianity with the sphere of secular civilization, it will first be necessary to have a clear understanding of the *meaning* and the *structure* of civilization.

3. *Meaning and Structure of Civilization and Culture*

To *civilize* means to refine; it points to our ability to transform the things of nature, to make them serve man, to make them articles of culture. *"Culture,"* on the other hand, which is derived from the Latin *"colere,"* "to till," likewise means to put a human stamp upon the things of nature. Hence both terms indicate that man takes hold of the raw materials furnished by nature ("la nature *inculte*" uncultivated nature, as the French call it) to beautify and ennoble them, or more exactly, to "humanize" them. We use the term "raw materials" here in a broad sense so that it signifies not only the objects of nature that *surround* us, such as wood, iron ore, flowers and trees, the vibrations of light which we transform into audible sounds etc., but also the human subject, the *self* with its corporeal and spiritual characteristics. Both terms, therefore, can be used in either a *subjective* or an *objective* sense, although these two senses can never be completely separated.

Subjective and Objective Culture

Civilization and culture in the subjective sense signify the refining and ennobling of the human subject himself, of man with his manifold corporeal and spiritual powers. In this sense we speak of body culture, culture of the mind and heart and, in general, say that some one is a civilized, a cultured man.

In the objective sense, civilization and culture refer to the totality of objective products by means of which man recreates his surroundings and makes them serve the purposes of his life and spirit. Thus he transforms them into a human *milieu,* into what we have called a "world," a world of culture which is man's creation, a product in which he expresses himself and in which he is mirrored. In this sense, language and writing, works of art and monuments, literature and scientific works, social and political institutions, laws and administration of justice are "objects of culture." Hegel called them the world of the objective spirit, that is, of the spirit which *expresses itself, objectivates itself* in objects.

These "spiritualized" objects are of supreme importance for man's life of the spirit. They make history and progress possible because they lie at the foundation of "intersubjectivity," i.e., the fact that human subjects, separated by time and space, are able to instruct and help one another. This interplay of learning and giving, of receiving and communicating, makes development, progress and history possible. Plato died long ago, but he continues to live in his work; and so, if we study philosophy, we can take him for our teacher and need not start "from scratch."

There is, then, a close connection between objective and subjective culture. Mankind must "express itself" to rise to a higher, nobler, more worthy humanity. As someone has said, "Man perfects himself only by perfecting the universe," he has to cultivate, to humanize the world if he wants to cultivate and humanize himself. Hence, culture, in the subjective sense, is the aim and purpose of culture in the objective sense. In short, culture is something *of* man and *for* man: the meaning and significance of culture lie in man and in man's growth in humanity.

Civilization, Culture, Humanism

We can now see why in ordinary language "civilization" and "culture," taken in a broad sense, mean almost the same thing.[6] Both expressions indicate the humanization of man and the world, and they are closely related to "humanism" when this term is taken in its broadest sense. "Humanism,"

[6] Sometimes, as on page 81, the term "culture" is taken in a narrow sense.

says Archambault, "is the constant concern, the respectful activity of man, for man and for everything that truly makes him a man."[7]

We see that "civilization" and "culture" are often used synonymously by the fact that we indiscriminately use the terms "history of civilization" and "history of culture." In the same sense we speak also of "ancient cultures" or "ancient civilizations."

Sometimes, however, the two terms are not perfectly synonymous but even somewhat opposed. Thus when it is said that to foster "the culture of the laborer" is one of the aims of the social movement, no one would replace "culture" by "civilization." Or again in the expression: "The Greek civilization is a thing of the distant past, but we still need to make Greek culture our own." It is difficult to determine why we spontaneously distinguish here between "civilization" and "culture" but the probable reason is that "culture" refers here to the spiritual aspect of this particular civilization.

However, it is not our intention to engage in linguistics, and we shall use the terms here as if they were synonymous. The thing that is more important is to examine the structures that are found in all civilizations and cultures and that ultimately rest on the structure of man's own being. Since culture belongs to the essence of man's being, we find echoes of our many-sided structure in all cultures. It will be useful to distinguish a horizontal and a vertical structure.

The Horizontal Structure

We understand by this term the above-mentioned *relationship between subjective and objective cultures,* which we must now examine further. This relationship results from our

[7]*L'Aube,* June 2, 1932. In a narrow sense the term "humanism" is often used for the humanistic ideal of the Renaissance, which had its origin in the rediscovery of classical or Greco-Roman antiquity.

bodily being, or more exactly, from the fact that to realize ourselves, to attain a richer internal life, we have to *"go out of ourselves,"* express, or *"exteriorize"* ourselves in an objective world of culture, the world of so-called "objectified spirit." In other words, we must transform our surroundings into a humanized milieu which unfolds all around us in an ever widening horizon of life. For this reason we speak here of an "horizontal structure."

Man exists as an *embodied spirit;* therefore, we should not look at the material world as an impediment to the life of the spirit but rather as an indispensable means to attain spiritual liberation and progress. It is impossible to accomplish even our most "immaterial" aspirations without the assistance of matter. No science is possible without laboratories; no esthetic sentiment has any value as long as it is not expressed in a work of art; there is no poetry without language; no philosophical life without books of philosophy; no social life worthy of man without social institutions and positive laws; no lofty moral life without good conduct, for good intentions alone do not suffice to turn us into good men. As we have already remarked above, there can be no culture in the subjective sense, that is, no self-realization of the human subject, without the ensemble of objective creations by which nature is transformed into a world of culture.

We see from all this that the relations between subjective and objective culture do not consist merely in a passive juxtaposition, but the two cultures actively influence each other. When man expresses his ideas, his sentiments and aims in objects of culture, these in turn will influence the ideas, the sentiments and aims of mankind. Thus, history will never come to a standstill. Every invention becomes the starting point of new research, every work of a philosopher is an invitation to further thought.

This mutual influence and interaction, however, does not run its course as a mechanical process. Man is not an automaton, and man's attitude toward the world is not that of a self-regulating machine in which everything *runs of its own accord.* If the artist produces works of art, the reverse is not true: works of art merely serve as *suggestions* for new artistic endeavors. Books of philosophy do not of themselves produce philosophical thinking; the work of Plato, for example, has to be personally studied if we wish to come under the influence of his personality.

Moreover, if objective culture is indispensable for the liberation of the human subject, it can also turn against man. Contemporary philosophy calls this the "ambiguity" of objective culture, which is like a two-edged sword. Man can become the victim of his own creations if he does not know how to make good use of them. For example, man's present ability to use atomic energy is an achievement without equal and contains the richest promises for the future, but it could also lead our planet to its doom.

The same truth applies to the highest spheres of culture. A flood of philosophical books and the multiplication of philosophical congresses can become an obstacle to sound and original thinking. Or to give other examples, *"Quid leges sine moribus"* says the proverb; "What is the use of having good laws if men do not keep them?" *"Summum jus summa injuria,"* i.e., a strict application of the law can in particular circumstances be cruel injustice.

Even religious life does not escape from the law of ambiguity. It is good for the Church to have at her disposition a number of religious and cultural institutions, such as schools, hospitals, youth organizations, trade unions, etc., if she wants to be fully efficient in her care of souls. But these same institutions can also lead to sociological stagnation and aloofness and become obstacles to the free preaching of the Word.

In short, in the world of objective expression everything is ambiguous. This is a very important point and is implied in the very nature of "expression." The fact that man's inner life of the spirit has to express itself and become embodied in the material world contains the danger of petrification. However, as long as man remains alert and listens to the voice of the spirit which has to "renew the face of the earth," history will continue to evolve.

The Vertical Structure

The structure we have considered until now is crossed by another, which we shall call *"vertical,"* because it is a consequence of the fact that there is in man a *hierarchy of spheres of life,* of *regions of truth* and *levels of values,* and these can hardly be described without the use of metaphors such as *"high and low," "superficial and profound."* We use, for example, the term *"super*sensible," as practically synonymous with *"spiritual."*

Why such imagery that originates in a vertical dimension (such as high and low) spontaneously arises in man is still a puzzle. Undoubtedly it is somehow connected with the bond that attaches his spirit to matter. Ultimately, we may connect it with the restlessness that characterizes his existence as embodied and limited freedom and constantly prompts him to "surpass" himself, to rise *above* himself. Man is, as it were, the meeting ground of matter and spirit, of heaven and earth. That is why he has been described as a "fallen deity" or again as "a sick animal," a dissatisfied animal that wants to *transcend* its animality. Man is polarized between two opposite tendencies, one trying to pull him *down,* the other striving to lift him *up.* As Simone Weil expresses it, "Two forces rule the universe: light and gravity."[8] Both forces come together in man.

---

[8]*Gravity and Grace,* London, 1952, p. 45.

Whatever may be the true reason for the important role which such imagery, borrowed from the vertical dimension, plays in human language, it cannot be denied that we find within the unity of our being-in-the-world a hierarchy of worlds, that is, of spheres of civilization, of fields of sciences and of values. This hierarchy corresponds to the hierarchy of levels of life.

The Sphere of Material Goods. First, there is the so-called sphere of material or biological goods, which we need to preserve and foster our biological existence: such as housing, clothing, comfort, care of health. All work of civilization begins with the endeavor to gain control over the raw and often hostile forces of nature and thus to make this world a better place to live in, to adapt it to man's biological needs and aspirations. It goes without saying that science and technology play the principal role in this matter.

The Sphere of Special Cultural Values. Secondly, there are what can best be called the particular spiritual or cultural values in the narrow sense. In everyday usage, the term "culture" does not have the wide meaning which we have attached to it above where we used it for the whole of creations by which man humanizes nature. In ordinary parlance the term "culture" indicates usually only a special sector of the whole which is distinguished from material and biological goods on the one hand, and moral values on the other. The sector in question contains the things that foster the free play of the mind. As such we may name science, not so much as a means to control nature, but as considered in itself, as the unfolding of pure, disinterested knowledge; philosophy, of which it is rightly said, "man must first live and then only philosophize"; art in its many forms, such as literature, plastic art, and the building of monuments; etiquette also and politeness in social conduct; in short the rich spheres of the so-called "useless" or "distinterested," which are sought for their own sake and not for any utilitarian reason. These we do not want to miss for anything in the world because they make life pleasant and beautiful, they bring sunshine, expansion and joy to our existence, for "man does not live by bread alone" (Matt. 4, 4). Accordingly, when we speak of a "cultured" man or a "cultured" people, it is to these particular spiritual values that we principally refer. We call them "particular" spiritual values because they foster only one or another form of mental life and therefore contrast with moral values which are also spiritual but have, as we shall see, a relation with the human person as a *whole*, as an "end in himself." A very cultured man is not necessarily a highly moral man or vice versa.

The Sphere of Moral Values. Thirdly, there is the sphere of morality or moral values. Why do we consider certain human activities to be morally good and others morally evil? In a broader perspective, why do we speak of a sound or high level morality or of moral decadence and deterioration, when we judge civilizations and their various institutions? What criterion do we use? Our norm is certainly not their material prosperity or their cultural refinement. Take, for example, the Nazi concentration camps. They were excellently organized from a scientific standpoint and were even used as experimental laboratories for physiology and biology. However, once we know that they used man himself as a guinea-pig, this fact indicates for us utter moral degradation. To use man as a thing or a beast, as a means for other things, goes counter to the dignity of the human person, and is condemned as immoral by everyone.

As Kant has stated it excellently in a formula that has become classical: "Never treat man, whether in yourself or in others, as a means but always as an end-in-himself." Here lies the fundamental principle of all morality. That which ennobles man, that which raises him above material things and the brute is the fact that he is a free and autonomous being, who has his own destiny and vocation, who is never merely for anything else, but an end-in-himself. In short he is a "person."[9]

Now there are some values which so intimately affect the person, which are so closely connected with the recognition of man as a free and independent being that to attack them is to attack the person. To facilitate matters we shall call them values that "constitute" the person, that "free" the person. The fostering of these values has always been considered a norm and standard of morality, so that they can justly be called *moral values.*

Prominent among those values are the following:

1. Respect for *life and death* (remember the world's revulsion from the concentration camps).

2. Love of *truth* and respect for the *honest search for truth.* For truth liberates man. Personal insight is the foundation of free personal activity. The human person is struck at the very core of his being and is treated as cattle when free search for truth is not tolerated or when it is replaced by lies, calumny, propaganda, and deceit.

3. A sense of, and love for *authentic freedom,* a freedom that rests on truth and understanding, that liberates man from the dictatorship of instinct and caprice, that renders him capable of assuming responsibility and remaining faithful to the voice of duty. When this sense for the seriousness of freedom fades away and is replaced by arbitrariness and

---

[9]"*Persona*" was the name given to the mask worn by the actor in the Roman open-air theater, hence it came to be used to signify the "role" played by the actor, finally to designate man as one who has to play an irreplaceable role.

levity, there is no longer any room for a social life worthy of man because the sense of responsibility has disappeared.

4. *Love,* in the noble sense of the term, that is, a love which loves the other for *himself,* because "it is *he*" and not merely because of his talents and qualities, for these can also be present in others. He who loves his wife, his child, or his friend only because of their talents or their money, or as long as he can draw profit from them, does not know genuine love. Love is unselfish, unconditional and faithful. This kind of love is the highest form of respect for the person and is, at the same time, a school in which reverence is taught; hence the importance for a child to belong to a family that is governed by love and fidelity. When love has lost that purity and seriousness in a society, the human person is in grave danger.

5. However, one cannot build a society with love alone. Respect for the human person must become embodied in more steady forms, otherwise the other's freedom will not be sufficiently safeguarded and will be abandoned to the whims and instability of sentiment. *Justice and law,* therefore, are necessary. These also are moral values. It is the purpose of law to determine and protect the sphere of what is "mine" and "thine," of what belongs to "us" and what belongs to "others."[10] "Mine" and "thine" must be understood here in a broad sense. It is not enough to be able to "possess" things; man must also have the power to "act," to play a role in the world (hence the right to work). It is not sufficient to have the right to dispose of some material goods; man must also have the liberty to follow the dictates of his conscience and to live his private and public life according to his religious convictions (freedom of conscience and of religion).

[10]The organization of ownership, as we shall point out further, is at the same time *private* and *collective;* in primitive cultures it was almost exclusively collective.

We do not claim that this list of moral values is complete, but it certainly includes the most important ones. Where these values are cultivated and honored, there exists, we say, a high level of morality; where they are trod under foot, there is moral decadence.

The Sphere of Religious Values. Finally, there is the sphere of *religion* and of *religious values.* That religious convictions exercise great influence on man's moral conduct needs no proof, but this does not mean that morality and religiousness are one and the same thing. It is not at all rare to meet unbelievers who have a great sense of responsibility, unshakeable honesty, and boundless concern for their fellow-men. A so-called "morality without God," or rather "morality without belief in God," can possess true ethical elements. Examples are the moral theories of Aristotle, Kant, Confucius, and Buddha.

Reversely, religiousness does not *of itself* produce moral virtuousness. The Christian religion imposes high moral requirements and is a powerful means for a good moral life, but this does not mean that religious belief and morality always and everywhere keep abreast; think, for example, of our Christian Middle Ages. It follows, therefore, that a religious education is not the same thing as a moral education.

What is it that characterizes the sphere of religion and religiousness? The typical element of all religious belief consists in this, that it attunes man to the Absolute, to the Holy, to what Professor Rümke calls the "deepest ground which man feels as the ground of his own ground."[11] The three previous spheres of values were related to my being-in-the-world, my relationship to the world and to the others in my world, and aimed at humanizing this being-in-the-world. My faith, however, directs me to the "Totally Other," to

[11]H. C. Rümke, *Karakter en aanleg in verband met het ongeloof,* Amsterdam. 1953, p. 18.

the awe-inspiring and fascinating mystery, the God or Divinity that transcends the world. This orientation takes place in an attitude of respectful fear, obedience, self-accusation and compunction, and surrender.

All this, however, does not mean that religious belief appears as a sort of *"superstructure"* on my being-in-the-world, nor does it necessarily take the shape of a flight from the world, a kind of *alibi,* a "being-elsewhere." Man remains an embodied ego even in his religion. He expresses his religious vision of life and the world in visible acts, such a rites and liturgical celebrations, in such objects as temples, icons, statues, sacred articles, and in moral acts. The history of civilization even shows us that religion more than anything else, has imprinted its stamp on the various cultures. The whole of Greek antiquity, for example, is mirrored in its temples, just as we find a reflection of the Christian Middle Ages in the cathedrals, and of Islam in its mosques. This is to be expected since religious faith claims to give an answer to the ultimate problem of life: What ultimately is man? In other words, it is an answer that gathers *all* human behavior and conduct into a single meaningful unity.

Interconnection of the Various Spheres

Much could be said about the concrete relationship and influence of the various spheres of truths and values. Let us restrict ourselves to point out that their interrelationship is dominated by a *twofold principle.*

There is first the principle of mutual *independence* or *autonomy.* Each one of the spheres of truth and value which we have described presents itself with a certain autonomy, develops according to its own vital rhythm and laws and, therefore, has, to a certain extent at least, its own particular history. Thus a man can be an excellent physician while having little feeling for art. There are civilizations whose technology is still in its infancy yet they possess a very refined artistic and moral sense. The reverse can also frequently be found. Accordingly, the history of technology does not completely coincide with that of art, of social institutions, of ethical and religious convictions and vice versa. Man is not a monolith.

Nevertheless, the autonomy proper to the various spheres of truth and value is not absolute. It does not mean that all these spheres are merely juxtaposed and that they grow or wither without influencing one another. If man is not a monolith, he is even less the sum of superposed blocks; he is rather a living symbiosis of insights into truths and value judgments.

Thus, alongside the principle of relative autonomy, we must admit the principle of mutual *interaction* and of the *ambiguity* flowing from it. For here also we find once more the important law of ambiguity. By ambiguity we mean that the mutual influence can be exercised in opposite directions. A particular value can equally foster or hinder the development of the other values.

A certain technique, for example, is indispensable for the creation of a work of art and new techniques may even open new artistic possibilities; nevertheless, art can also perish through too much technique, and this always happens when the artist becomes the slave of a particular technique. To give another example, pauperism has always been a source of much immorality and crime, but too much wealth and comfort can also foster sloth and heartlessness, and dull the sense of spiritual values. Likewise, as we have shown in the first chapter, the modern mentality can be advantageous to the faith, but it can also generate doubt about the faith.

This law of ambiguity is readily acceptable when we take into consideration that every value has the significance of a *situation* in reference to the other values. A world that is dominated by technology becomes a situation in regard to the philosopher, the artist or the religious man who dwells in this world and must deal with it if he wishes to accomplish authentic work. Much, however, will depend on the manner in which he conducts himself in regard to that situation, i.e., on the stand he will take. Every situation, then, is essentially ambiguous.

Guided by these principles, we shall now examine the question which was the starting point and the purpose of all these considerations: What is the relationship of Christianity and civilization? We shall first deal with the theoretical question, whether or not faith and civilization can in principle be reconciled. After that there follows the practical question of why it is that faith and civilization regularly come into conflict even though they are fundamentally reconcilable.

4. *The Encounter of Faith and Civilization: the Theoretical Question*

Christian faith has its source in divine revelation and, at least in the Catholic community, attributes to Church authority the power of determining the revealed truths of faith, that is, in theological language, to make dogmatic definitions; hence faith has a more or less explicit dogmatic character. We are thus led to ask ourselves: Can a faith that, as it were, comes from above and is led from above, be reconciled with man's *free, autonomous* and *ceaseless* search for truth, science and culture? And if the answer is in the affirmative, where and how does this meeting of faith and the creation of culture, of dogma and free inquiry take place?

The answer is readily available if we connect our conclusions regarding the Christian message of salvation to what we have said here about the meaning and structure of all human civilization. For, when we compare the analysis of the Christian Creed, on the one hand, to that of the vertical structure of civilization, on the other, we arrive at once at the two fundamental principles which dominate the whole problem of the relations of faith and the world and which we now intend to consider.

First Principle: Mutual Independence. "Revelation," which lies at the source of Christianity, is doubly divine. It not only comes from God, but its sole object also is the mystery of God and of God's work of salvation. Hence we have to do here with a purely religious revelation which as such, has nothing to do with secular science or the creation of culture and, therefore, in no way comes to disturb this world or will be disturbed by it.

Let us illustrate this by an example. Galileo was right when he said that he was unable to understand why the theologians of the Holy Office were opposed to his theories: What difference does it make for man's eternal salvation, he reasoned, whether the sun turns around the earth or vice versa?[12]

In fact, as Pope Leo XIII wrote almost three centuries later in his Encyclical *Providentissimus* concerning the Bible: "It could not have been the intention of the sacred writers, or rather . . . of the Spirit of God, who spoke through them, to instruct us about things that cannot be of service for the salvation of man, namely, the internal constitution of the visible world." And Pope Pius XII, in his Encyclical *Divino afflante Spiritu* concerning the significance of divine revelation as transmitted to us through Holy Scripture, specified further that: "Holy Scripture instructs us only regarding divine things, but it makes use of the ordinary language of men for that purpose."

The profound reason why religious faith, on the one hand, and free inquiry in the service of secular science and culture, on the other, are in principle not in conflict with each other,

---

[12]Descartes, the contemporary of Galileo, made the same remark in his famous *Discourse on Method.*

lies in the fact that we are here dealing with two different dimensions of human existence, dimensions of truth and of value, which, as we have shown in the previous section, do not belong to the same level. Science and culture want to subjugate the world of matter to man, to foster his being-in-the-world, i.e., to construct a world that is a dwelling place worthy of man. Religious faith, on the other hand, directs man to God, makes him free and fit for God, *"capax Dei,"* as Augustine expressed it. Now the Christian God is not a part of the things of this world. He is the Totally Other, the Transcendent, who, as we read in Scripture, "dwells in inaccessible light." To sum up, faith gives us "eternal life"; and this eternal life, this "life of grace," does not mean the endless extension of our earthly life through knowledge of biology, progress of medicine, and a greater control over the forces of nature. "Eternal life," as understood by theology, is the introduction of the believer into a community of life and love with the Eternal God, through adherence to God's Word and God's Spirit: "This is everlasting life," says Our Lord in St. John's Gospel, "that they may know thee, the only true God and Him whom thou hast sent, Jesus Christ" (John, 17, 3).

The ultimate basis of the possibility to reconcile secular civilization and religious belief must, therefore, be sought in the fact that both spring from *two distinct dimensions of existence,* or more precisely, from two distinct dimensions of freedom. On the one hand, there is the openness of existence that attunes us to the *world* and enables us to transform the power of nature over man into a liberating control of man over nature by means of work and culture. On the other hand, there is the even more radical openness of existence that attunes us to the Absolute, the "sacral," the awe-inspiring and fascinating mystery; in a word, the spontaneous religious "sense" which, with the help of God's grace, will enable us to make ourselves free for God and His work of salvation.

That there is question of two distinct dimensions of existence is of great importance for our subject, for it shows us that we really have to do here with an essential reconcilability. In other words, it does not depend on conditions of time or other circumstances, nor can it be destroyed by the progress of civilization or the development of Christianity. The one thing required is that each dimension remain faithful to its own nature and mission. Hence Auguste Comte and scientism were victims of an illusion when they imagined that science would eventually make religion superfluous, just as Marx and Lenin were mistaken when they maintained that the communist organization of society and its elimination of classes would automatically kill the religious aspirations existing in the world.

The religious dimension is not a prolongation of the secular dimension nor is religious faith a substitute for science or for an immature civilization. This might perhaps be true of archaic religions in which the exact frontiers between religion and magic, between faith and superstition, between the sacred and the profane are not yet clearly defined. The reason is that in these religions, God, or rather the gods that are worshipped without any idea of a Creator, are merely demiurges, competitors with man in his battle for control over nature. For instance, in the Prometheus' myth, Prometheus, prototype of man as discoverer and conqueror of nature's secrets through technology, is punished by Zeus, the supreme god, for having stolen the fire.[13]

Lenin is right to a certain extent when he writes: "The helplessness of the oppressed classes in their struggle against the oppressors leads as necessarily to faith in a happier hereafter, as the helplessness of primitive peoples in their battle against savage nature made them believe in gods, devils, and miracles." He seems to forget, however, that what he calls

[13]Cf. the following chapter.

"faith" is branded and rejected by Christianity as "superstition" and "misuse of faith."

This, then, is our first principle regarding the relationship between religion and the secular world. We could express it even more simply in this way. The Christian is a man like other men. The words which God spoke to mankind at the beginning of history, when there was not yet a distinction between Christians and non-Christians, "Fill the earth and subdue it" (Gen. 1, 28), are not cancelled or modified by the other divine words spoken by Christ to His disciples and in which He summed up the mission of Christianity: "Go, therefore, and make disciples of all nations, baptizing them in the name of the Father, and of the Son, and of the Holy Spirit, teaching them to observe all that I have commanded you" (Matt. 28, 19-20).

Second Principle: The Encounter of Religion and the World by Way of Ethics. When we wrote above that the Christian revelation, since it has a religious character, has nothing to do with the secular world of science and civilization, we meant that Christian revelation, as such, neither fosters nor impedes the development of science and our striving for control of nature. However, one should not conclude from it that we are dealing with two worlds existing and evolving in pure *juxtaposition.* Both meet *in man* and impose a task on one and the same human being. The Christian is and remains a man like everyone else. He must acknowledge and serve God in his capacity of man among men, that is, of one who is bound to the world and is the builder of a world. His religious life does not mean a flight from the world or from earthly existence, but gives it an additional depth and richer meaning.

The meeting within man of his faith and his secular task in the world takes place through what we have called the "third sphere of existence," the sphere of *morality* and of *moral values.* This is so because no culture worthy of man is thinkable without ethics, just as Christian faith would not be a living faith if it were divorced from Christian morals.

Without ethics no culture that is worthy of man is possible, for culture is something of man and for man. As we have already pointed out, science, technique, art and cultural refinement, when taken by themselves, are open to misuse, i.e., they can be used by man to oppress men. In other words, only then will they attain their full human meaning and value when they are borne and animated by an *ethical ideal,* that is, when they are put to the service of all mankind and work toward the genuine recognition of man by man.

There is, likewise, no living nor authentic faith in God without "works of faith"; and among these there is first of all that of caring for others "without distinction of persons." To the question of the Pharisees, "Master, which is the great commandment of the Law?", Jesus answered "Thou shalt love the Lord thy God with thy whole heart, and with thy whole soul and with thy whole mind. This is the greatest and the first commandment. And the second is like it: Thou shalt love thy neighbor as thyself. On these two commandments depend the whole Law and the Prophets" (Matt. 22, 36-39).

To love one's neighbor as oneself is not confined to satisfying, by means of charitable assistance, the most urgent necessities of our neighbor. It means also and above all effectively to desire for him what we desire for ourselves, such as health, education, civilization and culture; it means to wage an effective war for him against the evils which we fight to our own advantage; it means, therefore, e.g., to do our best to eliminate great economic and social inequalities and the oppression of man by man.

Hence, to be a Christian is not purely to serve God, but is also an ethics, a service of mankind; it is not merely a theology but also an anthropology. In the perspective of the Gospel message, the dignity of the human person acquires an excellence that has no equal in the previous history of civilization because even the least among men is the object of God's love; he is as it were a "sacrament"—to use the expression of Hans Urs von Balthasar—of Christ's presence in our midst. As Our Lord said concerning God's final judgment of man's conduct: "Amen I say to you, as long as you did it to one of these the least of my brethren, you did it to me" (Matt. 25, 40).

This lofty idea of every man's dignity has as its consequence that Christian morality presents itself as a high and demanding ethics and shows the utmost concern for what we have called the values that constitute the person. Christian faith greets the birth of a new man as a "blessing from God"; it approaches death with fear, for death marks the end of the earthly time of trial and the passage to the definitive Light: "May perpetual light shine upon him, O Lord!"

According to the Gospel, truth is something sacred for man, and trustworthiness is likened to the purity of the eyes and the straightforwardness of children: "Let your speech be, Yes, Yes; No, No," said Jesus. Since every man has eternal life and is thus worthy of an eternal love, Christianity honors the unbreakable bond of conjugal fidelity; and it does so as much out of respect for husband and wife as through concern for the child. For the human family—which is non-existent if there is no fidelity or love—is the first and indispensable school in which man must learn what it means to be a man, to be a being able to love unselfishly and to deserve similar love.

Hence also, Christian ethics demands tender love for the child, since a living human being, however helpless he may be, is a person. Likewise, since civil society exists for man and not man for that society, Christian ethics constantly underlines the personalistic character of all social action and, according to the words of Pius XII, it recognizes "truth, justice and love as the three foundation stones" of human society.

There is, then, no Christianity without a Christian ethics. Hence although Christianity is directed to the "beyond," it nonetheless influences our actions in the realm of the "here below," i.e., insofar as they constitute our being-in-the-world, foster science and promote civilization.

Doesn't this influence, one may ask, hinder man's free and autonomous search for truth, science and culture? The reply is in the negative. The fact that Christianity helps to direct and regulate human behavior by way of an *ethics,* is certainly no reason to accuse it of shackling freedom and progress, unless, of course, one wishes to identify autonomy with unhampered arbitrariness and savage lawlessness. It belongs to the very nature of a morality not to permit everything. Every ethics gives direction and norms and it would be erroneous to look at ethical norms as so many impediments in the way of freedom, for their purpose is precisely to make man's freedom possible. The driver, for instance, who observes the traffic rules shows that he is an autonomous and free man: he desires to keep the road open for everybody instead of driving wildly and becoming a danger to all. Likewise, Christian ethics does not permit us to murder our fellowmen, even though, as at Dachau, it be done for the advancement of biology and medicine; or it forbids us to enslave other peoples, even though it would be done to create "living room" for our own. Yet, who would claim that such prohibitions shackle freedom and progress?

Hence the question ought rather to be formulated in this manner: Is it true that Christian morality, since it is rooted in Revelation and claims eternal validity, is a static and unfruitful ethics, incapable of performing any creative work?

It is perfectly clear that Christian morality, if properly understood, does not deserve such a reproach. It certainly is not a complete code of minute and stiff rules of life which, once and for all, fixes all of man's actions. True it originates in an eternal, unchangeable core of value, in the fundamental fact of the absolute, inalienable value of the human person, or in theological language, the commandment of charity: "You shall love your neighbor as yourself." However, is there any ethical principle that has a more dynamic power, a greater creative value, a greater flexibility and inventiveness than love for our fellow man?

Thus, it would be entirely wrong for us to try to reduce Christian morality to a code of prohibitions. As in every other system of ethics, there are, of course, negative commandements such as, "Thou shalt not kill, thou shalt not steal." But these negative commandements are rooted in a foundation of positive values and norms, in respect and active concern for human beings. Christian morality, in that sense, has first of all a positive significance, and appears as a source of creative inspiration which must constantly animate, prompt and guide the actions of man as an I-with-others-in-one-and-the-same-world.

This creative and inspiring power contained in a well-conceived evangelical morality is not destroyed, as is sometimes maintained, by the fact that Christian religion appears in an ecclesiastical structure and by the fact that the Church claims the power of making pronouncements regarding faith and morals that have divine authority. For it is precisely the function of the ecclesiastical hierarchy to safeguard the soundness of faith and morals, to see to it that the Christian community remains faithful to the evangelical message. This the church authority does, among other things, through her authoritative pronouncements. These pronouncements either clarify disputed points of faith or put them in theological language, they define them *dogmatically*—or, when the integrity of Christian moral teaching is in danger, they help the faithful in forming their consciences. The authority of the church is, therefore, a religious authority, which is exclusively in the service of divine revelation, of a purely religious revelation. This prompts us to clarify the meaning of the term "dogma."

The word "dogma" generally does not have a pleasant sound for modern man. It makes him think of a taboo, a "forbidden" zone of research because he confuses two meanings of that term.

Firstly, there is a *secular* or *philosophical* meaning that makes "dogma" the equivalent of an irresponsible view. Its psychological, or in modern language "noetic," counterpart is "dogmatism." As Gabriel Marcel writes very appropriately: "Dogmatism is an attitude of mind rather than a doctrine. There is a kind of dogmatism of criticism, a dogmatic way of excluding dogmatism."[14] In other words, dogmatism is a certain attitude of mind, an unwarranted or arrogant positiveness of assertion. The inclination to dogmatism is a trait of the human mind and it is found everywhere, not the least in some milieus where religious dogmas are taboo and where, at the same time, anything that tears down religion is recklessly accepted and applauded without serious examination.

Secondly, the term "dogma" has a religious or theological meaning. As such, it refers to the religious mystery which has been revealed in Christ and to the formulation of the mystery that is proposed officially by the Church. For this reason theology refers to the final proclamation and formulation of a mystery of faith by the supreme ecclesiastical authority as a "dogmatic declaration" or "dogmatic defini-

[14]*Journal Métaphysique,* Paris, 1927, p. 315.

tion." The psychological correlative of "dogma," in the religious sense of the term, is not dogmatism but faith. "Faith" and "dogmatism" are not synonymous. Faith, for the Christian, is a free and responsible assent to God's revelation, an act of confidence in the liberating and saving work of God as revealed in the person of Jesus Christ.

For the Christian conscience, just as that of the unbeliever, there are no "restricted" zones of truth. On the contrary, even in theological matters there is a science whose task it is to reflect upon the truths of faith in order to get a more exact and more solidly established insight into the faith. For example, there is *Dogmatics* which seeks to determine the exact content of the faith, what precisely must be believed; there is the question of giving *a rational account of the faith,* or *Apologetics,* which seeks the motives that make faith a rational, free and responsible attitude of life; lastly there is *Moral Theology* which shows what faith demands of human conduct. This is why theology was defined long ago as *"fides quaerens intellectum"* (faith which seeks understanding). Theology is the endeavor of rational man enlightened by faith, to transcend the simple "faith of the charcoal burner" and rise to a mature and responsible life of faith through an evergrowing understanding and a stronger motivation.[15]

[15]Jean Jaurès, the socialist, was reported to have said before the French Chamber, February 11, 1895: "The thing that must be safeguarded before all else, the inestimable good which man has conquered amidst all sorts of prejudices, sufferings and struggles, is the idea that there is no such thing as a *sacred idea,* that is, a truth that man is not permitted to subject to a full investigaion. This liberty of the mind is the greatest thing on earth and it forbids that any interior or exterior power, any dogma should limit the human race in its perpetual effort and research."

A Catholic can agree with this demand for a free, ceaseless and never finished search in all fields. But what he rejects in the statement of Jaurès is his making "dogma" synonymous with "sacred idea" in the sense of a "truth that man is not permitted to investigate." The "sacred" in Jaurès' speech in synonymous with "taboo," and this surely points to an archaic concept of religion in the mind of the speaker.

We are certainly allowed to conclude from this analysis that a true Christianity, one that is open and not petrified, cannot be an obstacle to the progress of civilization. It gives, on the contrary, the best guarantee for progress that will tend to benefit all mankind and bring a little more love, joy and peace into the world. The reason is that Christianity assigns such a lofty place to man in the perspective of the evangelical view of life.

Atheism, on the other hand, can be dangerous for mankind, according to a frequent judgment of both believers and unbelievers, and that opinion is not completely groundless. For what is a "man-without-God"? According to atheistic materialism, in the *last analysis* the individual man is reduced to being a mere passing "moment" in cosmic evolution, a handful of molecules and atoms which fall apart at death. It is evident that where such ideas are accepted, the respectful fear for the "holy," the "admirable," and the great miracle which man himself is, is in danger and might even disappear altogether. When there is no longer any holy fear and everything becomes banal, there is danger that man himself will be treated as a mere handful of atoms. It is this thought that made Dostoevski tremble and caused him to say in *The Brothers Karamazov*: "If there is no God, then everything becomes permissible." And the words of Cardinal Saliège, "Unbelief ends by making man ferocious," have unfortunately been confirmed by history.[16]

5. *The Practical Question*

In principle, faith and civilization can live peacefully together, but in practice history reveals tensions and even conflicts between them. The Galileo case is perhaps the most

[16]Cf. Cardinal Saliège, *Menus Propos,* Vol. 4, p. 26. In all honesty, however, we must add that religious faith also has led to much fanaticism and cruelty; as is exemplified by the Inquisition and religious wars.

famous, but it is not an isolated case. It would be an endless task to go over and examine all similar historical facts in order to determine exactly what happened and who was responsible. What is of primary importance for us is to find out the source from which the conflicts usually originate and what we can learn from them, in other words, what their meaning is. Before doing this, let us make two remarks.

First, we should not exaggerate or dramatize these conflicts. When we look back and consider the twenty centuries that separate us from Christ, we see that most of the time the relations between Christianity and the world were rather good. Apart from periods of war and tension, we find mainly understanding, cooperation, and mutual fruitfulness. History teaches us the important role which the Church and Christianity have played in the "making of Europe" and the formation of Western civilization.[17] We can confidently say that the idea of freedom of conscience and the autonomy of the human person, which are perhaps the core of Western civilization, are the fruit of the long battle for emancipation which the Church herself has fought in opposition to the despotism of medieval emperors and kings.

Secondly, in regard to the conflicts themselves, it would be wrong to put all the blame on the Church. The secular lay community is not without guilt. If the Church sometimes failed to observe the word of Our Lord, "Render to Caesar the things that are Caesar's," the State and the temporal powers have frequently failed to "render to God the things that are God's." If there is a professional deformation of the clergy called "clericalism," there is likewise a professional deformation of the layman, called "anticlerical laicism." If the Church has unjustly condemned Galileo, how often haven't the men of science attacked the Church by allegedly scientific arguments? How often, for

[17]Cf. Christopher Dawson, *The Making of Europe.*

example, hasn't the theory of evolution been misused to make simple people believe that modern man can no longer accept the idea of creation?

All this shows that we must not exaggerate. From the historical viewpoint, tension and conflict are easily understood. But what deserves most of our attention is the meaning of these conflicts. How do they arise? What can they teach us? When these questions are asked, it is useful to make clear the distinction between the tensions that occur in the field of speculative truth between faith and science, and the others which directly concern the progress of civilization.

The Tension Between Faith and Science

Why can and do difficulties arise although the two fields of truth are distinct? The reason is rather simple. Conflicts will arise when either faith or science transgresses its own boundaries. We have just given the example of science combating faith with "scientific" arguments. But faith also has sometimes thwarted scientific work with improper interventions. How, we may ask, could this happen?

The proper object of faith is the religious mystery of salvation itself, the mystery of the living God, what He is in Himself and what He is and does for man. But to adhere to this mystery by faith, we need to represent it in a complex of concepts and propositions concerning God and His redeeming love. Although the mystery itself transcends all human concepts and representations, nonetheless, to a certain extent, it can be indicated and expressed in language; we know it and can make it known to others. If this were not so, the very idea of a divine revelation would evaporate and the preaching of the faith would be impossible (hence the importance of dogmatic definitions).

Now it is clear that we can distinguish two things in every representation of the mystery of faith. On the one hand, and this belongs to the essence of the representation of the faith, there is that which is necessary to designate the mystery in a correct and authentic manner. It is not possible to believe truly in God and creation without a correct concept of God and of creation. He who confuses God and the world cannot adore God "in spirit and in truth." The same applies to the Incarnation of the Divine Word and all other mysteries of faith.

On the other hand, a number of accessory elements can enter into a representation of the faith, elements which have nothing to do with the nature of the dogma. We mean the many secular, historical, cultural images and sentiments that inevitably creep into every representation of the faith and accompany its expression. Thus a child can have a true idea of God and believe in Him, although he represents Him in a childish fashion as a good Old Man with a beautiful flowing beard. This surely does not belong to the essence of the dogma. The film *Green Pastures* showed how certain Negroes represent God and creation to themselves. So also, it is now generally accepted that the Bible story of creation and the Fall must be read as a religious story with religious meaning, but a story which was conceived and written in a popular way.

Thus, we readily see how our concepts of faith are very often tainted with images and sentiments that have nothing to do with faith but are purely extraneous elements attached to it. Here lies the source of conflicts. Now it is precisely the task of theology to distinguish what is essential from the accidental and relative and thus reach a purer concept of faith, namely, a truer understanding of the mystery itself. For this reason, as we have noted before, faith is described as "faith that seeks understanding," as man's reflection upon the faith for the sake of a more authentic understanding of it.

It is easy to understand that such a work of purification is not accomplished without struggle or friction. Growth of faith, by which faith becomes more truly and consciously itself, is subject to the same laws as every other self-realization and self-conquest. No conquest is possible without struggle. We can thus say confidently that the famous Galileo case was not merely a great victory for reason, but that it was also a blessing for the faith and theology. Since the time of Galileo, we have a much clearer idea of what we ought to seek in revelation and what we must not look for. We understand better now that revelation has a much greater and more transcendent meaning than has sometimes been attributed to it. Revelation is a religious revelation of salvation, for it is fundamentally an unveiling of God's being and saving love. To speak of a revealed astronomy or biology is to profane revelation itself and prevents us from contemplating and accepting it in all its splendor.

The Tension Between Faith and Civilization

As we have pointed out at the beginning of our study, the conflicts between faith and science are now mostly a thing of the past, at least in the part of the world that does not live under the Marxist regime; for in the latter it is still commonplace to say that science has once and for all refuted the "naivetés" of religion.[18]

Hence we have a more immediate interest in tensions that directly affect the development of civilization because they occur on the level of social practice. Catholics, especially since the fall of the Old Regime have been rather slow in accepting the great revolutions occurring in the economic, social and political realms. It suffices to recall their first reactions to the democratic freedoms and religious tolerance,

[18]See below, Chapter Four, *The Prometheus' Myth and Contemporary Atheism.*

the social struggle for the emancipation of the proletariate and the establishment of what has come to be called "economic" and "social" democracy. But these conflicts did not originate from one side only, and it would be wrong to put all the blame on the Church. Nevertheless, it would be difficult to exonerate the Catholic community and to deny that it was guilty of slowness, lack of comprehension, and a certain conservatism.

In any case, it is important to remark that these tensions on the practical level generally differed in kind from the conflicts between faith and science, and also had a different origin. Their source must be sought in the realm where faith and civilization meet, namely, in the sphere of ethics. In fact, it would be easy to show that most of the tensions between Christianity and the world on the level of social practices have originated in ethical conflicts: a particular social ethics seemed to be against Christian ethics and thus led sometimes to a condemnation of it as sinful. We shall return to these conflicts in Part Three where we will deal with *Faith and Politics.* For the present we merely wish to ask ourselves why Catholics have shown such slowness and an attitude of reservation, especially during the last two centuries, in spite of the dynamic character of their morality, which is based on respect for one's fellow men without distinction of persons.

Various explanations can be given for these conflicts. They are, as it were, the reverse side of every ethics that draws its deepest inspiration from a religious revelation. It is indeed not an easy matter to live with one's heart in heaven and at the same time to keep one's feet planted on the earth. Christian ethics is neither a self-evident ethics nor free from dangers.

The Danger of Clericalism. First there exists especially in Roman Catholic milieus, a permanent danger of clericalism.

And this becomes more evident when we recall what power was actually exercised by the clergy in medieval society and under the Old Regime.

Clericalism is nothing but a vocational deformation of the clergy. Every calling is exposed to contracting its own specific deformation because it develops a sensitivity to particular values, so that certain values come to the fore whereas others fall into the background. The danger consists in this: that everything is approached and judged through that particular sense and scale of values. Let us give a few examples.

The priest or the monk who has never gone to see a movie or visited a theater will readily say that all this is a useless or dangerous pastime, because he either lacks information or nourishes a hidden resentment. He will find it hard to understand that some laymen attach great importance to those things. The cleric or religious looks at the relationship between subject and superior from the standpoint of his relationship toward ecclesiastical authority, which is of a sacred nature. Thus the superior becomes everywhere "one who rules in God's name." This, then, he applies not only to pope and bishop but also, without making the necessary adjustments, to the ruler in regard to his people, and to the employer in respect to his employees. In this way "Throne and Altar" are raised equally to the dignity of being symbols of God's sanctity and sovereignty. Submission becomes the best way to accomplish God's will.

It can hardly be denied that all this, to a certain extent, has played a role in the reactions of a part of the Catholic hierarchy and Catholic believers to the emerging political and social democracy. Moreover, many Catholics have not yet freed themselves from a certain paternalistic way of thinking. Frequently, for instance, we hear the remark that modern man has no longer any respect for authority. In my opinion this is not entirely correct, we should rather say that there is a new attitude toward authority. The modern student still preserves a very great esteem and respect for the professor who is well-versed in his field and works hard, just as the simple laborer continues to have an almost child-like admiration for a capable, understanding and just man of superior rank.

Clerical Morality. Secondly, the fact that, until recently, because of the scarcity of lay theologians, both the study and the teaching of Christian morals were almost monopolized by the clergy, has had the result that morality was studied and taught especially with an eye on the confessional. Consequently, the negative commandments, the things that cannot be done without sin, have been over-emphasized. As Professor Jacques Leclercq, of Louvain University, has often pointed out: until about twenty-five years ago the literature of moral theology consisted almost exclusively of, on the one hand, numberless treatises about sin and on the other, "treatises of perfection" for priests and religious, plus a few little books of devotions for the laity.

It is hardly surprising, therefore, that many Christians were satisfied with paying attention to the negative, the prohibitions, and neglected *social morality* whose task it is to create more just conditions, to improve inter-human relations through more equitable laws and sounder economic and social institutions. Through this neglect the morality of ownership was sometimes reduced to "You shall not steal, but respect the property of others." But this negative aspect of the ethics of ownership is but the reverse side of the positive ethical duty, of striving relentlessly for a better distribution of the goods of this world, for more equal opportunities to secure a decent living, and for a more genuine recognition of man by man.

Lack of Sense for History. The third factor that has played a role in the conservatism of a part of the Catholic community is a certain lack of historical sense. This also is connected with what we have called the clerical character of traditional moral theology. The specific role of the clergy is to be servants of the Eternal; they must direct men to the things that are above, making them see earthly life in the light of eternal and supernatural realities, which precisely, are the object of revelation. This certainly is a most sacred function. It has not only a sanctifying significance for man's earthly existence but also plays a hygienic role, for it fosters that spiritual freedom without which, as we have already shown, man so easily becomes a slave of his own earthly creations.

However, this function also has its reverse side and conceals a danger. It may easily happen that man forgets to pay attention to the *historical mobility* of earthly realities and makes some of them, such as particular social regimes and legal relationships, absolute when they are, in reality, only relative.

In principle, Christians enjoy a very great freedom of thought and action. There is no room in Christianity for dogmatic apriorisms in social and political questions. As Leo XIII repeatedly wrote, God has entrusted the economic and political organization of the world "to human reason and the institutions established by peoples."

However, when one carefully reads especially the older commentators of these social teachings of the Church, he gets the impression that in their eyes this freedom was very theoretical and abstract. As soon as there is question of changing from one economic or political regime to another, they suddenly show so much prudence and severity, and impose so many conditions before such a change can be made, that in practice there is not much else to do but to keep the existing regime with a few corrections. This severity has its source in a lack of historical sense and too static an interpretation of the idea of "common welfare."

6. *Conclusion*

To cut a long story short, the harmony between Christianity and civilization is not so much a theoretical problem as a practical program of life. Man's being, Heidegger has said, is a "having to be," a project and task for man. This is true for every level of human existence. It is also true in the matter of creating harmony between the various levels.

Hence everything finally comes down to a question of sincerity, fidelity and openness, both in our being-Christian and our being-man. The thing that is dangerous for the integrity of the faith and for the development of culture, is dogmatizing one-sidedness, "apartness," and closedness.

CHAPTER FOUR

THE PROMETHEUS' MYTH AND CONTEMPORARY ATHEISM

These reflections on the myth of Prometheus have no other intention than to shed a little more light on the special themes of the preceding chapter about *Religion and Civilization* by recounting some concrete data.

In Greek mythology, Prometheus is one of the most famous "Titans," the descendants of Uranos and Gaia (Heaven and Earth). It was he, so it is said, who stole fire from heaven, brought it to earth in a reed, thereby drawing the vengeance of the gods upon himself. Zeus, the supreme god, finally chained him to a rock in the Caucasus. He is considered the father of technology, the prototype of man who engages in a battle with the savage forces of nature by means of science, technique and civilization.

As we shall show more fully later on, the gigantic development of technology is the chief event of our own time. It determines and marks our twentieth century way of being-in-the-world, and of meeting this world in a whole of situations and tasks. No wonder that the ancient myth of Prometheus has been removed from oblivion and has become the symbol of our so-called "Promethean Age."

But, apart from this wonderful soaring of technology, and to a certain extent, in connection with it, our time is also characterized by a violent recrudescence of atheism. This atheism announces itself as the humanism of our era, the humanism of the Promethean man who has not only overcome nature but, like Prometheus, has dared to attack the gods and has managed to free himself from belief in, and subjection to God.

In other words, present-day atheism presents faith in God and the hereafter as an estrangement. By faith, so says the modern atheist, man, as it were, alienates himself, becomes a stranger to himself, to become the affair of the Other or God. Faith, then, would force a man to alienate the most essential feature of his nature, his task of humanizing himself and his world by means of work and culture, to another (to God), and to expect to be saved by him. Man thereby renders himself incapable of achieving the emancipation of mankind.

Especially in times of want, when man feels helpless in the presence of the brutal and blind forces of nature and is the plaything of historical events, he runs for help to God and his saints. Instead of making a profound investigation of the true causes of his misfortune and taking the necessary measures to prevent further calamities, he turns to the Lord with the prayer: "From plague and famine and war, deliver us, O Lord." It is not prayer but the progress of technique, of medicine and economics that has freed man from famine and epidemics.

In the sight of the modern atheist, recourse to God is but a cry of despair and a shameful capitulation, in short, a flight from one's earthly task. And this, according to the atheist, would explain why all religions, and especially Christianity, show a tendency toward conservatism. The existing conditions, such as the centuries-old social inequalities, and the so-called established order—which often is an established disorder—are considered signs of the Divine Will. Inevitably this leads to a "morality of resignation." No wonder, therefore, that "Religion is opium for the people," as Marx declared.

In this way, Prometheus is reinstated as the model and symbol of modern mankind. *"No More Chains for Prometheus,"* is the title of an article by Professor B. E. Bykovsky in the Russian review, *Nauka I Zhizn'* (*Science and Life*),

1957, no. 2. He claims to prove that modern civilization and religion are incompatible. According to this author, the battle for the conquest of nature has long been hampered by religion because religion always claimed to *know things better* than science and to *know better how to do things* than technology. Marxism, however, will *once and for all* free mankind from that domineering belief in God and free Prometheus from the rock to which he is chained, by announcing the gospel that God and the gods are dead. It is very instructive to note that modern atheism, and especially the Marxist variety, reintroduces the myth of Prometheus.

1. *The Meaning of the Prometheus' Myth*

A characteristic trait of modern thought, in particular in the philosophy of religion, is that the ancient mythologies are taken seriously. The modern thinker sees more in the myth than a childish fable, a foolish fantasy spun by peoples who had not yet attained logical thinking and mistook their dreams for reality. "In the last decennia," writes the famous Dutch phenomenologist of religion, G. van der Leeuw, "there has grown up an ever stronger conviction that the myth is not the product of a fanciful imagination nor a poetic license, but a very practical affair, which plays an organic and most important role in the whole life of a people."[1] Mircea Eliade, the great modern ethnologist of religion, writes similarly: "The myth is not a childish and aberrant creation of primitive human beings, but the expression of a way of being-in-the-world."[2]

The myth, in other words, is the attempt of primitive man to express in a *symbolic way,* namely, in a symbolic story, a

[1]G. van der Leeuw, in *Winkler Prins' Encyclopedie,* 1952, under *Mythe.*

[2]Mircea Eliade, *Mythes, Rêves et Mystères,* Paris, 1957, p. 19.

fundamental experience of his existence, that is, an aspect of his connection with the world or his relationship to the mystery of Being. Thus, the myth is not a foolish creation of the imagination devoid of all meaning or truth value. It even played an eminent role in the individual and collective life of the ancient peoples, for it expressed something important to them. We may compare it to the way the flag speaks to modern man, by making him see and feel a certain value, not by means of concepts but by the revealing power of a symbol. The myth, then, belongs to the world of symbolic thought and representation.

The Prometheus' myth in particular is a sort of pre-philosophical expression, in symbolic language, of the wondrous adventure that is the history of technology and civilization. We find in it, as it were, an attempt of early man to understand and represent symbolically the twofold paradox of technique. Let us see in what this twofold paradox consists.

Human Conquest and Gift of the Gods. First of all, technique appears to man undoubtedly as a human conquest, the result of his own daring initiative, but at the same time he sees it as a favor from heaven, a grace from above, a gift of the gods. In reality, man cannot claim that he "invented" fire. Fire was already there, as a power hidden in the heart of nature. "To invent" always means "to come upon" something, to discover something. It means, to a certain extent, to steal something; whence we speak of "robbing" nature of her secrets.

What is said here about technique applies to all human creation. Man is never a creator pure and simple, the absolute origin of his creations. Every work of man bears the imprint of a twofold finiteness, a twofold dependence. On the one hand, it has an intrinsic dependence on pre-existing materials of the external world, for to create, as applied to man, means to transform nature into culture. On the other hand, it means an intrinsic dependence on an interior and spiritual appeal which underlies, inspires and animates every great human undertaking. Everything great and beautiful and noble done by man is born of an inspiration. "Inspiration" means that man, as it were, discovers a Power in himself which makes an appeal to him. As G. van der Leeuw writes, when man "discovers Power in himself, it is 'other,' it is holy. In other words, man finds in himself something else than what he is himself, something foreign that is in him but not of him. . ., there is something or someone in him that is other or more than himself."[3] For instance, the idea of the "Muse" of the Romans and the "Daimon" of the Greeks. This is why every great work of man is felt and interpreted as being both result of personal initiative and a gift of the gods.

The Ambiguity of Technique.[4] Secondly, technique contains another paradox, the ambiguity inherent in every cultural creation. Technology frees man while, at the same time, it chains him; technology is both a promise and a threatening danger for man. How often in the course of history has man not become the victim of what he had created for his own liberation.

What the myth of Prometheus expresses is precisely the meeting of these paradoxes. Technique is, as it were, the ground where man faces a world of non-human and superhuman forces and gets involved in a struggle whose outcome is never a complete victory for man. Everything happens as if man's victory over nature brings with it the wrath of the gods: Prometheus steals the fire in a battle against the gods, but his victory is not complete; he is punished and chained to a rock.

---

[3]G. van de Leeuw, *De verhouding van God en mensch vroeger en nu,* Amsterdam, 1940, p. 26.

[4]Cf. Andrew G. van Melsen, *Science and Technology,* Pittsburgh, 1961, Ch. XII, (Tr).

If this is the meaning and the serious purpose of the Prometheus' myth it is not surprising that we find it again and again in most varied forms and under the most different names in almost all ancient religions. It represents man's first reflection on the great mystery of technique. At the same time, however, it mirrors man's reflection at an archaic stage of human thought, i.e., it represents a way of thinking in which the sphere of the *sacred* and the *profane* are scarcely distinguished. The reason for this is that there is not yet any idea of creation and no clear distinction between creature and Creator; hence the gods, even the highest among them, are only demi-gods, they rise above the world of man and nonetheless still belong to this same world.

The world of man, according to that concept, belongs at the same time both to man and to the gods. Man, in his struggle for the control of nature, meets the gods and must try to get them on his side. In the Old-Italian culture, mariners must dread Neptune who rules over the seas and appease him with sacrifices and prayers, just as the hunter must take account of Diana, the goddess of the forests. This explains why, according to archaic thought, technique is considered less a conquest of man over *nature* than a victory won over the *gods,* a rebellion against them, an invasion of the domain reserved to the gods.

Unquestionably, the Prometheus' myth brings us back to primitive man who, because he has no clear concept of divine transcendence, mingles and confuses the profane and the sacred, the natural and the supernatural and therefore also the *fabulous* and the *historical.* For it is also characteristic of mythical thinking to "negate temporal progress" and through the myth "to cling once more to a primordial event that serves as a model for man's daily conduct and acts as the authority upon which he bases himself. The myth has the nature of an exemplar: daily conduct has no value in itself, but becomes valuable only by repeating the mythical event [by means of religious and magic rites]. Everything in the myth is, as it were, eternal and belongs to all times.[5] For this reason, mythical thinking is irreconcilable with a clear realization of the historicity of human existence.

In short, the gods of archaic religions are but demi-gods who, together with man, rule over the world and, like men, are subject to Fate. Hence, man in a certain sense, competes with the gods and interprets his victories over nature as a defeat of the gods. In this way technique and religion are irreconcilable, for technique acquires the meaning of a rebellion. Man is thus faced with a dilemma: either he places himself on the side of Prometheus, the prototype of mankind's rebellion against Zeus, the supreme god, in order to make himself free and work out his own salvation, or man fears Zeus and chooses a morality of resignation in, and subjection to Fate.

All this, however, is meaningful only at the mythical stage of thinking, i.e., as long as man still confuses the profane and the sacred because he does not yet make a clear distinction between creature and Creator, he does not yet take into account the multidimensional character of human existence.[6]

The religion of Israel and of Christianity freed the world from the Prometheus' myth by introducing the idea of creation and the related idea of a transcendent and personal God. The ancient antithesis between technique and religion thus lost all meaning. Man is created "after the image and likeness of God." Just as God rules in heaven so man will establish his dominion on earth: "Increase and multiply and fill the earth and subdue it and rule over the fishes of the sea and the fowls of the air and all living

---

[5]G. van der Leeuw, *Mythe* in *Winkler Prins' Encyclopedie,* 1952.
[6]Cf. above, page 87.

creatures that move upon earth" (Gen. 1, 28). Such is the position of God and man according to the Bible. In this perspective there is no room for the above-mentioned dilemma: man, by subjugating the earth, fulfills God's own appeal to man.[7]

Together with this came a better understanding of the distinction between the profane and the religious, for God is not a part of the things of this world. He is the "totally Other," and man is not permitted to make graven images of representations of Him. The fabulous element of the myth thus automatically disappears to be replaced by a living reality of *history*. Because openness to the world and receptivity to the mystery of the transcendent God are two dimensions of our existence, history, at last, will provide the necessary space for both the sacred and the religious history of salvation and the secular history of culture.

2. *The Prometheus' Myth as Symbolic Expression of Atheïsm*

Taking all this into account, we may say that the weak point of Marxism with respect to religion consists in the fact that it still clings to the legend of Prometheus and in this matter continues to dwell on the level of the myth. In its critique of religious faith, Marxism makes no distinction between the gods of polytheistic religions and the Transcendent and thrice holy God of Christianity. Some may read this assertion with astonishment and suspect us of apriorism, but the texts them-

[7]It must be admitted, however, that ancient Israel did not immediately reach a pure idea of the position of God and man. Even the Bible shows traces of what we have called the Prometheus' myth; thus we read in Gen. 11, 5-9, concerning the tower of Babel: "The Lord came down to see the city and the tower which the children of Adam were building. And He said, 'Behold . . . they have begun to do this, neither will they leave off from their designs, till they accomplish them in deed.'" In other words, "this is only the beginning of their enterprises. If they are not stopped now, there will be no limit to their designs."

selves are too eloquent to be so easily disposed of. Commenting on Marx' famous statement, "Religion is the opium of the people," Lenin remarks that it is "the cornerstone of the Marxist idea of religion." "In fact," he tells us, "wherever the proletariate knows no other prospect than the unavoidable necessity to labor for others in poverty and dereliction, religion appears in the form of spiritual oppression. The helplessness of the exploited classes, in their struggle against the exploiters, inevitably generates in them a belief in a better hereafter, just as the helplessness of primitive peoples, in their warfare against savage nature, gave birth to belief in gods, demons, and miracles."

An Anthology of Marxist Articles on Religion. At the beginning of these considerations we referred to the article of Prof. B. E. Bykovsky, in the Russian Review, *Nauka I Zhizn (Science and Life)*, entitled *"No More Chains for Prometheus."* The purpose of the author was to show the radical impossibility of reconciling religion and technology. His reasoning gives evidence of incredible naïveté.

"When we compare science and faith," says that author, "we see that they cannot be mutually complementary and beneficial, for they are mutually exclusive, paralyze and fight each other. Science and faith are incompatible, not only in some specific conclusions and positions, but they are always and everywhere antagonistic by their very nature, by their idea of the object and the method of knowledge. . . . Religion makes use of the gaps still left empty by our scientific knowledge and it penetrates through every chink and crack that is still found in the modern scientific view of nature."

It is clear that in such a monolithic view of man's world of truth, science and religion are inevitably engaged in perpetual warfare, and religious faith will tend to reserve to itself all kinds of "forbidden zones."

However, continues Professor Bykovsky, in this it is not successful, for "even religious experience, the sentiments and psychic attitudes that are connected with religious faith, can become the subject of scientific investigation. The origin and development of religion and morality are subjected to scientific analysis just like any other form of collective and individual consciousness. Modern science has already made important contributions to the study of those phenomena." Professor Bykovsky forgets, however, that most of these "important contributions" have been made by Christian believers and theologians, and that the scientific study of the religious phenomenon occupies a very important place in every modern theological faculty.

The same review, *Science and Life* (1957, no. 2) published another study of the same topic, authored by a Mr. Jacovlef, under the title: *"Two Irreconcilable Views of the World."* Here the argumentation is even more arrogant. The author rightly complains that the faithful generally have a wrong and vulgar concept of materialism, seeing in it nothing but a mode of life that is wilfully closed to all that is spiritual. For many, a materialist is a man "whose god is his stomach." "The assertions of the faithful," says the author, "that the materialistic view of the world has an eye only for base, material interests and rejects all higher ideals and moral values, is pure calumny." We are glad to be able to agree, but it is equally slanderous to assert, as is done in said article, that "every advance in the scientific study of nature has always further undermined the foundations of religion," and that "it is only the hopeless misery of the oppressed that forces them to place their hopes in miracles, from which the theologians then conclude to man's so-called irrepressible need of religion."

Let us add one more example of this peculiar line of argumentation as found in another recent study published in that same monthly, *Nauka I Zhizn'* (*Science and Life*), 1958, no. 8. The article is written by a Mr. Goudojnik and deals explicitly with the relations between *Religion and Technology.* "Man's active intervention in the processes of nature and his systematic transformation of nature to make it become the servant of society have always been accompanied by a struggle with religious doctrine. The sacred books of all religions contain the idea that man is not permitted to change nature, since it was created by God and therefore must be perfect. Does not the Gospel say, 'Be not solicitous for what you will eat or drink? Look at the birds.' This is also the reason why religion is opposed to man's scientific investigation of the world, since the latter is so closely connected with man's productive and transforming intervention in the processes of nature. . . . It suffices to recall the biblical legend about the Fall. The first human couple was cursed and expelled from paradise because it had transgressed the prohibition of eating of the tree of knowledge of good and evil. Man is not permitted to possess any other knowledge than that which is revealed by God, for, according to the concept of every religion, knowledge is a privilege that God reserves to Himself."

And in regard to the meaning of work, Goudojnik has this to say in the same article: "Labor, according to the Bible is a curse, a punishment for sin. Hence we see how in the Bible the laboring slave is considered to be a despicable being, belonging to the same level as the animals. For instance, according to Genesis 12, 16, Pharao overwhelmed Abraham with presents so that he received sheep, cattle, he-asses, male and females slaves, she-asses and camels . . ."

Further on, the same author quotes the famous passage regarding the Tower of Babel (Gen. 11, 3-9) as another confirmation of that fact that, according to the Bible, technology and religion are incompatible. For God does not allow men to "build a city and a tower the top whereof may reach to heaven," for according to Yahweh, "this is but a beginning and later it will no longer be possible to stop them in their plans."[8]

Comment on These Quotations. We have purposely assembled this small anthology, not only to show the almost primitive logic used by popular Marxist atheism, but also to point out the contemporary importance of theology and especially of Biblical theology. It is difficult to escape from the impression that this atheistic literature deals with concepts of religious belief in God according to the rather superstitious and medieval popular belief of the rural population of Russia before the Communist revolution as we find it described, e.g., in the novels of Dostoewski.

One thing among others that we object to in these quotations, is that the authors claim to speak in the name of modern science, but seem to have no notion of what scientific exegesis of the Bible has accomplished during the last decades. Again, they do not make the least distinction between Christianity as love of God and fellow men on the one hand, and on the other, "the primitives' belief in gods, demons, and miracles" (Lenin). In other words, they do not distinguish between the nature of the Christian belief in God and the superstitions and religious humbug which Christianity also rejects.

Another objectionable thing is that these quotations confuse man's trust in technology for a greater control over nature with genuinely religious hope, the "theological virtue of hope" by which man puts his trust in God for the work of salvation that God accomplishes in the world through His Word and His Spirit. That is to say, these texts continue to confuse the spheres of the profane and the sacred, of na-

---

[8]Cf. our previous footnote, in regard to this article also.

ture and supernature, as was done in thinking at its archaic stage.[9]

The Church Has No Monopoly of Truth. For the sake of honesty, however, we must add that there continue to be some Christians who, consciously or unconsciously, speak and act as if they were still thinking after the manner of primitives or of the people of the Middle Ages. They seem to have no eyes for the many dimensions of human existence and readily place the profane and the sacred, positive science and religious knowledge, secular and sacred history, on one line. For instance, an otherwise excellent Catholic students' magazine wrote a few years ago: "The Church of Christ alone, in virtue of a divine privilege, possesses truth one and undivided." However nice and flattering this may sound, such a pronouncement has strictly speaking no sense and is merely apt to arouse antireligious feelings in those who think otherwise.

First of all the truth is not so "one and undivided" as one might think and as was more or less believed in the Middle Ages, when, in the absence of positive science, the study of nature was a section of philosophy and philosophy itself the "handmaid of theology." As a result of this, the Church, which guaranteed the supreme or religious truth, at the same time exercised control over the whole world of truth. But, since Galileo and Descartes, physical science, philosophy and theology have gone their own ways because they have come to realize that their respective foundations and their value for the disclosing of reality are different. True, these various realms of knowledge constitute a whole, and it is the task of man to seek for an ever higher and richer synthesis of truth, in which everything that has any truth value may be integrated. But this does not mean that he who is occu-

[9]It could also be expressed in this way: The articles place Divine Providence and social care on the same level, as if the latter could replace the mystery of God's Providence and vice versa.

pied with the "highest," or religious truth, is automatically in possession of all the rest and has a criterion for evaluating all truths. It is only too evident that the Church has neither the competence nor a criterion to determine whether the physics of Einstein is better than that of Galileo and Newton, or whether the latter excels that of Aristotle and Ptolemy. The reason is very simple: positive science is the result of a method of research invented and elaborated by positive science itself. It belongs to positive science, therefore, to evaluate its method and research.[10]

The Church Has No Monopoly of Cultural Development and Morality. If the Church does not have the monopoly of truth, neither does she possess the monopoly of cultural development and morality. The task of Christ's Church is that of watching over the faithful proclamation of Christ's Word, a word that comes from God and is spoken by God to men. Implied in this is the fact, which precedes and is independent of Christianity, that man has *by nature* the power of listening and learning, and can freely accept what appears true to him. To put it in theological language, the supernatural presupposes nature, and faith presupposes reason. For reason is fundamentally nothing but that openness of man which makes him an intelligent and free being by making him able to recognize the true and the good in their diverse forms and to weave them freely into his own life.

As we have seen, there are several regions of truth and of value. Moreover, man is also *by nature,* that is, as a rational being, not only a *creator of culture* but also a being endowed with ethical sensibility and ethical will. From this it follows that a non-Christian and an unbeliever can be highly ethical and endowed with a keen ethical sensibility. He may have, for example, a great sense of right and justice, and an energetic determination to bring justice into the

[10]Cf. below, Chapter Eight, *Truth and Freedom.*

world. The Christian believer should not reject such an "un-Christian" sense of ethics, for it is precisely his task to show great appreciation for every authentic truth, cultural value and ethical greatness, whatever may be their source, and to try to integrate all this into a higher synthesis, namely, the synthesis of faith, hope, and charity. This was the attitude of St. Paul, e.g., regarding all that was worthwhile in the ethics of the Stoics. It was also the attitude of Thomas Aquinas with respect to Aristotle.

That is why I consider it bad apologetics, which does the Church more harm than good, to point to the many contradictions that are still found in our world, e.g., the fact that in spite of the development of technology, there still are so much sickness, famine, poverty and suffering, economic and social inequality, and then to use it as an argument for the claim that the "salvation" of the world can be found in Christ's Church *alone*. When people speak that way, and there are still many who do, they forget to specify what kind of "salvation" they have in mind. Is it the earthly, temporal salvation, man's mastery over the savage forces of nature, the elimination of social inequalities, the battle against epidemics and famine, the restoration of peace among the nations? Or is it the supernatural salvation which delivers man from his sinfulness, which through faith in God's Word and receptivity to God's Spirit makes him worthy of God?

The fact that India suffers from famines is not the result of present unbelief or lack of organized religion, but it is to be attributed to the inadequacy of the present economy, and it is with economic measures that the evil ought to be combated. It is obvious, of course, that if there were more love of God and more evangelical love of our neighbor among men, earthly conditions would be better. As we have already pointed out, because of its high ethical norms, a genuine and lively Christianity will of necessity be of benefit to temporal civilization;

but this proof is not properly expressed when, without further distinction, one claims: "It is only in and through the Church that the world reaches its order and salvation."[11]

3. *Conclusion*

We are thus brought back to the conclusion of our previous study. The problem of religion and technology is not a dilemma for the Christian believer but it calls for the elaboration of a synthesis, a synthesis of Christian hope. Hope, as we have said before, is the soul of human existence and the driving force of history. The Christian, however, knows a twofold history, one is secular, the other sacred, and for this reason the hope of the Christian believer encompasses two dimensions.

The Christian believer is a man like any other man. As such, he shares in and helps to make the secular history of mankind of which technical progress, in a certain sense, is the foundation. But by faith he also takes part in a sacred history, which is rooted in an intervention through which God wants to liberate man from the power of sin and make him free for the mystery of God's love.

That is why Christian hope is a synthesis of, on the one hand, the general earthly hope of man that is based on technological and cultural progress and, on the other, the theological virtue of hope by which the believer puts his trust in God for the completion of the work of salvation which God is doing in the world through His Word and His Spirit.

These two dimensions of Christian hope must not be confused. At the same time they may not be simply juxtaposed,

---

[11]Cf. *Basic Text A,* a discussion guide used at the Second International Lay Congress, held in Rome, October, 1957: "If we wish to study the responsibility and the formation of laypeople in view of today's crisis in the world, we must first keep in mind the mission of the Church . . . and realize how the world finds its order and its salvation in and through the Church" (page 3).

for they should permeate each other in a fruitful synthesis. This synthesis lies in love of our neighbor and in the Christian ethics flowing from this love. It is this synthesis which St. Paul had in mind when he said: "The fruit of the Spirit is: charity, joy, peace, patience, kindness, goodness, faith, modesty, continency" (Gal. 5, 22-23). These fruits of God's sanctifying Spirit are gifts from above, and it is their first task to open the soul to the mystery of God and His redeeming work of grace. But they are on that account not less human values of inestimable price. They are the best protection of life in society and the most powerful defense against the possible dangers of technology.

PART TWO

TODAY'S WORLD

CHAPTER FIVE

HISTORY AT A TURNING POINT

"The war was not an interlude." With these words Cardinal Suhard began, shortly after the war, his famous reflections on our own time, entitled *Essor ou Déclin de l'Eglise*. "By that very fact," he continued "this postwar period should be considered as a prelude or preface, as the beginning of a new world-in-the-making."[1] In other words, we are at a turning point in the history of civilization.

A turning point is had when a road abruptly follows a new direction. We speak similarly of a "turning point" in history when it follows new ways, so that there occurs, as it were, a break between the past and the future. This takes place every time an *existing cultural situation* conflicts with what *could exist henceforth;* or to express is more exactly, with *new possibilities* that suddenly appear as a result of an important material or spiritual discovery. New truths then make their appearance, new *horizons for the future* are opened to mankind, man puts his hopes in them, and applies his best efforts in that direction.

Turning points are decisive moments in the history of mankind. They are almost always full of promises and yet pregnant with dangers. The danger is that other important values will be discarded and forgotten. Turning points are moments of crisis that can end ill or well. In any case it is of the utmost importance that man should realize what is taking place, so that he will not be taken by surprise but able to dominate and control them as much as possible.

The sudden and accelerated evolution of science and technology during the last decades has resulted in the fact that

---

[1]"La guerre n'est pas un entr'acte, mais un épilogue. Mais du même coup l'ère qui s'inaugure après elle prend figure de prologue: préface ou drame d'un monde qui se fait." *Essor ou Déclin de l'Eglise.*

we are now in the midst of an encounter, full of possibilities of conflict, between what *was* until now and what soon *could be* or *will be.* There has never been such a tension between the past and the present, from both the *quantitative* and the *qualitative* standpoint, as that which exists today. For, from the quantitative standpoint, it is not merely this or that group of people that is involved in the present conflict but the whole of mankind; and, from the standpoint of *quality,* man's world is in the process of undergoing a profound change.

Here again, we understand the term "world" as the world in which man works and dwells, the world as the whole of human situations and tasks, or, more correctly, the way man experiences and lives the four-fold relationship to *himself* (his past and his future), to the *things of nature,* to his fellow-men, the *others,* and to the universal, all-embracing *mystery of existence* in which he is rooted, by which he is surrounded, and in which he has a share (as Karl Jaspers calls it, *das Umgreifende*).

In this first study of today's world, we intend to describe that fundamental change in our being-in-the-world and in the sensitivity to value that it contains, in its *general traits* and *components.* We shall reserve for subsequent discussions a more detailed and close analysis of some particular components and values.

1. *Accelerated Technological Evolution*

Undeniably, the enormous progress of the positive sciences and the resulting technology of the last decades, is the fundamental fact of today's world. However, it is of the utmost importance to remark that, as a result of the development of technology, there has been not merely an extraordinary increase of *production,* of produced goods, but also of *productivity,* of the quantity of produced goods per hour of work. Perhaps even more important is the fact that labor itself has undergone a radical change. An ever increasing and more perfect mechanization has created a new relation between man and the raw materials of nature, so that the slave-like aspect of labor has more and more disappeared. The working hours have been shortened; consequently, man has more leisure time, and this makes room for cultural and spiritual values that lie dormant in every human being. In other words, technology has not only raised the *standard of living,* but also changed man's *way of life.* His relationship to nature has undergone a change. Technology has given man a greater dominion over the material forces of nature, and this dominion has become a liberating factor for his spirit.

It would, therefore, be erroneous to see nothing but material progress in the development of technology. We owe many spiritual and ethical possibilities to technology. Drunkenness and banditry have to a great extent disappeared from most western countries. This has taken place not through the conversion of the drunkards and the bandits, but through the elimination of pauperism and the general rise of the cultural level. The lengthening of the average span of life, the expansion of care of the sick and preventive medicine, the humanization of penal institutions and mental hospitals, all these were made possible by the development of the positive sciences and technology. And, last, but not least, many habits of superstitious thought and practice have gradually disappeared as the ordinary citizen acquired a more scientific understanding of reality.

Nevertheless, it is true that this accelerated progress of industrial technology also has its dangers and creates new and very serious problems. There is the problem of the proper use of the new leisure, of the democratization of education and its adjustment to the demands of modern science, the integration of the employee into the enterprise, conceived as an industrial society of human beings. Technology considered in itself, is an ambiguous reality. Although it is a liberating factor and power, it may also lead to new forms of slavery. One among others, is the dictatorship of a technocracy which reduces human labor to a meaningless mechanized movement in a gigantic system of machines; another, a dictatorship of bureaucracy and organization which reduces man to an anonymous functionary or even to a quasi-automaton.

If we find no solutions for all these problems, man will become the prisoner of a civilization which he created for his own liberation. This, however, is no reason for condemning modern technology and preferring past times to our own, for the new problems with which mankind has to battle have arisen precisely because technological progress has created new *possibilities for the life of the spirit.* It is undoubtedly more difficult to diffuse instruction and education more widely among the masses than to open an abbey school for the children of princes and high functionaries, as was done in the Middle Ages, or to create colleges for the upper classes as was the case in the sixteenth and seventeenth centuries. The complexity of the modern problem of schools and education is precisely the best proof that there exists now greater opportunities for the life of the spirit, and this happy result must be attributed to technology.

2. *The Unification of the World*

An immediate consequence of the accelerated development of technology is, as Cardinal Suhard expressed it in his above-mentioned analysis of our time, "the unification of our planet": we have become "one world." This unification means the gradual abolition of the distances that formerly separated men, peoples, and cultures. Those distances were of various kinds, so that the present unification of the world shows diverse dimensions.

First of all, the *space-time* distances are constantly shrinking. We often hear the remark, "There are no more distances." This means that man is now capable of reaching the most distant spots "in no time." And those who on account of financial conditions are unable to cross the ocean by jet, can daily meet the whole world through radio and television or newspaper in their own kitchen or office.

Secondly, technology has fostered *solidarity* among men and nations. The smallest product of culture that we use bears the marks of thousands of human hands and puts us in debt to numberless unknown human workers, without whose brawn or brain we would no longer be able to live or work. Science has become an international enterprise; the national economy can no longer be divorced from the world economy; wars become world wars, and peace is no longer conceivable except as world peace.

Unsurprisingly therefore, mutual understanding among men and nations has also grown apace. A few years ago a series of lectures was given in Brussels about the world of the Far East, the world of Islam and the African-Negro world. This series bore the general title: *Worlds of Today and Christianity*. Our time is fully mirrored in this title. In fact, the series considered worlds, some of which are much older than our Western world, older even than the Greco-Roman world of culture which has made possible the civilization of the West. And yet, paradoxically, those ancient worlds are suddenly re-baptized with the nice name of "worlds of today," as if they were the great novelties of our own times.

They are indeed *new* in the sense that they are henceforth lying within the horizon of our daily life. They have become for us a living "reality," with the result that we are now directly concerned with their development. Thus, our attitude toward them has completely changed within the last decades. We have only to compare our present mission magazines with those prior to the War to realize that our attitude toward Islam, Indian spirituality, Buddhism, or Bantu philosophy is quite different from that of the past. We now show more appreciation for all the valuable and profoundly human elements that are contained in these ancient cultures.

All this could be summarized in one thought: for the first time in history, *mankind as a whole has become the bearer and agent of history.* So-called "world history" no longer exists in its ancient form as a compilation of regional and continental histories: the history of the United States and annexed to it, a short history of Europe, of the East, of India, China, or the peoples of Africa. Whatever man accomplishes now, acquires a global dimension. The ancient urge for "universality," which characterizes man as a rational being and always has been the most powerful moving force of history—witness the numerous attempts to "dominate the whole world"—is suddenly faced with new potentialities, as well as new and extremely difficult problems. For there is a universalism that is *authentic* and a universalism that is *unauthentic,* one that liberates and enriches and one that is synonymous with superficiality, impoverishment and a leveling-down.

Unauthentic is the universalism of the lowest common denominator, of the residue that remains when all originality, personality and free creativity have been eliminated. Also unauthentic is the universalism of the one who knows something of everything but has no profound knowledge of anything.

Authentic universalism is of a different kind; it is great qualitatively, not quantitatively. It is bound up with originality and personalism. Hence it is that all great works of art and culture have a *universal* value to the extent that they are original and personal creations. Homer and Plato, Aquinas and Kant, Dostoevski and van Gogh are beyond imitation, and yet they attract the whole world. This they do, not through any pressure or violence, but because what they have seen and heard, what they have said and shown in their works belong to what is most profound, most universal, and essential in man. That is why they continue to speak to the whole world and still have a message for it; they are listened to and find a response in every one of us; they reveal us to ourselves and enable us to be better men.

In other words, the universalism that liberates and enriches us, that gathers us into a higher unity, belongs to the order of dialogue; the genuine dialogue, in which there is not only speech but also a mutual listening in order that each might learn from, and give to the other.

The crucial question then is this: in what way will the dialogue between peoples and cultures take place in the world of tomorrow? If the unification of the world were to lead to the establishment of some kind of cultural collectivism or a colorless and lifeless standardized culture, man would be terribly impoverished. A world that becomes too large contains a horrible danger, the danger that it might transcend the measure and the power of man, give preference to organization at the expense of personal creation, and level everything down to the nameless "mass."

3. *The Socio-Economic Revolution*

The rapid development of technology and the unification of the world have also resulted in the gradual disappearance of frightful socio-economic differences. Not that equality has already been achieved, but there circulates through mankind an urge for social justice and international equality of rights which justifies our best hopes for the future; even though a crisis of unprecedented dimensions will continue to plague international life for many years to come. What we said above about the turning points of history, is especially true in reference to the present-day distribution of goods. In this respect we face an acute conflict between the actual *situation* we have inherited from the past and the present *possibilities* that open up new horizons for mankind.

With respect to the actual situation, we find that, from the economic standpoint, almost sixty percent of the world's population are still undernourished and do not even have the necessities for living in good health. From the social standpoint, slavery has not yet been eliminated, in this sense at least, that the poverty of some, for example, of colonized or half-colonized peoples, still makes possible to a great extent the riches of others.

This actual situation is in conflict with the new possibilities offered by our present world. The development of the positive sciences, of industrial technology and the possibilities of economic organization give us hope that that situation will not last forever, but will change at a rather rapid rate. Mankind has awakened to the fact that modern technology has, or will soon have, the means that will enable all mankind to lead a life that is more in keeping with man's dignity. For the first time in history the idea gains ground that it is no longer utopian to expect that ever widening circles of society and the economically weak nations of Asia, Africa, and South America, will be able to share in the things that have been acquired by Western civilization and culture.

The working class is no longer content with being a second rank class of possessionless subordinates in the service of a higher class, with working principally for the purpose of having a minority of owners enjoy to the full the products of civilization, such as special medical care, a comfortable home, education, vacation and leisure. At the same time, the peoples of Asia and Africa have awakened. They no longer want to be in bondage to the West. Hence the inevitable struggle within today's world, a struggle for greater equality between classes, more justice and brotherliness, more prosperity and genuine liberty; in a word, a struggle for the recognition of man's dignity, which, after all, ought to be the soul and the purpose of every human community.

The fact that mankind at present seeks to establish an economic and social order that is more worthy of man, and to make this earth a dwelling place that corresponds better to the material needs and the spiritual aspirations of present-day humanity, is undeniably a far-reaching and most promising event. Immense reserves that lay unused until now, such as human minds, wills, affectivity, moral energy and religious potentialities, will thus be released. New values, whose significance and educational importance were scarcely known, are coming to the fore and beginning to play a role. For instance, the value of labor as the expression of human creative power and as a living link between the raw materials given by nature, and the world of civilization and culture; economic and social solidarity as the foundation and symbol of human co-existence.

For the first time in the history of the world, the Christian concept of neighbor, which in principle knows no frontiers, stands a chance of being actualized into human conduct. The word "neighbor" in the evangelical commandment of love toward our fellow-men, "Thou shall love thy neighbor as thyself," has an absolutely universal meaning. We must consider as our "neighbor" not only blood-relatives, those who live close to us, and our countrymen, but every man upon earth, regardless of language or color, for God is the Father of all. The Christian concept of love of our neighbor has the character of a mission now and is presented with an opportunity for its fulfillment such as it never had before.

Nevertheless, this social unrest, while it is ultimately the greatest event of our time, is not without danger for mankind. In any case it puts serious problems before man. Will this socio-economic renovation be accomplished in an orderly or disorderly fashion, by legal and peaceful reforms, or through the inhuman and murderous violence of a world-revolution, a third world war?

Again, will the social battle be fought in the spirit of Marxist materialism or with a more spiritual and freedom-loving view of the world and life? For we must not forget that the present socio-economical struggle for a better world and greater justice, considered concretely, cannot be separated from another fact of world-wide significance, the fact of Marxist Communism.

4. *Communism*

It would be undoubtedly wrong to reduce all modern events to the opposition between the communist and the non-communist world. Nevertheless, communism must be considered as one of the basic elements of the modern world. Any analysis of our world would be historically incorrect and would remain in the realm of abstractions, if it failed to take account of Marxist communism. Communism is not just one of the many realities in this world, but it is a phenomenon of planetary dimensions. This means that everyone who is interested in the future of mankind, must take communism very seriously, he must do his best to be as objective as possible in evaluating its significance for today's world.

Undeniably, Karl Marx is one of the greatest men of our time. One does not destroy this fact by showing a number of errors and mistakes in his economic works. There is, besides, this other factor that one third of mankind already lives under Marxist regimes and this seems to indicate that other things are found in his works than just a number of economic errors. Neither is it a sign of great seriousness to present a caricature of Marxism and then to discourse learnedly on the stupidities of Marxism. One such caricature pictures Marx as naively believing that he could transform the earth into a paradise. Another widely circulated caricature describes Marxism as a materialism that leaves no room for spiritual and ethical values and wants to lower humanity to a level on which it will crave only biological satisfactions, a humanity "whose God is its belly." Lastly, it is also a caricature to say that Marx's so-called "historical determinism" leaves no room for man's free intervention in history, for it proclaims almost the exact opposite.

What, then, is Marxist Communism? It is first of all an *atheistic philosophy* which reduces the whole existence of man to an earthly being-in-the-world, and thus attributes no other task and vocation to man than to make man's labor, civilization and culture serve all mankind. Man's ultimate foundation is man; he is the Alpha and Omega of the history of civilization, and nothing exists outside that history of civilization. The ultimate meaning of human history is to free man from every shape and form of economic and social slavery that oppresses him; to construct an economic and political world which will be the expression of a social life that is no longer driven and dominated by the anonymous power of money, but is based solely and exclusively on the recognition of man by man. This is the first point of Marxism.

Secondly, Marxism, in close connection with its anthropocentric metaphysics also wants to be an *historical ideology,* an *interpretation* of the concrete economic, social and political history of mankind. It wants to be an interpretation which, by means of a critical analysis of the past and of present social conditions inherited from the past, aims to discover the great laws, lines, and vectors of history; this, in turn, will enable man to intervene in a more purposeful manner in history, to intervene in order to direct it to its final goal, which is the more perfect recognition of man by man.

Thirdly, communism wants to be *the great revolutionary organization of power* which, while working in the light and in the service of the above-mentioned ideology, considers itself to be entrusted with the mission of guiding the history of mankind to its completion, by the establishment of a classless society.

Finally, communism is a system of *economics,* namely, the extreme form of the leveled socialist economy, which may, as in China, even reach the extreme rigidity and mercilessness that is typical of any war economy. The measures which in time of war are accepted as a necessity, become here, as it were, the permanent form of economic life, in a time of peace. The economic life is totally in the hands of the State, not only in regard to the choice of goods to be produced and the organization of production, but also with respect to the use and distribution of the products.

We have stated that Marxist communism simultaneously proclaims itself to be an atheistic metaphysics, an historical ideology, an organized revolutionary system of power, and the extreme form of a leveled and unified economy. All this, however, should be understood in the sense that these four aspects are conceived as sectors of a *single closed and indivisible synthesis.* It is here that lies the strength of communism, but also perhaps its weakness. It is its strength, for it enables Marxism to pose before the world as the herald of a new gospel of salvation, a kind of mysticism of salvation—albeit a mysticism without God—which tries to enroll the religious forces that lie dormant in mankind, in the service of a political ideology and especially of a revolutionary activity which will finally free man from all slavery. Communism, therefore, claims at the same time to take the place of religion, to represent the humanism of tomorrow, and to be the vanguard of the world-proletariat and of the colonized peoples in their struggle for freedom, truth and justice.

But this rigidity of the communist synthesis perhaps also constitutes its weakness, for it does not recognize the many dimensions of human existence, it puts the sacred and the profane on the same level, and confuses religion and economy. This unavoidably leads to fanaticism, harshness, and heartlessness, which in turn tend to provoke a reaction of man's innermost forces.

In any case, all this shows that communism is an essential element of the image of our time. It permeates the whole of contemporary events and gives to them a tragic and oppressive character, for it is the extreme expression of the *situation of conflict* which we have described above. This situation itself is the result of the enormous possibilities contained in modern technology as well as the reason why we are now at a turning point of history. But, if this is the meaning and significance of communism, we have to conclude that the only way to extricate ourselves from the impasse of communism is to accept the challenge of that situation of conflict from which all the trouble originates. In other words, we must in a decisive and systematic fashion remove the frightful inequality which still divides our world into a minority of the rich and a majority of the underprivileged.

5. *The Religious Situation*

Before we conclude this general analysis of today's world, we want to state that up to now we have confined ourselves to the description of the *cultural-historical* character of this world. This picture is, therefore, incomplete, since we have omitted the *religious situation* and have viewed things solely from the standpoint of *secular* history. It cannot be denied that our Western world, in which Christianity has grown up, is passing through a sort of crisis of the faith. A similar crisis, moreover, affects all religions. We have analyzed this religious crisis in the first part of our study and, therefore, will not develop this topic further here. However, besides this crisis of the faith, we also observe a *renewal of the faith.* Perhaps never in the history of the Church has the clergy been of so high a quality as today, and never has the layman shown such eagerness for a genuine life of faith, for authentic forms of social worship, for translating faith into action and taking a practical interest in apostolic concern with others. Our time, according to the beautiful expression of Father Yves Congar, is characterized by the *"volonté des gestes vrais,"* "the will to make true gestures." Modern man rejects sham, mere formalism and external make-believe in religion. External rites must find their source in, and be the expression of interior attitudes and desires.[2]

6. *Conclusion*

One fact certainly stands out. Our time is a time of greatness and character. Although it is only a time of transition, a turning point, it has nonetheless an enormous importance for the future of mankind and also for the Church. As we have constantly pointed out, it is a difficult and dangerous time, but also one that is full of promises and potentialities.

Besides, it is for us the *only real time,* the time in which *we* live. Everlasting wailing over the past, the good old times that are no more, but which are usually looked at through the spectacles of idealization, as well as apocalyptic fear for the future, are unworthy of a Christian or any noble-minded human being. Such attitudes originate in a flight from the reality of the present.

The worst thing that we Christians could do would be to lose confidence in man at the exact moment when mankind

---

[2]This religious renewal we do not wish to describe here, for we consider it in another small work entitled *Priest and Layman.*

is at a turning point of history. "The greatest mistake the Christians of the Twentieth Century could make," wrote Cardinal Suhard, in the above mentioned book *Essor ou Déclin de l'Eglise,* "would be to let the world develop and unify itself without them." Let us not forget that what we call "the world of today" is in fact nothing else but the living mankind of today, a mankind of which we ourselves are a part and with which we are connected by innumerable bonds of culture and civilization. One of the first duties of today's Christian is to feel a solidarity with today's world and, furthermore, to take his share of responsibility in it. For solidarity and responsibility are inseparable in regard to history.

CHAPTER SIX

SOLIDARITY

Solidarity, as we have noted in the conclusion of the preceding chapter, is man's first task and, is at the same time one of the most promising ethical values of our time. Let us see, therefore, what solidarity is.

We are not simply playing with words when we connect "solidarity" with "solidity." Both words are derived from the Latin *solidus* which means "whole." "Solidarity" at first sight makes us think that a man finds solidity, firmness, and safety only when he lives in a group and feels surrounded by others. This first impression, however, merits closer observation and greater precision.

A child, at the sight of an approaching dog, clings to his mother and buries his head in her skirt or apron. This he does, one would say immediately, because he wants to withdraw from the sight of the threatening animal; but the reason is much more that he wants to make himself invisible, to hide his threatened existence from himself, to forget his anxiety. During the war people took refuge in bomb shelters and every time they heard the approach of a bomber plane, they instinctively huddled close together, as if a compact mass could resist such attacks better than an isolated individual. In reality they clung together in order to disappear in the mass and, as it were, lose consciousness of their threatened bodily existence. Likewise it is a well-known fact that panic drives people together, it unites them in a compact group, a solid mass. But this solidity is not a true *human* solidarity, for instead of giving man back to himself and liberating his personality, it causes him to go underground and lose himself in the compactness of a crowd.

We do not mean to say that "solidarity" has no connection with "solidity". However, there are two kinds of solidities. There is the solidity of a lifeless thing, which we consider to be solid to the extent that it shows strength, sturdiness, durability. We speak in this way of a house that is "solidly built." There is also a *human* solidity, the solidity of a man about whom we say, "he is solid," he has a solid personality because we can depend on him, we can trust in his self-reliance, in his sense of responsibility, his fidelity to his word. We can "bank upon him," as we say colloquially, throughout the difficulties of life. With him we can build a true "we," a durable community of men, who can count upon one another and learn from one another, who can entertain mutual respect in mutual understanding; in short, a community of men who constitute a "solid" yet living whole which can withstand the corroding force of time. This "whole," however, does not have the characteristics of the closed and dead density of the thing, or the massive compactness of a herd, but consists wholly in a steadily renewed openness toward one another. Its motto is, "All for one and one for all." It is this that we customarily call "solidarity."

Human solidity is born of solidarity. "Solidarity" actually is a term borrowed from the realm of law. In law, "solidarity" is synonymous with right or obligation "in solidum," which means that every creditor can ask the whole amount from each of the debtors, or every debtor is responsible for the entire debt. Hence the idea of solidarity always contains the thought of a common responsibility. To have the feeling of solidarity means that we do feel responsible not merely for our own individual deeds but also for those of others and even, to a certain extent, for the right or wrong course of the world. Only from such a sentiment of solidarity with the past, the present, and the future can original and lasting work be born.

Faith and the World

1. *Solidarity With the Past*

Solidarity with the past means that we recognize and are grateful for what others before us have done—whether they are already dead or still alive does not matter here. An example may help to clarify this meaning of solidarity here. A young man wishes to become a philosopher and registers in a school of philosophy. This is his firm resolve, his "project," as our contemporaries like to call it. He made this decision personally, perhaps against the will of his parents who see only a scant hope of financial reward in philosophizing. The young man himself stands at the origin of this project and therefore is also responsible for it. Nevertheless, this is not entirely correct, for his decision was rather a reply to a call which he once heard when he came in contact with a philosopher, a call whose echo he often listened to, and finally followed after much hesitation. Before he made the decision, he was already in dialogue with those who had preceded him on the road to philosophical research and he felt that he was in fellowship with them.

At the university he will continue this dialogue with a holy earnestness. He does not want to repeat in parrot fashion what he reads in the textbooks but wants to arrive at a personal and original insight. Now here lies the marvel of human solidarity in the search for truth. We do not truly learn to philosophize by shutting ourselves up in ourselves but by sitting at the feet of the great masters of thought, of Plato, Aristotle, St. Thomas, Descartes, Kant, Hegel, Heidegger. It is only the dialogue of the great thinkers, the long, laborious wrestling with their work that leads us to personal and original thinking. It is only in the dialogue, says Heidegger, that the "logos" awakens in us, that we acquire the power of listening in person to the mystery of Being and of speaking originally about it.

This is true not only in regard to philosophical thought, but also in art, in scientific research and, in general, in regard to all that man does. Without the others, I am nothing and cannot accomplish anything. To begin with, there is my body that I have received and that enables me to maintain myself in the world. There is also the world itself and the way of dealing with the world so that I will not be crushed by it but will be liberated by it. All this I have also received as a gift. For the world in which I move, is not a crude world, but one that bears the marks of previous generations and thus meets me as "humanized" in many ways.

The flowers and the trees and the landscape around me, the starry heavens above me have something to say to me; they bring space and openness to me, because they have been sung by poets and have been recreated by artists. The clothes I wear, the house I live in, the language I speak, the education which has nourished my mind and my heart, are gifts to which thousands have contributed their efforts.

In regard to the socio-economic welfare which we enjoy and the political regime of freedom which safeguards our thinking and our actions, all are the tardy fruits of centuries of struggle against the tyranny and the arbitrariness of the mighty, for many have died in order that we today might live in freedom. Finally, there is also the faith that I profess, and which gives ultimate meaning to my life; it came to me through a long, unbroken tradition of fidelity to the original message of faith, often at the cost of life. To summarize: all that is best in the things that I possess binds me to the past; I owe these things to those who have gone before. To recognize this is a duty called "gratitude."

2. *Solidarity With the Future*

It would be erroneous, however—as happens only too often—to think that our solidarity with others consists solely in this that, in order to do our work well, we have to be attuned only to the past, by receiving and learning from our predecessors. Any meaningful action orientates us just as much to the future, or more correctly, it directs us to others in the future, for to act meaningfully means to act *for* others, with *an eye on* others, with the hope that others *will* benefit from our action.

This solidarity with the future is in a sense even more intimate than our solidarity with the past. Let us suppose that the world is nearing its end and that you, by a fortunate play of circumstances, are the last survivor. You are the sole heir of all that mankind has ever yielded, everything belongs to you and to you alone and forever. You are scarcely able to survey your kingdom and yet you are the poorest man that ever was on earth, for there is nothing more to be done. No longer are there any poems to be written, for no one is left to read them; no more lectures to give, for there is no one in the hall; there are no more classes to teach, for there are no more students, no more plans to be conceived, for there is no one to profit by them.

"It is more blessed to give than to receive" (Acts, 20, 35). We need the others not only to receive from them, but even more to be able to give to them, to open new opportunities for them, to become *some one* for them. He who has no one to love and to be loved by, finds life an absurd and unbearable burden. He no longer has any reason for existing, "he is superfluous" (Sartre).

3. *Solidarity With the Present*

Solidarity with the past and with the future does not mean that we must flee from the present. On the contrary, these two solidarities precisely establish us in the present, and give to our presence in the world its full force. "The past" means what is no longer, the "future" what is not yet. Hence only what I shall do *now* has real importance and ultimately deserves my greatest attention. Although this is perfectly correct, nevertheless, precisely in order that I may now philosophize, in order that my philosophical work may not become an empty, meaningless play with words, I apply myself to the study of, e.g., Plato, for Plato still has a message for me. This is true regarding any other pursuit that I may choose. Only by gratefully recalling what others have done for us in the past and taking an earnest interest in a better future for the benefit of the coming generations will there awaken in us a sense of earnestness in *regard to the present.*

We are, as it were, responsible, at every moment for the past and for the future of the world. What the world will be like tomorrow depends on what we are doing today; and if we fail to recognize and gratefully accept the past, the past will become proportionately valueless and die, for it depends on us whether or not the past gets lost in oblivion, whether or not the seeds which past generations have sown in labor and in pain, will bear fruit.

"It is one who sows the seed, and another who gathers the harvest," but if the harvester neglects his work, he renders the labors of the sower useless.

Human solidarity, then, is *a solidarity with and for history.* It is only when we recognize the past and care for the future that we accomplish true and lasting work; only then do we give to the present day its irreplaceable meaning and value for the liberation of men. In other words, only when our sense of solidarity accepts the historical dimension that we have described above, is there a chance for genuine freedom. We mean by this a freedom that frees not only ourselves but others also and that, at the same time, is experienced as selfhood in solidarity and openness.

4. *Christian Solidarity*

These considerations of solidarity have been made from the standpoint of philosophy. For the Christian this means that they have developed only a provisional idea. Christian faith gives to human solidarity another and more profound dimension. In the eyes of the Christian, God is the ultimate foundation who gives meaning to our manhood. He has gathered us in Christ to belong to a living and eternal whole and "has reconciled us to Himself through Christ" (Cor. 2 5, 18), and He will "re-establish all things in Christ, both those in the heavens and those on earth" (Eph. 1, 10). Hence solidarity received a new name in Christianity, "love," (*agapē*), the same name which the New Testament uses to reveal the mystery of God's profound Essence: "Beloved, let us love one another, for love is from God. And every one who loves is born of God, and knows God. He who does not love does not know God; for God is love (*agapē*)" (1 John, 4, 7).

When it is said that the Christian vision of faith gives a new dimension to human solidarity, this also means that it does not destroy this solidarity but strengthens it in its being by incorporating it in a higher meaning. Grace presupposes nature, integrates it in a higher synthesis and, in this sense, elevates it. Accordingly, all that we have said above remains true and is preserved in Christianity. Christian solidarity is also human solidarity and must satisfy the demands imposed by the above-described structure and nature of solidarity.

In other words, our belief in God may never become a flight from the world and from the history of mankind; it must, on the contrary, give a deeper meaning to our bond with the world and history. Solidarity with history here becomes the sacrament of God's saving presence in our midst. "I was naked and you covered me; I was in prison and you came to me. . . . As long as you did it to one of these, the least of my brethren, you did it to Me" (Matt. 25, 36-40). So will the Son of God speak to us on the day of the Last Judgment, which will inaugurate the final liberation.

We thus find once more a theme that we have frequently underlined as being of great importance for our time. The Christian is a man like any other man, with and amidst other men. The words spoken by God at the beginning of the great human adventure, "Increase and multiply, and fill the earth, and subdue it" (Gen. 1, 28) were addressed to all mankind when there was as yet no distinction between Christian and non-Christian. That word still holds for all men without distinction and beyond all boundaries. That word has even become more actual than ever because the world has effectively become one. Now, more than ever, must the Christian feel his bond with all mankind, especially with the great multitude of the poor, for whom the hope for a more dignified human existence has become the soul of their suffering and their struggles.

Self-isolation and the petrification of Christian groups are the greatest dangers of twentieth century Christianity. We are so accustomed to look upon our Christian community as one that is apart and specially chosen by God that, when we meet with any great work or a great man, whether he be a thinker, an artist, or a politician, we spontaneously ask, "Was or is he a Catholic?", implying by this that whoever is not a Catholic is thereby less a man. John Smith is a very clever mayor, he governs the city very well, is honest and is anxious to take good care of his people, *but* . . . . we add, "he is a socialist" or "he is a Protestant." Why do some introduce that little word "*but*"? Why should we not simply feel joy and satisfaction that some one is doing good?

The fact that the Christian has a "special vision" about the meaning of life is not a good reason for isolating himself from the rest of mankind. Rather the contrary is true. Let no one, however, interpret me wrongly. I do not mean that Christians should never organize themselves separately, that they should not have their own schools, universities, hospitals and cultural institutions. However, these institutions should not lead to *separation,* to *"apartheid."* Hence they should not become identified with the Christian community, covering it so completely that there finally are two worlds in mere *juxtaposition,* a Christian world *alongside* a non-Christian world. The question that may be legitimately asked in this connection is: Is our presence *in* the world of today sufficiently efficient? Do we not live too much *alongside* this world, more concerned with our own group than with being an inspiring and constructive force in this world? More especially, is our presence in the world truly a *dialogue* with the world? Do we not often speak a language which those who think differently simply cannot understand?

However, it would be just as wrong to conclude from what we have said that our solidarity with, and our presence in the world of today demand that we henceforth consider our Christian belief and our Christian way of life as a purely private affair, and that we ought to keep hidden under the bushel whatever distinguishes us from non-Christians. This would be directly contrary not only to the nature of Christianity, which is essentially a witnessing and a message, but would also be in conflict with the nature of our "being-together-with-others." To live together and to work together, as we have already pointed out, is an exchange of *receiving* and *giving,* of *learning* from others and *imparting* knowledge to them. Christianity needs the world, just as the world needs Christianity.

Henry Bergson, in the last chapter of his *The Two Sources of Morality and Religion,* entitled, "Mechanics and Mysticism," makes the famous remark that the world of tomorrow expects a "supplement of soul." He means by this that tomorrow's world will be in need of more "soul," more "spirit," more morality, more mystic power, to counterbalance the all-pervading and overwhelming power of standardized technology and anonymous administration. It goes without saying that Christianity could and should make a substantial contribution to provide this "supplement of soul."

CHAPTER SEVEN

HISTORICITY

1. *Statement of the Problem*

Man alone, among the many realities in the world, is an *historical* being. He is the only being of which history is written because he is the only one who makes history.[1] When we remarked above that our time is characterized by its being a turning point of history, everyone must have understood immediately that we were speaking of man and not of atoms and electrons, ants and robins. For the latter there are no turning points. They have no freedom; hence they cannot take an autonomous attitude regarding the situations in which they find themselves, nor do new horizons open before them for the future, for they always react in the same way. Therefore, when we study their behavior, we can abstract from the past, the present and the future, since we can with certainty determine what their future will be by studying their past. Water always boils at 100° Centigrade; when spring returns to our region, the robins also come back and once more build their nests as they have always done. In a word, they do not make history since they do not create a civilization, and therefore, they are not studied by history but only by physics, biology and the many branches of research called "natural sciences."

The fact that man alone is the bearer and actor of history, is rooted in the *structure itself of our being-human.* Modern philosophy expresses this idea by saying that man is a *history-making existence,* or that historicity is an essential characteristic of man's existence. A sharpened consciousness of his-

[1]Note that the word *history* has two meanings: the historical events and the historical descriptions and study of these events. The term "historicity" refers first of all to the historical event.

toricity is precisely one of the main characteristics of our time. It is one of the chief aspects of the way contemporary man experiences his being-man.

We do not mean to say that formerly man was not historical. Man is that by his very nature, but he was formerly not so keenly aware of the historical nature of his existence. For example, the ancient Greeks were dominated by the all-pervading idea of Fate, which determined everything with an iron necessity, and this Fate repressed their consciousness of historicity. The so-called "necessity" imposed by Fate, is, of course, a pseudo-idea, the product of man's spontaneous inclination to transfer the inevitable character of the past to the future. For, truly, what has happened can never be undone. This inevitability of the past, however, is purely *consequent,* i.e., its necessity merely follows the actual events. It would be wrong to conclude from it that these events were also antecedently necessary and inevitable, that they were inevitable at the time when they were nothing but future possible events alongside numberless others. Yet, man likes to endow possibilities with inevitability. Thus, when a student fails in his test, he consoles himself with the thought that "it had to be." In reality, it did not have to be. If he had worked harder, or if he had had better "luck" at the examination, he would not have failed. Now that he has failed, there is nothing that he can do about it and he must make a virtue of "necessity"; that is, he has to take into account his present situation, change his plans for a vacation, and begin anew to prepare for a successful test.

The Christian Middle Ages had, of course, no room for the pagan idea of Fate, which was replaced by faith in divine Providence. And yet, the idea that man makes history was not fully taken into account, probably because medieval man had but little control over nature and was regularly the victim of terrible natural catastrophes such as floods, famines, and epidemics. Consequently, he was strongly impressed by the fragility of earthly life and liked to repeat the Scriptural dicta, "Vanity of vanities, and all is vanity," and "there is nothing new under the sun." Resignation was a characteristic trait of the medieval attitude of life. This resignation was to some extent fostered by certain ideas concerning divine Providence which were not always far removed from the ancient idea of Fate.

An example may show that this lack of historical awareness did not quite disappear with the waning of the Middle Ages. Not many years have passed since the following argument was used in numerous Christian circles for indiscriminately condemning the social class struggle. A class struggle, so it was claimed, that aims at removing the inequality among men must be wrong, for it is a struggle against the will of God. For the fact that there have *always* been great inequalities among men, classes and peoples, points to a root in human nature itself, and therefore must be considered to be a sign of God's will who has created man's nature. Here, then, "what *has* always *been*" serves to support a conclusion, by way of an appeal to God's will, with respect to what will be in the future. However, another conclusion can be drawn from the same premises—the one that is now usually drawn: since all men are equal before God and we must love everyone as ourselves, it is in line with God's will that we try to eliminate the existing inequalities as much as possible, that we strive for the establishment of an economical and social world which provides for a more equal distribution of opportunities for all.

This transition from present inequalities to a greater equality does not occur without struggle, yet this struggle should always retain a human character, it should even take on a Christian character, but it may never degenerate into class war and class murder. Where, we may ask, lies the difference between the earlier and the new line of reasoning? It lies in the fact that man was formerly much more impressed by the "inevitability" of the past than by the possibilities opened by future horizons.

Now it is characteristic of the spirit of our time—caused in part by the influence of the enormous development of science and technology in our Promethean world—that man has recognized that the proverb "there is nothing new under the sun" expresses only one side of what is taking place in the world. Man now realizes that it is equally true that great changes are occurring and that they are to a great extent the work of man himself; he realizes that it is man's task to construct this world, to subjugate nature and, if necessary, to re-create the social structures. Our modern awareness of historicity is directed to the future rather than to the past and puts emphasis upon the fact that man not only "undergoes" history, or finds himself in the midst of history, but that he has also a responsibility for it. In other words, today's awareness of historicity is closely connected with the awareness that the world, in a certain sense, is man's work, the fruit of his labor, as creative of culture. Merleau-Ponty, the French philosopher, has said very well: "Man is a working being, and labor, the *foundation of history, . . .* is not merely the production of wealth, but is, in general, the activity by which man projects around himself a human milieu and transcends what nature provides for his life."[2]

To transform the raw materials of nature into a truly human milieu that is worthy of man, is the task of man, of the "worker," that is, of man as the builder of culture, of a world. Consequently, man is also a *historical* being, for wherever there is civilization there is also a history of civilization.

---

[2]*Sens et Non-Sens,* Paris, 1948, p. 215.

Reflection, therefore, on man's contemporary awareness of historicity is necessary if we wish to understand today's world and cooperate in its construction. This is most important especially for the Christian because he has to reconcile this sensibility for the historical with a sincere belief in divine Providence. As we have pointed out in our chapter on the Prometheus myth and modern atheism, this reconciliation is not always very easily accomplished.

2. *Pre-philosophical Experience of Historicity*

We must seek to define the *nature* of historicity, ask the question, What exactly is historicity? It is actually the task of philosophy to discover the *nature* of things and express it in a clear definition. But where does the philosopher obtain his knowledge? Like anybody else, he gets it from the daily experience that is common to all and which for this reason is called *pre-philosophical experience.*

Historicity is a structure that belongs to every human being as part of his essence. In other words, that man is and knows himself to be a historical being, is contained in the way man experiences, pursues and accomplishes his being-man every day. In some sense, therefore, no one, not even a philosopher, can *teach* you what historicity is, just as no one can teach you what it is to be man. You know this from your experience of being-man, although you may perhaps not be able to give immediately a clear and precise answer to the questions, What is it to be man? and, What is historicity? But there are many things which we know without being able to formulate and define them clearly. Moreover, if a definition of sadness, of joy, of love means something for us, it is because we, as it were spontaneously, realize that the given definition agrees with what experience has already taught us. In this sense Socrates, the great Greek philosopher, said that man's learning process is in many cases a sort of remembering; man becomes more clearly conscious of what he already knew implicitly. Expressed in modern terms, when we reflect upon our being-man and the meaning of being-man, when, for example, we want to bring to light its historicity—which precisely is the task of philosophical thought—, all we do is clarify and make more precise a kind of pre-philosophical understanding which is contained in the daily experience itself of our being-man. What we are going to do now is to follow this procedure. We will start with our pre-philosophical experience of historicity, an experience which we have had thousands of times.

We have perhaps first experienced what historicity is when, many years ago, we learned from our parents how to call things by their proper names: What is this? a spoon; and that? a fork; and that? a chair.

What happened when we learned these names? We were taken into the home-world of father and mother (a world that was there *long before* we were around); in other words, we were established, made *present* in that world, so that *from then on* we would conduct ourselves in its regard as becomes those who have to live together, to understand one another, "meet one another" through the many things which we experience as being "the same." When mother now asks me for a spoon, I will no longer come back with a fork, and when father wants a chair, I will not bring him a broom. It is as if a secret agreement had been made between father, mother, and myself: they can henceforth depend on me and I on them. I have been admitted to a tradition which I myself take over, and this means that the horizon of my life has expanded in the threefold dimension of the *past,* the *present* and the *future.* Every human product, however humble, a fork, or a spoon establishes us in history by the fact that it is experienced as a center of reference to others; these references point to those who are no more but who have put their stamp on them, they point to the many with whom we live together or to those whom we shall meet later through the instrumentality of these same products.

Later, when we went to school, we were made familiar with the history of our own country, with Europe, and the world. Of course, we became acquainted only with high points or outstanding events of history: the propagation of Christianity, the Barbarian invasions, wars and peace treaties, the lives and deeds of great men whose names have been preserved for us because they accomplished great things in one or another realm of culture, such as those of art, military science, the establishment of law, or statesmanship. In this way, on the level of explicit conceptualism, the term "history" gradually became synonymous with "a series of dateable events of the past."

Nevertheless, beneath this clear but rather superficial definition of history another much richer and more original concept of "historicity" was at work; for otherwise, how would we have been able to speak of "highlights," "turning points," of "great men," "heroes" and "men of genius"? Why did we call some events "great"? Because something great had "happened" there, something that had decisive importance for the course of future events. We learned, for example, that the discoveries of gun powder, of printing, and the New World, had been "turning points" in the history of European civilization. Whom did we call "great men" if not those who had known how to use the situations to prepare a better future for their people, those who instead of "undergoing" events, had helped to "make history"?

At the university, the student comes into contact with the great masters of culture in a more direct and personal way. Instead of mechanically repeating what he finds in textbooks of philosophy, he tries to get a personal philosophical insight and for that purpose he goes to school and sits at the feet of

Plato, Aristotle, St. Thomas, and Kant. Philosophy becomes a dialogue with the past by means of the work of these great masters, and he hopes to learn true philosophizing by means of this dialogue. He learns through this contact with the masters in a personal way what history truly is, what is meant by expressions such as "the history of philosophy," "of art," "of social institutions." He learns why man uses here the term "history" in preference to other terms that are more or less related to it, such as "becoming," "growth," "evolution"[3]; and he realizes especially what is meant when we say that now and then "something happens."

When I give my usual course on Special Metaphysics every Thursday, or publish an article about philosophy, little or nothing "happens." But when Descartes wrote his *Discourse on Method*, when Kant published his *Critique of Pure Reason,* and Heidegger gave the world his *Being and Time,* so much happened in the realm of philosophy that whoever earnestly occupies himself with philosophy must henceforth take notice of these "events." Every great work of art, of culture, or of the mind is an "event," that is, it has a universal and lasting significance for mankind. Uniqueness, originality and universality here walk hand in hand. No true history would be had without such major events. They make it possible that the history of mankind in general does not run idly by, that even outside those "high points" something happens; that, for example, the average man also makes contributions to true science, art and philosophy.

Man knows what "historicity" is because he "is" a "history-making" existence, even when he might not know it with the clarity and precision of a philosophical definition. He knows what history is because he lives in history and has a responsible share in it. In this original experience of his-

[3]All those terms, "becoming," "growth," "development" are borrowed from the world of nature. History implies choice, decision; in short, freedom in regard to given situations.

toricity is rooted all that man, including the philosopher, can ever tell about "historicity."

3. *The Three Components of Historicity*

From our past discussions it is evident that we must look for the nature of historicity *in the essence of our being-man* itself, that is, in that which makes us experience our existence as the existence of a human being, as an existence worthy of man. There could certainly be no question of history if man lived in a closed self-centered consciousness that is incapable of coming out of itself and showing itself to others; or in philosophical language, if he were a Cartesian kind of *Cogito*. Nor would there be history if he lived all alone on earth and if, like God, he were an eternal, unchangeable and timeless being. In other words, that man makes history is a consequence of the following three essential characteristics of his being-man:

1) Man is neither a pure spirit nor lifeless matter but an *embodied spirit.*

2) Man is never alone in the world but always experiences and unfolds his being-man as a being-together with others. Modern philosophy expresses this characteristic by the term *intersubjectivity.*

3) Man *lives in time.*

These three properties of our being-man constitute the three components of historicity; but they are so intimately connected, that whenever one is mentioned, the two others are also implied. Let us consider this more closely.

Man, as Embodied Spirit. As we have explained fully in the third chapter, man is not a pure spirit, nor a lifeless body, but *an embodied spirit, a besouled bodily being.* Materiality is not an obstacle to the unfolding of his life or the spirit but rather is the way by which the spirit expresses itself, in the threefold sense that is always attached to that term. This threefold meaning is: 1) it exteriorizes itself, comes out of itself; 2) it shows itself to others, comes in the open; 3) it realizes, completes itself (in scholastic terms, "it passes from potency to act"). To be man is to become man, or rather, it means to take our being-man to heart in freedom and responsibility.

Man therefore, is not a raw datum of nature, but he is a task, a great program that is never finished, a "theme" or a "motif," as one speaks of them in music, something that returns and is taken up over and over again, because it can neither be sufficiently expressed nor uttered with satisfying beauty. In short, man is a "work" of, a task for man.

The term "work" (*oeuvre*) must be taken here in a very broad sense. A smile, a gesture, speech, technology and art, poetry and the philosophical essay, social legislation and charitable deeds, all of these are expressions of man's "work"; they are an encounter of the human spirit with matter, with the materiality of our own body and that of the outside world. In and by means of this encounter man puts his stamp on matter, he humanizes matter and reveals himself, he shows himself to himself and to others, and becomes a reality for them. Man thus mirrors himself in his work and only through this mirroring he completes his being-man. This work is both the product of his freedom and at the same time an objective situation for a new free action. For this reason man, and man alone, is the bearer of civilization and culture. To humanize himself, man must humanize the world, he must re-create the crude materials given by nature into a world of civilization and culture.[4]

---

[4]Cf. the chapter *Christianity and Civilization.*

Man's Being is a Being-Together. All this is true not only of man as an individual, but also of mankind as a whole, for "to be" for man always means "to be together with" that is, a mutual giving and receiving, listening and speaking by means of "work." It is first a *receiving and listening.* The best of what I own I have received from others, beginning with my bodily being which enables me to maintain my earthly life; the clothes that protect my body, the pen with which I write, the words I use, all these I owe to others; even my openness-to-the-world that makes the things that surround me speak with meaning and love to me, all these to a great extent I owe to the warm affection with which I have been surrounded from my tender years.

But "to be together with" also is *giving and speaking.* Man is likewise always directed to others in his conduct and creativity. What he does, he does in the name of others, for others, in the sight of others, as if to say, "What I think, say or do, is good and has value; therefore, act as I do." He who lives in accordance with God's commandments, bears witness to those commandments in the sight of others, it is as if he were acting in the name of all men. "By choosing himself," Sartre justly remarks, "man chooses all men."[5] That is why human life has the significance of a testimony, a "profession," i.e., a public declaration.

Since man expresses and manifests himself only in his "work," realizes his being and his being-together-with in his "work," this "work" is the *meeting place* of mankind. It is the place where the dialogue with the past is freely continued with an eye on the future; it is the place where facticity and idea meet in a dialectical tension, without ever fusing into a lifeless unity; it is the place where tradition is taken over

[5]J. P. Sartre, *L'existentialisme est un humanisme,* Paris, 1946, p. 25; "There is no act of ours which, in creating the man we want to be, does not create at the same time an image of man as we believe he ought to be."

and reappears on the scene after being re-created. In short, it is man's "work" that makes history possible. In this sense Merleau-Ponty speaks truthfully about "work as the foundation of history."[6]

Man Lives in Time. The meeting of man with others through "work" takes place *in the course of time.* What time actually is, is one of the crucial questions of philosophy, and it is not our intention to delve into that question here. The following will suffice.

Our experience of time undoubtedly contains a certain awareness of transitoriness, of a succession of temporal moments, a continuous flux. This is why we are always inclined to represent time as an endless series of loose, successive moments that can be divided into three sections: the innumerable events of the *past,* the endless series of events that will constitute the *future* and, the in between, the *fleeting now* of today, which, as soon as it has presented itself, immediately disappears into the past and makes room for a new *now.* Strictly speaking, this is a wrong picture of time; it is the result of a projection of time in space, which by no means corresponds to our original lived experience of time. "Lived time" is quite different. It is primarily an experience of *presence.* What we call the past, is something that once was *present* and which we, from the standpoint of *our present* now, recognize, preserve, and retain as *past.* What we call the "future" is something that we, again from the standpoint of the *present* now, expect as a possibility that some day can or will become a *present* reality. Hence the experience of an open presence lies at the foundation of the ideas of past and future. The experience of presence takes precedence over the past and the future, because it encompasses, as it were, the other two; but this presence is not the fleeting *now* with its total lack of extension.

[6]*Sens et non-sens,* p. 127: "le travail sur lequel repose l'histoire."

Time, according to Husserl is, in reality, presence (*Gegenwart*), more correctly the "life-stream of presence." (*lebendig strömende Gegenwart*). It is a kind of presence—we may say, the only mode of presence we human beings know—the endless presence which is always a tension between absence and presence, in the sense that the negativity of the absence contributes to the positivity of the presence. In other words, the experience of existence that makes us human, that enables us to experience ourselves, to maintain and realize ourselves together with others in a real world of real things, is an experience and an exercise of a presence which exhibits a temporal structure; it contains a reference to the past and to the future, and, therefore, also to the others in the past and the future.

In fact, what do we call "real"? How does reality appear to our consciousness? In contrast with the unreal phantasies of dreams and so-called "contents of mental consciousness," we call real whatever we meet in an experience of presence 1) as being already there (which points to the past); 2) as an object of possible projects for me or others (which points to the future); 3) as a meeting place for a possible encounter with others in a common situation and a common task.

A thing that belongs *exclusively to my world,* that cannot be recognized by anyone else, or, what comes down to the same thing, that cannot be shown to anybody else, will never be able to impress me as fully real, as an objective and real being, but it will impress me as a subjective experience. The same idea could also be expressed by saying that reality for man is the correlate of an encounter, of an experience-of-presence which contains in its very nature a reference to the past, the future, and intersubjectivity. That is real which appears to consciousness as something with which something still can be done, either by me or by others, albeit only that it can be examined and studied.

We thus arrive once more at the conclusion of our previous chapter. Our analysis of the idea of solidarity had led us to the idea of historicity. Now the study of the latter leads us back to the idea of solidarity. As we pointed out, solidarity should not be reduced to a vague feeling of gregariousness, but ought to produce a true "we," a lasting and fruitful community of persons, who recognize and treat one another as free and autonomous beings. Genuine solidarity must possess a historical dimension, and this was even the principal theme of the preceding chapter. "Human solidarity is solidarity in and for history," we said. To be solidary and feel solidary with mankind means that we are ready to take our place in *contemporary* history. We want to take our place with gratitude for what our predecessors have given us, with zealous care for the *future,* for we know very well that any meaningful action is action for others, an action done with the hope that others will draw profit from it.

All this makes us understand better why a more lively awareness of historicity together with the sense of solidarity characterize the world of today. And how could this be otherwise, for the world is becoming one and mankind suddenly sees itself confronted with the greatest task ever, the task of building an economic and social world in which there is *room* for *all,* a world in which there is more truth and more freedom?

CHAPTER EIGHT

TRUTH AND FREEDOM

Perhaps never before in the history of the world has there been so much talk of truth and freedom, so much suffering and struggle for truth and freedom as in our own day. And yet, has there ever been so much doubt about them and so much sinned against them?

In regard to truth, we are all aware of the vast amount of work that is being done to foster knowledge and study. Enormous sums are set aside for research. International congresses of scientists and philosophers constantly grow in number and scope, as if the disinterested search for truth and science were the only field in which mankind can still meet in a peaceful dialogue. Yet the result of the dialogue is usually small. The loudest cry resounding in these congresses echoes the old question which Pontius Pilate addressed to Our Lord: "What is truth?"

Almost the same can be said about freedom. Freedom is considered more and more as the great collective task of our generation. As we have seen, faith in a large scale liberation of individuals and peoples is the driving force of modern history and the reason also why we are at a turning point of history. Nevertheless, we notice at the same time that human freedom is called into question by many, and not the least by those who talk most about the emancipation of man. This attitude of skepticism is the result of the influence of physiology, especially endocrinology, psychology, particularly depth psychology, and the social sciences. Moreover, the world has become hopelessly divided in the name of freedom and the liberation of mankind. What in one camp is hailed as freedom and emancipation, is branded as slavery, dictatorship and imperialism by the other and vice versa. What is perhaps even worse, a refined technique of publicity is more and more replacing the calm practice of the art of persuasion. Hence we can undoubtedly say that truth and freedom are passing through a severe crisis.

It would, nevertheless, be wrong to conclude, as is often done, that the urge for truth and freedom which pervades the present world, is not sincere, or is sincere only on one side (ours, of course, the Western, and especially the side of those who accept Christianity), whereas on the other side (those who think differently, especially the Marxist world), there is nothing but lies and deceit. As long as we do not take a less radical, a more objective attitude, our world will not be able to free itself from its present impasse, for no dialogue is possible under such conditions.

The sole aim of our present study is to obtain a better insight into the paradoxical situation in which truth and freedom are today. The question that will principally occupy our attention is the following: What is the situation of freedom and truth in our present world? Why is it that mankind is so hopelessly divided, while at the same time it asserts that it is using its best efforts to foster truth and freedom? This question is not only important for everyone who is interested in the present world, but is important most of all for the Christian who believes in the liberating force of Christianity and who asks himself not without anxiety: What should be the role of Christian truth in the present struggle for freedom? Did not Christ say, "The truth shall make you free"? If we wish to cast some light on all these questions, it is most necessary to keep in mind what freedom is, what truth is and what the relations are between the two. This suggests to us the sequence of the following considerations.

1. *Nature and Structures of Human Freedom*

Man's first task as a free being, is to liberate freedom itself, just as it is the first task of man, as a rational being, to develop his reason. Now, it should not astonish us that mankind in its zeal for freedom does not agree on the very meaning of freedom itself, if we keep in mind that a finite and embodied freedom like ours is a complex reality with various aspects and components. The fact that the meaning of the words "freedom," "free," and "liberation" can vary in the ordinary language of the people expresses this complexity. As we put the emphasis on one or the other aspects of human freedom, we at once are dealing with different interpretations of it. Some fundamental truth is usually contained in these various interpretations of freedom. However there is always a danger of one-sidedness, an inclination to reduce the whole human life of freedom to one of its aspects. Let us see, therefore, the most important meanings attached to this term, "freedom."

Wrong Meanings of the Term "Freedom"

Freedom as Arbitrariness. There are a few meanings that are often met with, but they are, strictly speaking, a misuse of the term "freedom." First of all, there will always be an inclination to confuse liberty with *arbitrariness* and *absence of all obligation.* "To be free" is taken to mean that man can and may do as he pleases, that man is allowed to give free rein to his instincts, may satisfy his lusts unhampered, and is not bound by anything or any one. In other words, what is understood by the term "freedom" ought to be called "arbitrariness" and "caprice."

It is the freedom of the unfettered dog that "freely" runs around wherever it pleases and minds nothing and nobody. People who have no higher ideal of freedom than this show that their level of life does not rise much above that of the animal.

Freedom as Security. There is a second concept of freedom that we cannot accept. Many people understand by freedom the absence of all worries and burdens, thanks to a perfect system of social security which protects them, as it were, automatically against all future concerns. They dream of a super-socialized state in which man will be free from all worry, where there will be no more need for initiative, and where no one will have to take care of wife and children.[1] Such an ideal of freedom is but the freedom of the infant that has not yet any responsibility, because it is cared for by father and mother, the "freedom" of the soldier, who receives his ration daily, and at the end of the week, his pay; or also, to name the utmost carefree existence, it is the freedom of the prisoner who no longer has anything to care for and lives at the expense of the community.

What we say here, evidently, is not meant to condemn a sound system of social security. We merely wish to underscore that security is not synonymous with freedom. Security must be a means of enabling man to rise to true freedom.

Three Authentic Meanings of the Term "Freedom"

We can distinguish three essential aspects in human freedom and these, in turn, have led to the distinction of three fundamental meanings of the concept of human freedom. For our purpose here, it is of the utmost importance to distinguish these three meanings, but without losing sight of their interconnection.

Freedom as Ideal of Existential Perfection. First of all, there is the meaning which in all probability is the source of all the others and to which all others refer, namely, that freedom is the ideal of existential perfection, autonomy, and personality. Man experiences his freedom first and above all as an *ideal of his existence,* as something which gives meaning

[1] Let us honestly acknowledge that this is not the concept of freedom as it exists in socialist regimes, and it is surely not the concept of freedom in Russian or Chinese communism.

to his being-man.[2] For it cannot be denied that man, as an individual and as a collective reality, feels himself driven by an inexhaustible urge for self-realization, autonomy, maturity, independence, or whatever one may wish to call it. Now, the word "freedom" has always been used to express this ideal of autonomy, of "self-hood", by which man, on the one hand is *freed* negatively from the many estrangements that oppress him, and on the other, is made free positively for a *full, autonomous life and creative activity*. Let us try to illustrate this with a few examples.

Think of the expert craftsman who knows his profession, who has really mastered it. He exercises his knowledge and skill freely and in a sovereign way. There are, as it were, no longer any obstacles nor difficulties for him. He is, as we say, a "master" in his profession. The apprentices, on the contrary, are like slaves who merely imitate what is done by the master. They depend on the master for what they do. They are slaves even of the tools they use, and experience them as impediments rather than as subservient instruments to be freely and sovereignly governed with a masterly hand.

The same could be said of the accomplished artist. In a free and autonomous way he creates his work of art, he completely dominates his technique and, as it were, "plays" with it.

We could also take examples from the field of knowledge and science. Consider, e.g., the difference between an intelligent man who reflects personally, who speaks from *personal* insight, who knows what he says and why he says it, and, on the other hand, the superficial man who thoughtlessly repeats what "everyone" says.

Man has always used the idea of "freedom" especially to refer to the summits of *moral* and *religious* life. In fact the

[2]The term "meaning" refers here to that to which our being-man is directed.

hero and the saint look less upon the good as a command imposed on them from without than as an inner appeal which, as it were, identifies itself with freedom and gives it its inexhaustible creative power. The "spiritual man," says St. Paul, is above the law, he has the freedom of a child of God: his soul lives in harmony with God's love, for he has been re-created by the Holy Spirit and made free for the mystery of God and God's work of salvation. To express this spiritual maturity, which makes man free for religious and moral values, St. Augustine used the term "freedom" (*libertas*) rather than "free will" (*liberum arbitrium*).

These examples suffice to show that freedom, as ideal of spiritual autonomy and maturity, has no relation to caprice and arbitrariness, and that it is, likewise, foreign to sickly narcissism, i.e., the spirit of self-sufficiency and self-satisfaction which shuts man up in himself and condemns him to unfruitfulness. Man is not a "capsuled" Cartesian *Cogito,* as we have already remarked, but he is, in his deepest being, openness to the world and to the others who are in the world. It is only through this openness to others, by which man makes himself free for others that he attains true autonomy and self-possession, and becomes irrevocably and freely "some one." It is sufficient to recall here the great "names" in the many realms of human life, the great men of science, artists, and philosophers, the social thinkers and pioneers, the heroes and the saints. Their "names" are synonymous with personality, autonomy, renewal, creativeness, liberating freedom.

A thirst for more freedom and liberation for all, both individuals and nations, is the great animating and moving power of our time. It is clear that the terms "freedom" and "liberation," as used in such expressions, must be understood in line with that first and most fundamental meaning of the concept of freedom. This does not mean that we want to make everybody a genius or a hero, but we want to give to individuals and peoples a greater autonomy and right of self-expression, to free them from numerous estrangements, and to give them opportunities for a fuller development of the spiritual potentialities that are dormant in them.

There can be a profound difference of opinion, even on this level of the individual and collective aim of freedom. It is quite evident, for example, that what St. Paul means by "the freedom of the children of God," or St. Augustine by "freedom," are not the same thing as what an atheist or a man like Marx means by liberation. This difference does not mean that the atheist does not aim at making man really free and autonomous, but the concrete content of the terms is not identical or is only partly the same for the unbeliever and for the believer. The former reduces human existence to his being-in-the-world, whereas the latter acknowledges also a deeper dimension of truth and freedom in man, the religious dimension, by which man is made free for God Himself and the saving work of Him "whom to serve is to reign."

But whatever may be the concrete content or meaning given to man's liberation, freedom as the ideal of autonomy and maturity is for man a goal that is attained only with difficulty, slowly and then only in part. This brings us to the second concept of freedom.

Psychological Concept of Freedom. Freedom as free will (*liberum arbitrium*) means man's power or ability to work freely at the development and the liberation of his existence. To be free means to be fully responsible, to know what one is doing and why he does it. In other words, freedom is the ability that every man has to give a *meaning* and a *direction* to his life and his work, to say autonomously "yes" or "no" with respect to the numerous possibilities and values that constantly present themselves. Freedom in this sense is a quality of man's willing. It is a result of the fact that man is endowed with reason, that he can reflect before he acts, that he can judge and weigh the significance or the purpose of his deeds, that he can work freely for the unfolding of his own personality and the liberation of mankind. In this sense freedom, as free will, is not an ultimate goal but rather a means, a power of liberation.

When we reflect further and see that our actions obtain meaning to the extent that they embody values and develop the realm of values in the world, one can say that the freely chosen activity is fundamentally nothing else than a conscious and purposeful judgment of value which becomes embodied and is completed in a concrete action. What psychology of the will calls motivation, decision and execution, are not so much distinct moments, having their individual place in time, but rather related components of one same process of conduct. Let us take note, in fact, that these three aspects permeate one another. He who truly appreciates a value is ready to do something for it, to translate it into purposeful deeds and to foster it in the world. By this very fact he gives *meaning* to his life.

This shows once more that true freedom, freedom that truly liberates us and others, is in no way related to caprice or arbitrariness. It does not consist in doing anything that comes to the mind, in blindly following the promptings of instinct, in discarding all responsibility. Far from sowing whims and disorders in our life, freedom appears on the scene as a principle of order, purposefulness and regularity. It prevents us from being tossed hither and thither by circumstances, but, on the contrary, invites us to use all situations to foster the values to which we have consecrated our lives. This, at the same time, explains why freedom does not disturb the order and the law of nature; on the contrary, it constantly needs this law and order.

Indeed, if the world in which we live and of which we form a part were only a disorderly succession of happenings and phenomena, if any phenomenon could be preceded and followed by any other phenomenon, in other words, if at any time anything could become anything else, then there would be no possibility of undertaking anything in such a "world." In such a world there would be nothing fixed to anchor our knowledge or our action, for things would be without fixed properties, and no fixed attributes could be predicated of anything. Lead, iron, water and the rest could in no way be defined, they could not be distinguished from other things. They would not be recognizable, they could not be pointed out and designated by a fixed name, and thus it would be impossible to understand one another, since we would never know whether we were talking about the "same thing" as the others.

A fortiori we could not make use of anything, we would not be able to count upon anything, we would not be able to make a single project, nor could we give meaning and value to our behavior, since nothing would then serve as a means for anything else. In short, our freedom, which is an embodied and historically situated freedom, could not accomplish even the least useful work. Freedom and determinism are not contradictory realities but two complementary sides of man's existence as being bound to the body and the world.

Sociological and Political Freedom. In this way we arrive at the third concept of freedom: freedom in the sociological and political sense of the word. We are now thinking of the physical and social conditions that are necessary for the concrete exercise of our freedom. Hence in this third sense we usually speak of freedom in the plural; e. g., the "democratic freedoms."

Human freedom is not an unlimited power of creation. It is essentially finite and, because of our bodily being, situated in time-and-space and in history. In all that we do we depend on our physical and social surroundings. For the man who is born blind, there is no such thing as the art of painting; that is, his realm of freedom is less extensive than ours, since the entire visual section is missing. For a man who has never heard about Christ, there exists no freedom to accept the Christian faith and to give a Christian meaning to his life. At the beginning of the Industrial Revolution when it was the custom to employ young children, even six year olds, for work in factories, "freedom" and "liberation" were empty words and unattainable dreams for large segments of the people.

These examples illustrate what we have called the sociological meaning of the word "freedom." The term is used to designate the whole network of economic, social and political conditions of life that are necessary for the concrete exercise of freedom and for the effective liberation of the potentialities dormant in every man. It is precisely the role of the State, in so far as it is charged with the common welfare, to insure greater equality of opportunities for the citizens, by means of wise and appropriate laws. This sociological concept of freedom unfolds further in two directions.

First of all, there is a kind of freedom which is very closely connected with "natural law" and partly even coincides with it. "Freedom" or "freedoms" in the sense of natural rights refers to a whole series of freedoms, of possibilities to act freely, to exercise one's freedom without hindrance. These are so closely connected with human nature, or more correctly with the dignity of the human person and the harmonious development of man's personality, that they may on no account be taken away by the fact that man lives in a society. They, as it were, belong to man before he enters society, as a kind of inalienable rights. Society is never allowed to hinder those freedoms but, on the contrary, has the task of fostering them. Examples of these freedoms are: freedom of conscience, i.e., the ability to act freely according to one's conscience, freedom to marry or remain celibate, freedom to choose one's profession, to take care of one's health and preserve the integrity of one's body, to provide in person for the upkeep of wife and children. Freedom in this sense is very often synonymous with right, and this should not astonish us, for every right brings with it a whole series of actions which one should be able to perform freely and without interference by others.

Alongside this concept of a freedom by natural law, there is, secondly, the concept of freedom by positive law. In this sense, we speak, for example, of political freedom and freedom regimes.

No society that really cares for the welfare of all can attain its end without order and organization, without authority and legislative power, without sanctions and penal laws which serve to guarantee the observance of the law.

Every law restricts freedom of action and movement; it restricts freedom to the extent that freedom expresses itself outwardly. Traffic laws, for instance, do not permit us to drive as we please on the highways. The aim, however, of this restriction is to keep the roads free and open to all. Likewise, if we want to foster health and bring the necessary means within the reach of all, we must introduce regulations which restrict the liberties of some, for example, that of physicians.

Freedom of movement and of action, therefore can, be restricted to a greater or lesser extent through positive law. In this way there arises the idea of a "regime of freedom." It refers to a political regime which has the following aims:

1) To leave as much freedom as possible according to the principle: "As much freedom as is possible for all and as much restriction as is necessary for the freedom of all."

2) To guarantee especially the freedoms of natural law by means of positive legislation.

3) To create the conditions of life that are necessary or favorable for the liberation of all.

It is evident that democracy, which is characterized by the free "voice" and participation of all in the government of the State, is practically the only means that can establish a regime of great freedom.

These, then are the three basic meanings of the word "freedom." All three are indispensable, for they correspond with the three fundamental components of our freedom. Hence they are also intimately related and refer to one another by virtue of a logical connection and order in this fashion. Freedom, as autonomy and maturity, is the very *purpose* of our existence; freedom, as free will, is the *subjective* way to the goal, that is, the way which the human subject himself must trace and follow; social and political freedom, which point to the *objective conditions of life* that are necessary for liberation.

All this shows again that human freedom is a complex reality and a difficult task set before man. It is, therefore, at the same time a fragile and threatened value. The danger always exists that man in his struggle for more freedom and liberation will make one of these three components absolute and divorce it from the others. For instance, socialism, especially at its inception, showed a tendency to expect man's liberation almost exclusively from the objective conditions of life, such as the raising of standards of living and economic and social reforms. But conditions of life are only conditions, means, circumstances which are indeed necessary for the development of freedom but cannot *of themselves* make man free. What, for example, is the use of raising the wages of a laborer if he is left in cultural and moral ignorance and without any taste for the things of the spirit.[3]

The opposite danger also is present. The material and objective conditions of freedom may be underestimated, and freedom reduced to a kind of idealism or liberalism. It cannot be denied that such an idealistic concept of freedom is still at work among certain groups of wealthy Christians.

A liberating freedom is one that both strives for a high ideal of spiritual maturity and takes into account the concrete situations. In short, it is a freedom based upon truth.

2. *The Nature and Structure of Human Truth*

"Not by bread alone does man live, but by every word that comes from the mouth of God," we read in Scripture (Matt. 4,4). "Bread" is the symbol of all that nourishes the living or animal body. "Word," on the contrary, stands for all that speaks to the mind, that sets free the life of the spirit, and helps its development. Expressed in philosophical language, man, unlike the brute, is not *chained* to his surroundings by a network of instinctive and fixed patterns of behavior, but he moves freely, autonomously and creatively in his world. He builds his world by the fact that the things around him *speak* to him or, what comes down to the same thing, he *"recognizes"* them for what they are, and then deals with them in an understanding, judicious and meaningful way. In other words, man's freedom is an immediate consequence of his intellectual power, of his ability to recognize beings *as such,* i.e., for what they are, to distinguish them from one another, instead of confusing them, to understand their respective meaning, their role in the totality of beings. Briefly, the intellect is the power that enables man to discover meaning,

[3]It is undoubtedly the great merit of H. de Man in his book, *Au delà du Marxisme,* to have emphasized the importance of the subjective and spiritual elements in the struggle for freedom.

order and interconnection in things and thus to act with and toward them in a competent manner.

In fact, what is it that distinguishes man from the irrational and non-free animal? Among other things, to use just a very simple example, it is the fact that we can recognize a fountain pen as a fountain pen; we can recognize it as something that is constructed in a definite way and serves as an instrument for writing. Likewise, we recognize a watch as a watch, as something that makes us know what time it is; we can understand and use it, as, in general, we are able to discover the specific purpose of every tool.

A dog cannot do that and, therefore, has no meaningful relations with things. What we have said about the world of tools and instruments is true also of the world of natural things, such as trees, flowers, fruits, the earth under our feet and the sky above our heads. It is particularly true of the world of intersubjectivity. In the look of a child, the smile of a mother, the handshake of a friend, the work of an artist, the word of a poet and of a philosopher, the other appears to us *as other,* as another "I"; he speaks to us, we are introduced into his world, are made *free for* his world. In a word, space, openness and freedom enter into our existence by the fact that we are more and more capable of grasping all these being for what they are, we are able to evaluate, judge, respect, disapprove or admire them in truth.

Accordingly, man's capacity for truth is nothing else than the power to meet reality itself in an understanding, judicious and meaningful way. A discussion of the ultimate nature and the basic potentialities of this power, of the innermost essence of truth, lies beyond our scope, for it would demand philosophical considerations. The only question that interest us here is the following: What is the situation of truth in today's world? Never before has so much been done to foster truth and science, nor have men suffered so much for the truth or have so many sinned against it. How is that possible and how should we approach this problem? Two things above all should be carefully kept in mind: on the one hand, man's world of truth has a multidimensional character; on the other, every human truth is limited or rather incomplete.

The Multidimensional Character of the World of Human Truth

In the preceding pages we have frequently referred to the multidimensional structure of the human world of truth without examining it very closely.

Truth, no doubt, has unity, and man in his striving for knowledge and truth is driven by a desire for synthesis and unity. Truth and unity, says St. Thomas, are two interchangeable concepts. For to understand, to comprehend, means to discover interconnection and order, to reduce multiple data to a unity of order.[3a]

But this unity of the truth which always remains more an ideal of man than an achieved result, must not make us forget the multiplicity of diverse levels or realms of truth. For instance, we may distinguish the truth of the everyday practical world, the truth of modern positive science, the truth pursued by philosophy, and the truth we attain and cherish in religious faith.

The Truth of the "Everyday World." This truth is principally a practical truth. It arises from our daily contact with things in *prescientific practice*. For instance, we call "warm" the objects whose nearness causes us to experience a "feeling" of warmth; by "chair" we understand an object to sit on; by "fountain pen" we mean an instrument used for writing.

The Truth of Positive Science. Quite different is the truth of the so-called objective, positive or empirical sciences, whose

[3a]"To comprehend," a French philosopher has remarked, "is always a certain way of taking things together."

first foundations were laid by Galileo, Descartes, and Newton. This truth is called "empirical" *par excellence* because it not only starts from empirical data, but also aims at an explanation and understanding that can be verified and controlled by any one and anywhere through empirical examination. As Claude Bernard, the founder of experimental medicine expressed it: "The experimental method, as a scientific method, rests entirely on the *experimental verification of a scientific hypothesis.*"[4] In this, positive science differs radically from philosophy. When the philosopher endeavors, e.g., to prove the existence of God or the immortality of the soul, he too starts from empirical data, taken in the broad sense, but he cannot test his conclusion by means of a new experiment.

On the contrary, when the physicist constructs a theory about the atom, this theory has no value if it cannot be directly or indirectly verified and controlled through scientific research. In other words, for the scientist to "explain" means to discover the regularity and interconnection of phenomena, and still more, to determine functional relations between variable magnitudes, which relations can then be expressed in mathematical formulae. Positive science moves within a world of phenomena. Hence within this science it is meaningless to appeal to factors that are beyond the reach of experiment, such as the intervention of God or of other supernatural and preternatural powers, because such an appeal is contrary to the nature and the very purpose of the scientific method.

The fact that positive science, as Claude Bernard says, "rests entirely upon the experimental verification of an explanatory hypothesis," gives to it a prestige which cannot be attained by any other method of knowledge. Scientific truth alone is strictly controllable truth. This gives it the

[4]Claude Bernard, *Introduction à l'étude de la médicine expérimentale,* Geneva, 1945, p. 409.

priceless privilege of creating unanimity among scientists without much difficulty, and of putting at their disposal a language that is the same everywhere. But there is also another side, for that very method of control and positive scientific testing causes the field of scientific truth to be essentially limited. In other words, the fact that objective science uses a method that can be described objectively and can be controlled at will, limits the realm of reality to its *objective and controllable aspects* and excludes whatever cannot be "objectified," whatever cannot appear in objective and controllable forms.

For example, scales can very accurately determine the weight of my body but no research instrument can register that this body is my *personal* body, a body that belongs *to me,* and which has priceless *value for me* since it is this body, as mine, that enables me to live in the world, to realize myself by means of that world. This "mine-ness" of my body has neither weight or color nor any objectively-perceptible phenomenal form, and yet, for me it is its most special characteristic since it constitutes me as a "subject."

Let us take another example. The neurologist can study the conditions of my brain by means of an encephalogram and know what is taking place in it when I am joyful or anxious or am making efforts at philosophical reasoning. But all this leaves him ignorant of the content and the meaning of my joy and my anxiety, nor can he determine whether my philosophical reasonings are true or false. Not only does the encephalogram tell us nothing about all this but no objective experiment exists that can reveal such things, for the *meaning* and significance of my feelings and the *truth value* of my thinking do not belong to the world of "objective," controllable phenomena, but to the world of the inner and personal experience of my subjectivity.

Accordingly, it is important to note that some aspects of reality and, therefore, also some problems concerning reality are *by definition* beyond the reach of positive scientific investigation and lie beyond the competence of science. Among these problems we must name, first of all, those that consider the first origin and the ultimate meaning of the universe and which culminate in the question of the existence of a transcendent God. Indeed, scientific investigation will never be able to give evidence concerning the first beginning of things, for science presupposes the existence of things with their scientific intelligibility. As Einstein has said, what is unintelligible to us is the fact that the world is intelligible, that it lends itself to scientific understanding.

Alongside the problems about the beginning, the end, and the ultimate meaning of all things, there are also many questions regarding the value of things and the foundations of value, especially the questions about the truth value of our ethical conduct. This does not mean that positive science is not permitted to occupy itself with values, but, when it does, it confines itself to the viewpoint of positive science, to the standpoint of the purely *objective facts* science contains, as is done, e.g., in statistical research. In this way science can record that delinquency increases or diminishes in certain sociological conditions because of their connection with definite factors leading to crime; that monogamy predominates in some cultures, and polygamy in others. But science is not competent to determine why monogamy is ethically superior to polygamy, nor can it tell us why stealing and murder must be condemned as ethical misdeeds.

This also is easy to understand. The investigation of positive science tells us what are *the facts,* but not what human conduct *ought to be* in order to have *value.* Science records how men actually think and act, but not who is right and who is wrong. It teaches us which forms of propaganda and publicity are most efficient, but tells us nothing about the truth and the value of the things that are publicized. For the ideas of "truth" and "value" always contain the idea of a norm and an ideal which are used as criteria in the judgment about the truth and value of facts.

All this explains also why positive science is unable to deal with the real problem of freedom, for, as we have shown above, a free action is fundamentally a deliberate value judgment embodied in concrete deeds. Let us give an example to illustrate the point. A man grabs his gun and shoots a fellow man. For objective physiological and physical science, there is nothing but a series of physical and chemical phenomena, which can be explained by natural science. The pulling of the trigger is the result of muscular contractions and relaxations, and the amount of energy used in the process can be calculated by science. The scientist can also describe and explain the trajectory of the bullet according to the laws of ballistics, the weight of the projectile, the aim of the gunner, and the amount of energy released by the explosion of the gunpowder. The death of the victim, from the purely objective standpoint, is nothing more than the breaking up of a particular physiological structure of protoplasmic mass through the action of the projectile. Objective biology cannot tell us much more than this. However, the shooting of a man has a *meaning* and significance, it represents a *value* or a *non-value*. It might be the case of a soldier who risked his life for the defense of his country. But it could also be a cowardly murder inspired by hatred or jealousy. Biology knows nothing about that and is not concerned with judgments of value.

No doubt, the psychologist and the sociologist will go a step further and say that, to explain the affair, one should take into account the reasons and motives that were involved in it. But those motives are but objective factors for these men of science. Positive psychology and sociology know nothing about the value of the motivation, about that which gives ethical value to heroism and makes cowardly murder a non-value. Moreover, strictly speaking, they are not even permitted to claim that someone has been the *victim* of an *attack*. For, if these words have meaning, it is because they contain a twofold judgment of value: to speak of a "victim" means that the protoplasmic whole, which was attacked, is the body of a particular *someone,* is a value that *belongs to him and is for him.* Likewise when one speaks of an "attack", he considers the other protoplasmic organism which fired the gun, as an "assailant," as the *responsible* agent of the deed, as someone who is supposed to be a free being.

What must we conclude from all this? That objective science, because of its very method, does not consider the whole of reality and cannot reply to all the questions which inevitably arise when man reflects and wishes to give meaning to his life. There are questions that by their very nature escape from scientific investigation. These are questions concerning the first origin and the ultimate meaning of the world around us, the value of life, the dignity of the human person, the meaning of freedom, the ultimate foundation of moral values. None of these questions can be solved with the methods of objective research; they belong to a different order, the order of philosophy and theology.

Philosophical Truth. Alongside and outside scientific knowledge there is room, therefore, for philosophical truth. This truth also is based upon experience. The experience, however, to which philosophy refers is experience in the broadest and most comprehensive sense—namely, the experience of our existence as an embodied I, which realizes itself in intersubjectivity by means of the world. This explains why philosophy appears as a return to the concrete, why it elaborates the highest syntheses and asks the ultimate questions: what ultimately is man? and, what in the last analysis is the value of man's life?

Religious Truth. Philosophy itself does not claim that it is able to explain in a satisfactory manner the riddle of human existence and of the universe in which we live. For us Christians, to the great questions of life, a final answer is given on the religious level, in faith in God's Word, which was revealed in the course of history in the person of Jesus Christ. This means that we possess, besides philosophical truth, a truth of religious faith. It is the truth that makes us free for the mystery of the living God and his saving intentions in relation to man.

Dogmatism. Human truth is thus indeed a complex reality. Man in his thirst for clarity and understanding is always inclined to simplify truth and to make one realm of truth control the others. He then sins against the truth and lapses into so-called "dogmatism," since he forcibly wants to reduce all truths to one preconceived type. Dogmatism, however, can take many forms. Religious and clerical dogmatism enthrones the truth of faith as the highest and sole criterion of all other truth. The dogmatizing positivism of science or scientism refuses to accept any other truth than the truth of positive science. This dictatorship of positive science is just as dangerous and harmful as the dictatorship of clerical dogmatism.

In addition to this simplification of truth which tries to reduce all truth to a single type of truth, there exists another way of sinning against the truth. It is to maintain that truth is complete and finished, that no more progress is possible.

Truth as a Never-Finished Project

It is important to note here that we are referring to incompleteness in both the horizontal and the vertical line.

There is not only room for numerous new discoveries which constantly enlarge the horizon of our world of truth; progress in depth is also always possible because, in a certain sense, we have never said the last word about anything. All the concepts and principles we use, even those that are most self-evident, unshakeable and fundamental, lend themselves to further reflection and greater depth. Hence human knowledge advances not only horizontally, by new discoveries and conquests, but also vertically or more precisely, it advances according to a circular and spiral movement, because it regularly returns to its first principles and, as it were, renews itself in and through these principles.

The Exact Sciences. The experience that human knowledge can be developed in this circular way is one of the most important happenings of our time. It has given rise to the idea of a *crisis of the sciences* and has sharpened our awareness of the fact that all human truth is a living motion and an essential openness. Let us explain what we mean by this statement.

To everybody's astonishment, positive physical science and even mathematics have, especially in the last century, developed in a totally different way than the one that had been predicted by Galileo, Descartes, and Newton, who had laid the foundation of science. Until rather late in the nineteenth century the Western world still dreamt of a kind of "universal science" or "mathematics," of a science which, starting from a handful of eternal and unshakeable evidences and first principles, would gather the whole universe of phenomena into a single great, all-embracing system. But things have run quite a different course. The development of the objective sciences has not taken place in a straight line but rather in a spiral curve. The results of constant experimental research forced the scientists to re-examine their scientific principles, obliged them to revise the so-called unshakeable evidences from which they had started. Concepts which for centuries had been considered self-evident, such as those of individual and motion, of continuity and discontinuity, time and space, mass and energy, causal determinism, and the postulates of Euclidean geometry, were put into question one after another and underwent an inner crisis. Science was, as it were, rethought and reconstructed up from its roots. This is why the modern man of science is so careful in his statements and readily acknowledges that not a single scientific theory must be considered as a definitive picture of things. Scientific truth appears henceforth to man's consciousness as a project that to a great extent is still incomplete and requires constant renewal.

Modern Philosophy. Modern philosophy has also come under the influence of this concept of truth. No doubt, the philosopher is still occupied with the highest syntheses, he still aims at expressing the whole of reality. But no one any longer believes that the whole of reality will ever be expressed in a definitive and exhaustive way. Man is convinced now that, to paraphrase Shakespeare, there are more things in heaven and on earth than are dreamt of in all the philosophies of the world.

The modern philosopher does not want ready-made answers. To philosophize means for him a "relatively independent rethinking of the eternal problems which have always occupied the thinking man."[5] To philosophize means to question over and over again, to continue the struggle against numerous so-called "obvious" truths. The reason lies in the conviction of modern man that the last word has not been said about anything and especially not about the great riddle which man himself is. The arrogant self-complacency and self-certainty, which characterized philo-

[5]William A. Luijpen, *Existential Phenomenology,* Pittsburgh, 2nd impr., 1962, p. 2.

sophical thinking from Descartes to and including Hegel, has been discarded to a great extent by modern philosophy, not because of an empty skepticism, but because of a desire to get closer to reality and to authentic life, because of a love for truth itself.

Theology. The same assertions must also be made about modern theology. It also is much more modest, less dogmatizing, *precisely out of respect for the dogma of faith and the mystery of faith.* Whereas formerly there existed a great tendency to deduce ever more distant and more complicated conclusions from the premises of faith—which conclusions finally had very little relation to the faith—there is now much more interest in bringing out the full value of the mystery of faith itself and to show better how ineffable it is. At present, theologians are especially on guard lest their theological consideration give the impression of taking the place of faith and of substituting for the mystery of faith conceptual structures which are foreign to life. In this sense the greater contact with reality of present-day theological thought is something we can greet with joy.

Such an attitude is an excellent aid in ecumenical thinking, for, in regard to the things that divide us, it enables us to distinguish better what actually does constitute a difference of faith and what should be considered only a difference of theological perspective and theological formulation. As a consequence, it becomes increasingly apparent that one and the same belief is often hidden under a variety of theological formulae. It can be said, especially in the realm of faith and theology, that authentic theological truth, since it is the reflection of the faithful upon his faith, is an open truth which is never complete and which needs the ecumenical dialogue in order to rise to a more authentic truth of faith, one that is more faithful to the faith.

3. *Compenetration of Truth and Freedom*

What we have seen thus far shows clearly how intimately truth and freedom are interwoven. They are two values that cannot exist independently, they are inseparable and refer to each other. We may add even that they are constitutive components of our existence as human beings, that is, of our spiritual "*space*" and "*openness*." As such, they are the foundation of each other and fuse into each other.

As we have repeatedly remarked, what distinguishes us from lifeless things and from irrational non-free animals, is the fact that the world of nature and culture, the great human community of which we are members, and the mystery of existence that bears us, are not *closed books* for us. They are, on the contrary, eloquent realities that constantly tell us many and ever new things. For this reason we are able to deal understandingly, judiciously and meaningfully with all those beings. In a word, we can *move freely* in the world, full of respect, gratitude and good will toward all that *is*.

"*Connaître*" (to know) as Paul Claudel has poetically said, "is fundamentally a kind of "*co-naître*" (to be born together). It is a way, even the only true way, of arising and existing together. What we do not know is, so far as we are concerned, non-existing. Here lies the reason why the ideas of *space* and *openness* play so great a role in contemporary thought and speech. That the world and everything in it, is no closed book for man implies on the part of man a limitless and inexhaustible *openness* and *receptivity* to all that *is*. For St. Thomas "the soul in a way is all things," it, as it were, contains and encompasses everything. Modern thinkers, especially since Heidegger, have attempted to express this same idea by the terms *space, openness, omnipresence,* or encounter.

"The being of man," says Heidegger, "is *Da-sein,*" that is, a being that breaks through the material "closedness" of lifeless things; it brings space, openness and freedom of movement into the world. The *"Da"* (there) which makes us *Da-sein* is not a mere standing-here or there-in-the-midst-of-things, as a chair stands in the middle of a room, but it is conscious and free contact with things by the fact that these beings reveal themselves to us as they are. They, as it were, "show and announce themselves," leave their concealedness and come into the open. Existence, as *Da-sein,* means for man that he causes a "circle of openness," to arise around him.[6]

But whatever may be the way of expressing it, whether we use Thomistic or Heideggerian language, truth and freedom are so intimately connected that they are each other's foundation. There is no freedom without truth, but also no truth without external and interior freedom. Our Lord's words, "the truth shall make you free," do not merely express the essence of the Christian message, the mystery of the kingdom of God, but are also full of philosophical wisdom, wisdom for the whole of mankind.

There is no true liberating freedom that is not grounded on truth. Unless there exists love and care for truth, man will not be able to attain that interior autonomy, that sense of responsibility and resilience without which freedom unavoidably degenerates into capriciousness, arbitrariness, unbridled greed, ambition and lust for power. What is then called autonomy or personality is only a caricature, only self-centeredness, coupled with a total closedness to others. Whether it takes the form of paralyzing narcissism or that of aggressive hardheartedness and brutal drunkenness with power, it is ultimately an expression of self-satisfaction, the idealizing of the ego, which is just the opposite of openness and liberating freedom.

On the other hand, however, *there is likewise no truth without a climate of interior and exterior freedom.* Truth for

[6]Cf. W. Biemel, *Le concept de Monde chez Heidegger,* Louvain, 1940, p. 81.

man is, as we have seen, a complex reality and a project that is never completely finished. It presupposes a great willingness and receptivity (which is a form of interior freedom) in regard to the many realms of truth constituting the human world of truth; it requires a courageous determination not to allow any truth to get lost, whatever may be its source. Lastly, truth presupposes great openness to further progress of all sciences. That is why all true thinking is marked by the restless search of reflective thought. To reflect means to think anew and further about things; it means to separate oneself from the conventional patterns of thought, to go beyond the trusted formulae in order to discover their true meaning; it means to penetrate beyond so-called "obvious" truths, and to gather the results of the various sciences into a higher synthesis. Reflective thinking, therefore, is to think in freedom. This, of course, does not mean to think with anarchical licence, but with an interior openness of the mind to all that is.

This inner freedom or openness itself, however, is not possible, at least in general, without a climate of *external* freedom or tolerance. History teaches that to assure the victory of an idea by means of arms, social pressure or hypnotizing publicity has always been a short-sighted policy. However eminent a truth might be, if it is imposed at the sacrifice of freedom, it loses its significance and value because it does not obtain an interior agreement, but is accepted only with the lips without transforming and feeding hearts. Such a truth quickly degenerates into a meaningless juggling of soulless formulae and into purely outward forms of behavior, which man will soon throw overboard as useless ballast.

The internal compenetration of truth and freedom enables us to understand better the liberating power of Christian truth. This does not mean that Christianity claims to be a kind of "universal mathematics," or to possess the monopoly of truth. When Christ tells us, "I am the way, the truth and the life," He immediately adds, "No one comes to the Father but through me" (John 14, 6). His truth is not of this world but comes from above and is designed to deliver us from the darkness of a sinful and false existence, for sin is a flight from light. His truth aims at letting us walk in the light of God's Word, "He who follows me does not walk in darkness" (John 8, 12) and at making us free for God and His work of salvation. "If you abide in my word, you shall be my disciples indeed, and you shall know the truth, and the truth shall make you free (John 8, 31-32).

Nevertheless, the truth of God's word is not without importance for secular or profane truth. For there is no liberating truth, no truth that really fosters the liberation of man and brings more truth and justice into human society, without *ethical truthfulness and sincerity*. Even with respect to the realm of truth it is in *ethics* that the religious and the secular meet. Rightly does Holy Scripture consider the lie, both the lie against others and the lie against oneself, as the source of all social evils; and rightly it praises faith in Jesus Christ, the Word of God, as the liberating force of the secular life of human society. "You were once darkness but you are now light in the Lord. Walk, then, as children of light, *for the fruit of the light is in all goodness and justice and truth.* (Eph. 5, 8). How much more joy and peace, truth and justice there would be in the world if men were faithful to Christ's words in the Sermon on the Mount, "Let your speech be 'Yes, yes'; 'No, no' " (Matt. 5, 37).

CHAPTER NINE

THE SOCIAL PROBLEM AS A CULTURAL-HISTORICAL PROJECT

The term "social" can have more or less extensive senses. Take, for example, the expressions "social psychology," "social psychiatry," "the social nature of man"; and on the other hand, "the social problem," "social politics," and "social encyclicals." In the first three examples the term "social" points in general to man's life in community; in the three others it points to a particular and recent phenomenon in the life of the human community, namely, the striving of modern society for a more equitable distribution of cultural goods, for a greater and truer freedom for all, both individuals and nations. This social aspiration, which pervades the modern world, is one of the great events of our time and perhaps the greatest social event of all times. It will be our task in the following analysis to examine the nature of this phenomenon and lay bare its inner structure.

We are dealing here with a social event, a cultural-historical fact. This statement suffices to note that the term "problem" does not have a purely theoretical meaning here. In other words, we are not dealing with something that resembles a problem of chemistry or philosophy. What we call here a problem is rather a great longing, a gigantic purpose that has risen in the hearts of millions of human beings, workers and intellectuals, and has united them to form the greatest power history has ever known.

1. *The Origin of the Social Struggle*

As everybody knows, the social evolution or revolution that is at work in our present world has its source in the socio-economic evils of the last century. Some may be inclined to remark: Why go back and scrutinize the past? Why recall and rehash the evil conditions and the abuses that belonged to the liberal period, when many no longer even know that those evils existed?

It is indeed a dangerous temptation for man to allow himself to become obsessed with the past, especially when the past has been very harsh and can generate great bitterness. But this danger is not very great if those who revert to the past, have not personally suffered from its evils. Looking back to the past is even a necessity for them if they wish to understand the feelings affecting some of their contemporaries.

If at this time there are still many intellectuals who take little interest in the social problem, is not one of the reasons precisely the lack of knowledge of the past? They do not know the crying misery and want of the proletariat that prevailed during the last century, and most of them have merely read or heard vague general statements about it. They forget that many of today's laborers have been trained for the struggle by their parents and older comrades and that they still carry all these memories deep in their hearts.

Another and more compelling reason for the study of the past is this: we want to penetrate into the heart of the social problem. Now this problem is not a theoretical question but an historical fact, and a far-reaching cultural phenomenon. Like all historical events, it has a definite origin and its content cannot be separated from this origin.

The Concept of Origin

It would be useful to begin our inquiry by examining the term "origin," which plays such an important role in historical writing. A couple of observations, however, will have to suffice. The idea of "origin" contains not only the idea of the "past," but also that of "cause."

That a fact belongs to the past is not sufficient to make it the origin of what followed after it. History is not a mere succession of independent events that have no other connection than that of sequence in time. In other words, in historical writings "origin" has also a causal meaning. However, the causal bonds connecting historical events that are studied by the science of history are of a totally different order from those that belong to physics and chemistry. For man is not a lifeless thing of nature, and human conduct does not present the fixed, invariable regularity of physical events. Hydrogen molecules behaved a hundred thousand years ago just as they do now. Not so man, for man is alive, feels and thinks; he is able to appreciate values and defend them; he can either accept or reject conditions of life. In a word, he can make a project of the future, that is, as it were, "cast it before him," and gradually build what he has projected. For, as we have shown above, man is an 'historical' being, a being that makes history.

For this reason, the term "origin" has a very special sense in history. Here "origin" means the point of departure, the ground from which mankind at a certain moment leaps forward to something new. This point of departure and foundation for what is to follow later, consists mostly of three elements which are not simply juxtaposed and independent from one another but have influence on one another. They are the following.

1. There is a definite condition or, to use modern philosophical terminology, there is a *situation,* a whole of material, cultural, economic, and social conditions of existence, in which the men of a particular time live without having chosen them.

2. There is a growing consciousness of values, connected with this situation, that awakens new aspirations in man and prompts him to pursue a new line of action in order to change the existing situation and create better conditions of life.

3. There are social theories and even world views, whose aim it is to analyze and justify this growing awareness of new values, to throw light on the new aim, to devise means for its attainment, and give directives for action.

Those three elements are present at the origin of all cultural changes and of all great historical events. Let us take the French Revolution as an example. There were evil conditions in the Old Regime; the values of freedom and equality were discovered; and there were the new social theories of Jean-Jacques Rousseau and others. Taken separately, none of these three factors can sufficiently explain the French Revolution and its enormous influence on history. The three constitute one whole, and only this whole can be called the origin of the French Revolution. However, the core and the center of gravity of this whole is the growing consciousness of values. Although the conditions of the Old Regime are now a thing of the distant past and the social theory of Jean-Jacques Rousseau now appears antiquated, we cannot fail to see that the values brought to light at that time are still alive and continue to inspire our present society.

What we have said about the French Revolution applies with equal force to the social revolution that is taking place in our world. Here also we find the same three elements—namely, the social evils of the liberal period and the widespread poverty of underdeveloped countries; numerous social theories and world views; the discovery and growing awareness of new values. We will have to pay special attention here to these new values.

This digression in regard to the idea of "origin" has not been a waste of time. To our mind, it is of great importance if we wish to arrive at a correct understanding of both the origin and the object of the social problem. Origin and object are in reality inseparable. He who has a one-sided view of the origin, will also form an incorrect and one-sided picture of the object, and his attitude toward social developments will be influenced accordingly. The truth of this assertion manifests itself constantly. For instance, there are many for whom the origin of the labor struggle is to be reduced to the social evils of the last century. Since these evils have largely disappeared, these people think that the social revolution has come to an end.

Others reduce the whole social development to Marx and Marxist dialectics. What has happened and will continue to happen since Marx, they say, is and cannot be anything else than the inevitable unfolding of Marx' ideas about society and history. The film drawn by Marx, is now being unrolled. Therefore, if mankind wants to make further progress, it must put on the straitjacket of Marx' conceptual structure with its Hegelian background.

All this shows the importance of reflecting on the origin of social events.

The Emancipation of the Laboring Class

In 1886 a Belgian industrialist made the following declaration before the Belgian Labor Commission: "Industrial science consists in getting the maximum work out of a human being while paying him the lowest possible wages."[1] This man gave expression to what was then the common concept and custom. In the socio-economic organization of industry in the second half of the nineteenth century, the laborer was reduced to a purely economic value. He was a production factor alongside the machine and a burden on the budget. In England and the U. S. A. the terms "sweating-system" and "sweat-shop" eloquently expressed this new regime of slavery.

A report of the Belgian Royal Academy of Medicine dating from the same period gives us a bleak picture of the con-

[1] A. Muller, *Nos responsabilités sociales,* Paris-Brussels, 1924, p. 42.

ditions of that time: "The average working day for the industrial laborer is between thirteen and fifteen hours; here and there it is seventeen hours. The same situation exists in England, France and Belgium. Children are employed from the age of six or seven. In 1843, one third of the laborers in the Belgian weaving mills were children, and fifty per cent of these were between the ages of six and a half and ten."[2]

The French economist Jean-Baptiste Say, who traveled to England in 1815 to study the conditions of factory workers wrote that a laborer earned only one third of what he absolutely needed to support his family even when he worked at the maximum of his physical capacity.[3]

Today we ask ourselves how such a thing was possible. Why did the workers tolerate such inhuman conditions? Why did they not go on a strike? But the right to strike and even that to form a union did not yet exist. When the first strike took place in Lyons, police fired on the strikers and their leaders were condemned to prison.[4]

We should not forget that, if in many countries the standard of living of the laborer has considerably improved during the last years, this has not taken place without much blood, humiliations and persecutions. Want, misery and the struggle for life, have united the workers and given them class consciousness. When Karl Marx presented his Manifesto to the world with its fiery final formula, "Workers of the world unite," his battle cry fell upon fertile soil. The social struggle

---

[2]L. Bertrand, *L'ouvrier belge depuis un siècle,* Brussels, 1924, p. 134; J. Leclercq, *Leçons de droit naturel,* IV, Part II; *Travail, Propriété,* Namur, 1946.

[3]Gide et Rist, *Histoire des doctrines économiques,* Paris, 1922, p. 202.

[4]A good concrete example of the impact of a strike in a more peaceful atmosphere is given in the Mémoires of the French novelist, Jean Guéhenno, who was an employee of a shoe factory at Fougères when a strike of several months' duration took place in the winter of 1906: "That strike of 1906 sticks in my mind as the greatest human trial I have ever witnessed." *Le Figaro littéraire,* Jan. 21, 1961.

arose from man's most elementary instinct: his inborn desire of self-preservation, of freedom, of a life that is worthy of man.

The Emancipation of the Underdeveloped Nations

It is still the same "struggle for life" which today spontaneously drives together the poor peoples of Asia, Africa and Latin America, and gradually unites them into a collective power. What is now taking place in the so-called "underdeveloped" continents, is a continuation on a worldwide scale of what began in Europe a century ago. It is the entrance into history of what has sometimes been called the "fourth estate," although it would be more exact to speak of the great anonymous class of the poor and the socially oppressed, who, as a famous author wrote, "plant rice to feed those who have not planted."

In fact, individual and collective *poverty and want* have not yet disappeared from our increasingly wealthier world. The theme of the misery that is predominant in underdeveloped countries has even become the favorite topic of modern economic and political literature. Father P. Lebret, the leader of the association *"Economie et Humanisme"* recently undertook a comprehensive study of that subject under the eloquent title, *Suicide or Survival of the West.*[5]

In 1953 the Belgian statesman R. Scheyven made a report to the General Assembly of the United Nations in which he said: "59½% of the world's population is still underfed; the average life-span in India is 27 years, against 68 in Sweden; in some countries 80% are still illiterate; the average income of an Indonesian is $25 a year, in contrast to the $1,800 per capita of the American citizen. What makes the situation so hopeless and so tragic is the fact that the world's population increases by 80,000 per day, or by thirty million persons per

[5]*Suicide ou Survie de l'Occident,* Editions Ouvrières, Paris, 1958.

year, and that this increase occurs mostly in the parts of the world that are plagued by poverty."

But there is more than poverty; there is also *economic slavery,* and this is even more important. For, as Hegel so realistically described it in his famous dialectics of "the master and the slave," poverty as such does not act as a revolutionary force in history, but rather the poverty that is experienced as slavery, that is, when the slave whose labor supports production and creates riches receives almost no share in this wealth. Economic slavery can easily exist with political autonomy. The nineteenth century workers in liberal Europe, by law, enjoyed the same rights and freedom as other citizens, but that freedom was more theoretical than real. It is precisely because of that tension between the ideal of liberty, equality and fraternity proposed by the law, on the one hand, and actual conditions of economic inequality and slavery, on the other, that the social revolution was born.

The same situation exists today on a world-wide level. There is no more dangerous an illusion for the Western World than to imagine that everything this side of the Iron Curtain constitutes a "free" world since the process of decolonization continues and the emancipated peoples are, one after the other, becoming members of the United Nations. Economic slavery is just as dangerous for world peace as political domination, and the yoke of this slavery still lies heavily on most of the underdeveloped countries, not because they are poor and do not own anything,[6] but because foreign powers control and exploit their natural resources for their own advantage.

[6]Note that technological development has so greatly changed man's relation to the natural resources existing everywhere, that there are almost no more "poor" countries. Even the Sahara has immense wealth buried under its sterile surface.

It is not so much the inequality between the poor and the rich that lies at the source of the numberless social tensions and conflicts that have afflicted the world for more than a century, but rather the inner contradiction of a situation of political freedom coupled with economic dependence.

The situation could be expressed also in this way. Since the rise of vast industrial enterprises man has become conscious of the decisive significance of the *economy* for the liberation of mankind. As Marx correctly judged, philosophy can spin the most beautiful considerations about liberating man, but it is the economy that brings about this liberation on a large scale. The important point is to lend a hand in driving economic slavery out of the world and to make the *economy* serve *all mankind.* In this way a new idea has entered the world, the idea or rather the ideal, of what is usually called *economic and social democracy,* in contrast with purely political democracy. As in every democracy, it is basically a question of an *ethical ideal,* that is, a question of bringing more truth and justice, more equality, more freedom and fraternity among men; but, in contrast with nineteenth century democracy, the accent is now placed upon the socio-economic reorganization of social life. Let us consider this social ideal more closely.

2. *The Social Ideal*

From the preceding pages it is evident that the social problem is more than a question of wages, and that the social struggle aims at something more than mere material improvements for the working class and the underdeveloped and retarded countries.

Yet such a "materialistic" interpretation of present day issues is still very common, even among those who are not unfavorable to social progress and like to be counted among the adherents of a spiritual philosophy of life. They readily admit that evil conditions have formerly existed. But, they add immediately, there is no need to continue to recall the past; the worker's lot has greatly improved during the last years; the economy cannot work miracles; it is high time to go in reverse; and, as was done in the good old times, we should not try to run ahead of possibilities. In other words, economic factors must be given again priority over social concerns. For otherwise the whole of society, both employers and employees, will end in ruin.

Social progress is undoubtedly conditioned by the economy and in that sense the economy has priority over the social. Even the most progressive social leaders, including Karl Marx, do not deny that. Perhaps nowhere in the world is the priority of economic production so brutally affirmed as in the countries that are dominated by Marxism. Unfortunately, it must be added that even many laborers give rise to the impression that their movement has a higher ideal than their antagonists ascribe to it. They often forget that the nearer they come to the attainment of their ideal, the heavier their own responsibility becomes, that the more rights they acquire, the greater and the more sacred their obligations will be.

It is equally true that it is very dangerous to entertain utopias in the realm of economic and social life, and we must unfortunately add once more that some workers and popular demagogues now and then give evidence of being extremely naïve in their economic ideas. They seem to believe that a country's wealth is inexhaustible and that prosperity for all would come about at once if the so-called "huge" gains of the capitalists and managers of factories were taken away from them and distributed among the people. However great and exaggerated those gains sometimes may be, they represent but a small portion of the total economic earnings in comparison with the sums that are paid to the mass of workers in the form of wages and social security.

It goes without saying that the economy constitutes the basic condition for social progress, but a condition is but a prerequisite and not an ultimate goal. In other words, the social struggle is not merely a struggle for higher and more just wages, and the social problem is not a mere "problem of justice," in the ancient sense of the term. The medieval lord was also obliged to observe law and justice in regard to his subjects. The aim of today's social struggle is not so much to obtain higher wages within the frame of an existing socio-economic system, but to cause the renewal and reorganization of this system itself and, in general, of interhuman relationships. Mankind, at the present, is perhaps going through the most profound revolution of all times; a new socio-economic order is being born, civilization enters into a new phase.

A New Phase of Civilization

The mighty development of the positive sciences and the huge progress of industrial technology are no doubt the most characteristic and influential factors of present-day Western civilization. They make the West stand out greatly in contrast with the Middle Ages and with the East of today. The soaring flight of science and technology are the reason why, in popular language, "Western" and "modern" have become synonymous. When it is said that China, India or Africa are on the way to modernization, this means in the first place that they are taking over the scientific and industrial progress of the West together with the limitless possibilities of production therein contained. It is almost impossible to calculate the influence of technological progress on the material, cultural, social, national and international appearance of the world. Only in the light of this fundamental fact, can we understand our time and fully realize the significance of the contemporary social development.

The development of industry inevitably brings with it a parallel rise of the intellectual and cultural level of the common man. It could not be otherwise. A great capacity of production presupposes an equal capacity of consumption of the produced goods, otherwise it could not be maintained. For example, there would be no use for a well-organized press if the mass of the people were unable to read. Technological progress goes hand in hand with the development of man's awareness, the more so because technology makes distance meaningless and fosters the unification of the world. The whole world, as it were, belongs to him, and he cannot see why there should exist privileged classes or peoples in the world.

For this reason the working class has become aware, on the one hand, of the enormous possibilities technology offers for the material and cultural betterment of the masses, and on the other hand, of the important role the worker plays in modern society and the power he wields. The steelworker or teamster knows very well that when his union calls a strike, the whole economic life of the nation is paralyzed.

This, then, is the greatest event of our time: because industrial development has opened up almost limitless possibilities, because also the working class has become aware of its role and place in society, there has arisen for the first time in history the idea that it is possible for the masses to share in the achievements of modern culture. The concept of a strictly limited class of privileged owners and, on the other hand, the great masses of non-owners no longer belongs to our time. This concept will gradually have to yield before the ideal of greater equality in regard to opportunities of life, a more equitable distribution of property and the participation of all in the fruits of civilization. This ideal is no longer considered utopian, but it is thought of as a possibility, a goal that can be attained, a program for the future. The idea of "common good," of social welfare thus acquires a new content and structure. It is evident that a realization of this new "common good" necessitates a greater participation of all in the administration and control of economic, social and political life, as well as a greater mutual solidarity and co-operation of all peoples. All this we find re-expressed in today's slogans: freedom, equality, emancipation, and democracy.

A Renewed Democratic Ideal

It is quite possible, of course, that the above-mentioned slogans are sometimes improperly used. Nevertheless, they indicate the heart beat of our own time. This is not the heart beat of an anemic, exhausted world, as is sometimes maintained, but rather the heart beat of a humanity that has become aware of the opportunities and possibilities offered to men through the high development of technology.

Freedom and Democracy! Of course, the issue is not the philosophical or psychological question of free will, whether man has genuine freedom of choice. Neither is it a question of purely political democracy or equality before the law. What is at stake is the whole of material, economic and social conditions of life that are necessary for the free unfolding of man's powers, for the liberation of his mind and his whole personality. A few examples will serve to explain this more fully.

When we are ill, we are less free, we are handicapped in the full exercise of many of our activities. If we are wealthy we can obtain relief by means of an expensive operation or take a long rest, all this with the hope of regaining our freedom. In many countries those means are not at the disposal of the ordinary worker. When sickness enters his home, it is a catastrophe for himself and his family, a sort of enslavement from which he is unable to free himself. In view of the progress of medicine, such a situation of inequality in regard to the most elementary of all values, health, is no longer tolerable. Another example. How often does it not happen that a promising boy, the first in his class, is the child of a worker. His companion, less clever and less proficient, is the son of a physician. Nevertheless, in many countries the son of the worker has to go to the factory at sixteen, while the other, though less gifted, can continue his studies through college and perhaps the university. The first does not have the opportunity to make his talents bear fruit, but the other does.

It is this excessive inequality in *actual freedom* that the modern world has in mind when it advocates liberty, equality and democracy. Unlike the time of the French Revolution, the question is not now so much one of equality before the law or of fundamental liberties, for these are guaranteed by all modern constitutions. But it is rather a matter of greater social equality, more social freedom. Since all this is to a great extent conditioned by the economy, it implies a more effective participation of the whole community in economic, social and political life. In short, it is a matter of *economic and social democracy*. But what, one may ask, is the difference between political and socio-economic democracy?

Political democracy refers to the political regime that was born of the French Revolution and is characterized by the equality of the citizens before the law and the great individual freedoms which have been written down in every modern constitution, such as freedom of the person in regard to the judiciary power (no one can be punished except in virtue of law), freedom in regard to property and dwelling, freedom of worship, opinion and the press, of education and political assembly.

Socio-economic democracy, on the other hand, refers to a socio-economic regime which guarantees more *actual freedom and equality of opportunities of life,* and this, of course, is not possible without a more equitable distribution of wealth and a more effective voice of the whole community in the control of the economy.

It would be wrong and dangerous to consider these two forms of democracy as opposite terms. Yet this is done implicitly when it is said, as actually happens in some circles, that the socio-economic democracy should be honored as the *true* democracy, whereas the other is a *purely formal* one. The opposition of "true" to "formal" can give the impression that political democracy is a lie, that it does not contain any truly liberating value. This is most certainly incorrect. It will always be necessary to have political freedoms in order to prevent the socio-economic democracy from becoming a political dictatorship, as is certainly the case of most of the "popular" democracies behind the Iron Curtain. Both forms of democracy should be considered to be essential and complementary elements of integral democracy, that is, of the democracy that is fully worthy of man.

Taking all that into consideration, we can now draw this conclusion: the social problem is more than a question of wages; it is a struggle of individuals and peoples for a life that is more worthy of man. What is happening in our present society is a cultural development, a slow birth of a new phase of civilization; it is the gradual formation of a new socio-economic order, which will be characterized by the primacy of labor in its manifold forms, by a more balanced distribution and a more social ownership and administration of the goods of this world, by a greater equality for all in regard to the development of personality, by truer solidarity among peoples and an increasing economic unification of the world. In short, the present social struggle wants to bring more truth and justice to men at a moment when the world is becoming one as a result of technical progress. In this sense the social struggle is, in its deepest essence, a struggle for an *ethical ideal,* in which the *whole of mankind,* employees and employers, individuals and governments, poor and rich continents, are all involved, over and above any philosophical and religious differences that might separate them.

The first and most important task of our time, is to enlist, around this ethical ideal, the great masses of men of good will. On its success or failure will depend whether the social question will be solved in a human or in an inhuman way. Of course, great difficulties will be encountered, especially if one is dissatisfied with vague purposes and determined to use effective means for the attainment of the goal. Great differences of opinions will always arise when it is a question of choosing and organizing the particular socio-economic system that will best serve the social ideal. But this is not so bad, provided the aim itself is not sacrificed and the divergences do not lead to fanaticism. One and the same goal can be served in many ways and the cooperation of men of good will can assume many forms. Let us consider this question now.

3. *Co-ordination of the Social Forces*

There are divergences that are in principle unbridgeable. Communism and Christianity, for instance, will continue to consider each other as irreconcilable powers as long as Communism continues to consider its atheistic view of life to be inseparable from its socio-economic ideas. But not all divergencies are of this kind. It happens only too often that a cooperation which in principle would be possible and fruitful, is made difficult because of a confusion of ideas. Some think in too "monolithic" a fashion and neglect the multi-dimensional character of social reality. Everything we have said above about the structure of the world of human truths and of human values can be applied here also.

One of the dangers that threatens every form of human cooperation, is the dogmatizing one-sidedness that attempts to reduce the complexity and mobility of life to a rigid theoretical structure of concepts or an ideology. We must, therefore, examine the importance of social theories in the social struggle.

Social Ideologies and Social Study

It is certainly not our intention to deny the importance of theoretical study and reflection, for the sole liberating activity is one built on truth. However, a distinction must be made between diligent study, the perpetual search for truth and insight, and grandiose theoretical constructions, so-called ideologies. Study and reflection are never complete, for they are life and movement. Ideologies, on the other hand, always resemble a finished product; they usually present themselves as aprioristic constructions and closed systems to which nothing more ought to be added. Study searches for a solution; an ideology claims that it is a solution. When ideologies are not carefully handled, they often result in dogmatism, misunderstanding and intolerance. They become the aim of the struggle and at the same time, its principal weapon.

If this happens, the question that should guide every purposeful social action: "What, in particular concrete circumstances, is the best plan, from the standpoint of short range and long range, to promote the people's welfare?" is then replaced by this: "How can we secure the quickest victory for our theory about the organization of enterprises, the planning of production, etc.?" Much misunderstanding would be removed and a great step in the direction of a better relationship would be made if we simply asked ourselves what exactly we want to attain, instead of making comparisons between ideologies. It may, therefore, be useful to pause for a moment and consider the significance of theory in regard to social developments.

Two things must be kept in mind here. First, it would be erroneous to reduce present-day social developments to the two factors of theory and practice. There is a third factor, that of a growing awareness of value and concern for value. We have already called attention to this factor. What lies at the origin of the French Revolution and the democratic movement which it caused throughout the world, is not so much the theory of Jean-Jacques Rousseau concerning man and society, but rather the discovery of political equality and freedom as indispensable means for the emancipation of man. The same is true of modern social developments. There are innumerable social theories. All say worthwhile things but none have said the last word. More important than these theories themselves are the values which they desire to foster. The theories are less values in themselves than attempts to throw light on man's growing value-consciousness, attempts to analyze these values and seek their foundations, to guide man in his leap toward new goals and devise means for their attainment. A theory can change; it may be based even on false metaphysical grounds; yet the value with which it is concerned may continue to operate and attract man.

Secondly, within any theory a distinction must be made between its economic, social and political content and its metaphysical infrastructure or superstructure. The fact that this distinction is often forgotten undoubtedly makes it very difficult, even for men of good will, to enter into a fruitful dialogue.

Although, as we have seen, man's world of truth is one, yet it is not undivided. Thus it is not necessary to first solve the ultimate metaphysical questions regarding the mystery of human existence, e.g., that there is a God and that the soul is immortal, before one is able to distinguish a precious work of art from a worthless canvas, an economy that leads to prosperity from another that will end in disaster, a social and political regime that is not worthy of man from one that safeguards freedom, peace and justice.

Even an unbeliever can realize that freedom of worship belongs to the most elementary rights of man and that a true democracy must not only respect this freedom but should positively make it possible. In short, it is possible to foster spiritual, personalistic politics while adhering to a non-spiritual metaphysics in the realm of philosophy.

Personalism and spiritualism are terms that have a twofold meaning. A first meaning is related to the level of *the immediate experience of existence and description of existence.* We experience in ourselves a manifold spiritual life that constitutes our being-men, for "not of bread alone does man live." All values, both spiritual and material, are thus also experienced as being of and for man, as means that are in the service of the human person, for the human person is an end-in-itself. All this can be recognized as well by the unbeliever as by the believer. But another question may come up: What happens to man after death? Is man immortal or not? This is a metaphysical question which is not solved by means of a mere description of the experience of existence. He who replies in the affirmative gives a higher and richer content to the terms "spirit," and "person"; we are then dealing with a "spiritualism" in the *metaphysical and religious* sense of the word.

It seems to be characteristic of the old European continent to approach economic, social and political questions from the highest metaphysical viewpoint, whereas the Anglo-Saxon countries prefer to consider experience as *the* great teacher, and let it give guidance to action. In this way, Continental thinkers easily identify the strictly social and political content of a theory with its metaphysical infrastructures and superstructure. They find it difficult to understand that a materialistic metaphysics can be coupled with a spiritual ethics, and also the reverse, viz., that a spiritual and theocentric metaphysics can possess a genuine sense of temporal and material values. Clearly, such an attitude is the source of much misunderstanding and dogmatism. The confusion of religion and politics is also closely connected with it.

Let this be properly understood. We do not hold that a conviction regarding the meaning of life is not important for the proper course of social and political life. A spiritual metaphysics is no doubt a great safeguard for the spiritual values of society. Unbelieving materialism, on the other hand, can constitute a danger for social life, as we have already shown. When one sees man ultimately as nothing but a cluster of atoms which disintegrates after death, one can easily be led to deal with man as a mere handful of atoms. That is why Nietzsche, the great atheist, was so concerned about the growth of unbelief. He was convinced that mankind would have to pass through a severe crisis before it would be able to live, without God, a life worthy of man. What we mean, then, is only this: an unbeliever, who calls himself a materialist in the realm of metaphysics, can be very sensitive to, and have a great interest in the things of the spirit and therefore work for an economic and social system of politics that fosters the things of the spirit. Divergences in the realm of philosophy and religion in regard to the meaning of the world are not necessarily obstacles in the way of sincere and fruitful cooperation. Moreover, this kind of cooperation exists in most Anglo-Saxon countries. Why could it not be possible elsewhere too? But this presupposes that we take account of still another distinction which we have frequently met in our previous considerations, the distinction between the objective side and the subjective-ethical side of every human undertaking.

Social Structures and Social Ethics

As we have said, the social struggle is basically a struggle for an ethical ideal. This, however, does not mean that it has no other aim than to spread better feelings toward our fellow-men in the world. Feelings of good will alone are not sufficient to liberate mankind. Human freedom is bound up with matter and with the world, and it could never reach maturity and autonomy without appropriate *objective* conditions of life.[7]

It goes without saying that the *first* and *immediate* purpose of the social struggle lies in the realm of objective social structures and achievements. This follows from the very concept of the social struggle. The immediate effect of a co-ordination of all socially-minded forces, is not the inner liberation of man—for this is the task of education and personal effort—but the humanization of man's objective conditions of life; for instance, the improvement of working conditions and of human relations in great industrial enterprises, a more carefully planned organization of the economy, the democratization of education, better laws in the realms of public health, housing, and pensions.

However, as we have repeatedly said, the objective conditions of life are only means, they are not the ultimate goal. The final goal is man himself considered individually and collectively, that is, the rising of man toward a better, more ample life that is worthy of man, with more justice and fraternity among men. What would be the use of constantly stressing the primacy of work if the laborer himself no longer highly esteems and loves his work, has no longer any pride in his work? A more equitable social legislation can raise everyone's opportunities for a better life, but even then it remains necessary that individuals will use these opportunities. This

---

[7] Cf. above, Chapters Three and Eight.

no law can guarantee. The abolition of class differences can bring about more solidarity among men, but it can also harden interhuman relations, foster jealousy, ambition and egotistic individualism. To constantly improve social *legislation* and to *educate men in a better social spirit* are two different things.

We should never forget that the socio-economic reorganization of society presupposes a parallel cultural and ethical re-education of its members. Or again, a renewal of the economic and social system must go hand in hand with a renewal of man himself. The ancient saying, "what value have laws without morals?" (*quid leges sine moribus?*) is perhaps more to the point than ever before, now that "laws" increase constantly in complexity and demand more and more of us.

Our next question, therefore, is: In connection with the distinction between the objective and the ethical side of the social struggle, how should the cooperation of men of good will be planned and fostered? Particularly in our Christian organizations, it is considered almost self-evident that cooperation with men who hold divergent views is possible only on the level of objective achievements, but that such cooperation is completely out of the question as soon as it becomes a matter of the cultural and ethical formation of men, e.g., of the workers and especially youth.

I ask myself whether this viewpoint is really so "self-evident" and whether a milder attitude would not possess a greater educational value, provided everything is done with care, the autonomy of the respective organizations is not endangered, and the differences in the philosophy of life are not buried under the bushel. A genuine social education is, after all, hardly thinkable without an understanding of those who think differently. Moreover, no mutual understanding is possible without effective and sincere contacts, even though at the beginning this contact might exist only between the heads of the educational institutions concerned. Moreover, the great problems encountered by young workers in their daily lives are almost the same whether they belong to a Catholic trade union, a neutral or socialist organization or none at all. Many of those problems are crucial for the spiritual health of the people and are so complicated that they can be solved anly through the cooperation of all who are competent in the matter and of all men of good will. Such men are found wherever work is done for the education of youth and not only in one's own group.

The International Dimension of the Social Problem

We can never sufficiently insist upon the fact that at this time the social problem has taken on an international character and that the struggle's center of gravity lies no longer in Europe but in Asia, Africa and South America. Awareness of this international character of the social struggle could be a powerful incentive toward a better understanding among socially-minded men. Divisions within one's own country should not prevent cooperation on the international plane.

The question may be asked whether small countries like Belgium, Holland or Switzerland are able to exercise influence upon world events. Although one may be inclined to belittle their influence, it must not be underestimated. Several possibilities of action present themselves.

Firstly, there is the country's own foreign policy and the possibility of assistance given to underdeveloped countries. It often happens that progressive social politics for the interior of a country are coupled with a very conservative and unsocial attitude in the matter of foreign policy. Here lies a field of social action even for small countries.

Secondly, there is the possibility of promoting the unity of Western Europe. The social attitude that will be adopted by a unified Europe could have great significance for the future of the world.

Finally there is the formation of public opinion. In this field there are such works as *Pax Christi*, assistance to Latin America, the action of Father Pire, winner of the Nobel Prize, the World organization of Catholic Young Workers, the "Building Order,"[8] the Review *World Justice* of Louvain, the study center *Economie et Humanisme* of Father Lebret, O.P., to mention only a few of the works inspired by Christian thought. All these are very important and deserve powerful support. Their influence on world opinion and, via world opinion, on the politics of the United States, could prove greater than one might suspect. Among other things, they can aid in enlisting the great international community of the Christian faithful—which certainly is not a force that should be underestimated—and mobilize it for the service of the social ideal. This in turn brings us a new series of problems which are related to the significance of Christianity in today's social development.

4. *Christianity and the Social Development of the World*

"Religion," Karl Marx said, "is the opium of the people." Christianity, on the contrary claims to be the most solid foundation and the strongest guarantee of a renewal of the temporal order that will be worthy of man.

However, the great significance of Christianity for today's world is almost completely obscured when, as often happens, Christianity is presented as a socio-economic ideology alongside many others, or as the strongest antagonist of the Marxist concept of society. Marxism, to the extent that it identifies itself with godlessness, cannot have a more powerful enemy than Christianity; but as a defender of a specific economy, of

[8]The Building Order is a kind of Catholic Peace Corps. It was started in the post-war years. (ed.)

the extreme form of planned economy, its antagonist is not Christianity but capitalistic liberalism. For Christianity is not an economic theory but a religion and an ethics of religious inspiration. It is not impossible that in particular circumstances, a far-reaching planning and "collectivization" of economic life might not be almost the only way to make underdeveloped countries attain a relatively high degree of prosperity in a fairly short time. In any case, the question is not a religious but an economic problem and is to be solved not by theologians but by economists. The only thing faith demands is that whatever economic policy a country may choose, it must respect man and recognize the inalienable rights and values of the human person.

The widespread representation of Christianity as the antagonist of the communist social system or even of the socialist organization of society, is very dangerous. It creates the impression that the Christian faith is primarily a negative and conservative force in social matters, that it is the strongest bulwark of the capitalist concept of society and the distribution of wealth. Christianity thereby loses much of its creative value for the proper solution of the social world crisis.

This loss is very unfortunate, especially when one reflects upon the enormous positive power that Christianity could wield for the improvement and reorganization of our profoundly shaken world. Yet this force can be effectively applied only when Christianity pays heed to the true causes of the social disease and fights the evil in its roots. Not communism is the ultimate source of today's crisis but the crying economic inequality and enslavement of which we have already spoken, and for which communism claims to have an answer. So long as these conditions continue to exist, peace will be impossible in the world and we must expect the worst.[9] The question

[9]Father Lebret rightly says that we find ourselves in a dilemma: *Suicide ou survie de l'Occident?* Paris, 1958.

therefore is: How can Christianity foster social justice in the world of today? What are the conditions that are required for this purpose?

Christianity as a Moral Force

The social struggle is fundamentally a struggle for an ethical ideal. Its ultimate end is to bring more truth and justice in the world, to put the riches of nature at the disposal of all mankind, to humanize the relations among men, to bring about a more just distribution of wealth; in short, to construct a world that is not governed by money but by a truer recognition of man by man.

Now, as we have seen, Christianity is essentially a message of love, whose first task is to reveal *God's love to the world in the concrete form of effective brotherly love*: "Beloved, let us love one another, for love is from God. And everyone who loves is born of God, and knows God" (John 4, 7).[10] Hence love of God and concern for mankind are inseparably united: "For how can he who does not love his brother, whom he sees, love God whom he does not see?" (I John 4, 20). And Our Lord tells us in the Gospel that "You will know the tree by its fruits." Now, the fruits of God's Word and God's Spirit are: "love, joy, peace" (Gal. 5, 22). There is no peace, however, without justice.

All this means that perhaps Christianity has never had such great opportunities as in our own day. But it also means that the Christians will never have committed a greater treason than now if they remain aloof from the struggle at this decisive turning point of history, if they act merely as neutral onlookers who prudently wait for further develop-

[10]Note that to "know God," as used in Scripture, never means a mere theological knowledge; it does not mean the same as when we say that a child knows its lesson. "Knowledge of God" in the Bible means a nearness of God by which God becomes a living reality for man.

ments of the struggle, or, what is still worse, if they play the conservatives who through clever sophistry help to maintain falsehood and injustice in the world.

We have already quoted Cardinal Suhard's words: "The greatest fault that Christians of the twentieth century could commit would be to let the world organize and unify itself without them." This unification of our world means more than a geographical unification by the narrowing of geographic distances; it means, first of all, a social unification, a gradual elimination of the enormous social and economic inequalities which still continue to divide mankind into two groups: the small group of the rich and the large group of the poor. Nothing worse could happen than that the moral sensitivity for values of today's Christian community should not be in harmony with the sensitivity for values of the present world. The most striking characteristics of this sensitivity have been described in the foregoing chapters: they are the sense of solidarity, of equality, of historicity; in a word, sensibility for *social* justice, for *creative* justice.

It is, therefore, of the highest importance for our time that we become more conscious of, and give greater emphasis to the *positive dynamic character* of Christian morals. A Christianity that is understood properly cannot adopt a petrified attitude of life, which is the enemy of progress, adaptation and creation. Is there any power on earth more dynamic than loving, watchful concern for man? Of course, Christian ethics, like any other ethics, contains prohibitive commandments, as "Thou shalt not steal," "Thou shalt not kill." But these negative norms themselves are in the service of a positive sense of values and practice of virtues: "Thou shalt love they neighbor as thyself," and do for him what you would want him to do for yourself. Hence, Christian ethics contains the positive obligation of rethinking our attitudes in regard to property, the care of health, the dissemination of education, and, in general, of the objective social structures in line with economic development and in view of a more equitable distribution of wealth and a greater equality of opportunities for all.

Characteristics of Christian Social Action. The fact that Christian ethics always and everywhere aims at man and subordinates everything to man and to the fundamental values and rights of man, endows the social action of the Christian with a number of characteristics which by that fact offer great safeguards for our time.

First, the Christian does not go to work in an aprioristic and dogmatizing way. He accents the distinction between ends and means. He knows very well that a more genuine recognition of man by man pre-supposes, in the order of means, many and profound reforms affecting the economic and social structure of the world. But he does not believe that there exists an *a priori* solution for all these problems; experience and expertness must remain the principal teachers in all those matters. This distinction between end and means is of great importance for mankind. The confusion of end and means is the sign of a petrified and dogmatizing spirit and the source of fanaticism.

Secondly, because Christian ethics starts from a great respect for man, it spontaneously prefers order to disorder, law-abiding evolution to revolution and terror. Moderation, understanding, patience, and respect for the law are very important ethical values. To sacrifice whole generations in order to establish a new world in the shortest possible time, is inhuman and dangerous, for terror calls forth more terror and lowers man to the level of the brute. There is then great danger that the long awaited new world will ultimately lead to worse evils than the old order ever knew.

Thirdly, since the Christian believer attributes a religious dimension to human existence, he puts certain moral values in the foreground and pays special attention to them. For example, his social action will quite naturally be more explicitly personalistic;[11] it will stress the rights, values and freedoms of the human person, because in the Christian perspective man is an object of divine love and, therefore, has a limitless value and truth. Another consequence is the fact that Christian ethics is more demanding than many other ethical systems in regard to the morals of marriage and the family, for it sees a religious and sacramental meaning in the marriage bond: "this is a great mystery in Christ and in the Church." For the Christian, the consent by which man and woman bind themselves is a great and holy mystery because it is confirmed by God, symbolizes Christ's love for His Church, and inaugurates their mission in that same Church. Sickness and death have also a sacred significance in Christianity and are therefore treated with a holy respect. This the Christian believer cannot keep out of his mind when he enters the field of social health and the nursing of the sick. Finally, because the Christian believer recognizes an ecclesiastical community of faith alongside the community of the State, he wants a social order in which there is sufficient freedom for the proclamation of God's Word, the exercise of worship, the practice of charity, and the Church's spiritual task of education.[12]

In short, the Christian views of life and of the world have their repercussions on the Christian believer's ideal of the human society, and on his endeavors to realize it. For this reason there exists a "Christian social doctrine."

The Christian Social Doctrine

It is customary to call "Christian social doctrine" the expression of Christian ethics in the realm of social life, social

[11]Cf. for example, L. Janssens, *Personalisme en Democratisering,* Brussels, 1958.

[12]See Part Three, *Religion and Politics.*

action, and the organization of society. It is not easy, however, to determine its exact meaning. Moreover, when this meaning is not stated with precision and prudently handled, it can easily lead to conservatism.

What do we understand by "Christian social doctrine?" It means a theory about society that is inspired by Christian ethics. In other words, it is a unified whole of principles, designed to indicate the *conditions that a temporal society must necessarily fulfill,* in regard to both man's sense for subjective and ethical values and the objective structures of society, to make this society be in harmony with the ideas sanctioned by Christianity concerning the human person, his fundamental rights, freedoms, and values. Just as Christian ethics itself, the social doctrine of Christianity is an *open and dynamic* doctrine, or more exactly, it is a *whole of imperatives* regarding the ordering of society; but it is not one of the many economic and social systems in the technical sense of the word, such as the liberal, neoliberal, socialist and communist systems.

For example, Christianity does not honor any definite regulation of property, but could live in harmony with many different regulations, on condition that they respect certain fundamental principles. The same can be said in regard to the policy of employment, the structure of enterprises, social security, the organization of medicine, and public health. In all these fields, two ways are usually open, one more individualistic and liberal, the other more collectivistic and planned. In between, there are many different mixtures of the two. Faith does not indicate which form is best for specific circumstances. Nor can it be said *a priori* of any purely economic and social regime that it is specifically Christian, but every regime must observe certain requirements to be in harmony with the Christian concept of man and society. Thus we can understand that in some countries, like England, most Catholics favor a socialistic organization of society; whereas in others they prefer a more liberal or neoliberal organization.

Evidently our intention is not to develop here a Christian social doctrine. We merely wish to call attention to a few ideas which readily give rise to misunderstandings and sophistical arguments.

The Concept of "Social Principle." Christian social doctrine, like any doctrine about society, starts from general and abstract principles. Social principles, however, are not like mathematical axioms whose universality and perpetual validity suffer no exceptions; such as, two plus two is always and everywhere four. Social principles are mostly *affirmations of value* that are generally valid, and like any accepted value, lead to a *universal norm of conduct.* This norm of conduct indicates how man ought to behave generally in order to give practical recognition to some definite value and foster its application in the world. Now, even when we are in the presence of a value that must be universally accepted and is inviolable, that is, a value that must be respected and fostered in all times and places, this does mean that the corresponding *norm of conduct* must likewise be universal and inviolable. The reason for it is very simple: no concrete human action can simultaneously serve and foster all values. Every human action and undertaking is limited and even ambiguous; that is, it favors one value and is harmful to another. Moreover, a hierarchy exists among values, and this implies that sometimes one value must temporarily give way before another. A couple of examples will clarify this matter.

Life and health must, no doubt, be reckoned among the most fundamental and universally accepted values of life, to which every man has a right. This is expressed in a well-known norm of conduct, which forbids us to kill or to injure the health of another person. This rule of conduct is universal and yet exceptions can be thought of, as for example, in case of lawful self-defense.[13]

In the matter of medical care, "free choice" is rightly considered a universally and inviolable value; it, therefore, must be taken into account in the organization of social medicine. By "free choice" is understood the patient's liberty to choose the physician and the medical institution of his preference, and on the other hand, the liberty of the physician to exercise his medical art according to his own judgment. Free choice, like any other value that man desires, is a sort of ideal; hence man can come more or less near to it but, but because of his limitations, man can never completely achieve it. The ideal form of free choice, when we consider it from the standpoint of the patient, would exist if *every* man, in *all* circumstances, were able to make a *completely* motivated choice from among *all* physicians, and choose the one whom he considers *the best.* But this is evidently impossible except perhaps for a multimillionaire. The free choice is rather extensive for some; for others it is very limited, and there are still plenty of people in the world who because of their financial condition have no choice whatsoever.

Hence the question: How can we give a maximum of choice to everyone? This will require organization and regulation. Regulation means that the freedom of some will be curtailed in order to give greater liberty to others. For instance, travelling on the left hand side of the road is forbidden to keep the road free for all. In a similar way it could happen that unlimited freedom of choice in regard to social medicine is financially impossible or leads to countless abuses. Regulation thus becomes inevitable and the question then is: How should the care of health be organized in order that in these specific circumstances and with these available

[13]In other words, its universality is not like that of an axiom of mathematics.

means the best care possible will be put at the disposal of all, while at the same time a maximum of freedom of choice will be guaranteed?

To summarize, we can say that social principles are in the first place *affirmations of values.* But all values cannot be simultaneously and equally fostered by every social action and regulation. The precise task of the social worker and the politician is to construct a social order which 1) takes into account, in these specific circumstances, the hierarchy of values, especially those that are essential and indispensable conditions of life and to which every man has a right; 2) gives as much liberty and opportunity as possible to everybody; 3) and for this purpose introduces as much restriction as is required.[14]

Catholic Doctrine of Property. Another important point in the Church's social doctrine is that which concerns property. If the Catholic teaching regarding property is not properly explained, it may give the impression that the Church desires especially to protect the existing wealth of the rich, whereas on the contrary she desires a wider distribution of ownership and a more equitable division of wealth, so that "all may be able to enjoy the benefits of ownership" (Pius XII). On the other hand, this does not mean that the Church condemns the powerful concentration of capital without which a modern economy is impossible. However, the formation of capital can come about in many ways and can go together with a widespread distribution of wealth.

The Catholic doctrine regarding property is very simple and comes down to the following:

The riches of the earth are for man, and not vice versa. Originally, says St. Thomas, and as they have come from

[14]Cf. L. Janssens: *"De taak van de Staat," 23de Vlaamse Sociale Week,* Louvain, 1950.

the hands of the Creator, the goods of this world belong to no one in particular, but they exist for mankind.[15] And Jacques Leclercq writes that "the whole of the goods of the earth is destined for the whole of men."[16]

However, this final destiny of earthly goods would remain meaningless if ownership were not regulated in any way. In this regulation we always find a sphere of *private property,* in the strict sense of the term, alongside the sphere of *collective ownership.* If anyone for any reason were allowed to seize anything he wished, a free, peaceful and prosperous social existence of men and nations would be impossible. We must add that exclusively collective ownership would not suffice. Man cannot fulfill his task in the world if there is no sphere of goods that he can consider his own, as something which he can dispose of at will and freely. Otherwise, not only is the incentive for labor removed but it is even impossible for him to construct his future freely and autonomously, to exercise his duties as a father of a family, to assume responsibility for his functions, and to play his role in society. A definite sphere of private ownership is therefore required by nature and should be guaranteed in any system of property; this, in fact, is what generally happens. Stealing is forbidden, even in communist regimes.

Hence the principle of law, "to every man his due," the distinction between "mine and thine," between "ours and theirs," have a permanent ethical significance. This is expressed negatively in the commandment, "Thou shalt not steal." But the doctrine of property also has a positive side, which flows from the fundamental destiny of earthly riches. It is nothing else than the demand that, as civilization advances, the system of ownership be adjusted to new possibilities, that the socio-economic regime be constantly im-

---

[15]*Summa Theol.,* p. 22, q. 66, a. 1, ad. 2.

[16]*Leçons de droit naturel, t.* IV, Part 2 ,1946, p. 95.

proved, and that man come ever nearer to the ideal of justice and fraternity, viz., to distribute property as widely and as effectively as possible.

Evidently, this doctrine represents an open and dynamic conception of property. It goes without saying that the positive significance of the Christian doctrine of property is not brought to light by emphasizing only the negative aspect: "Thou shalt not steal."

There is, however, a second way of being one-sided and presenting a false picture of the Catholic concept of ownership. This happens when one gives so much priority to private property that collective ownership is considered almost a necessary evil, a sort of invasion of private ownership; and it is then considered to be permissible only when there is no other way, or, as is expressed in the traditional formula, when "the general welfare absolutely requires it."

Yet, since man is by nature a social being who can live only in society, private property and collective property are equally *primary*. We may add that these two formulae concerning ownership have always existed together in history as two complementary elements of every system of ownership that is worthy of man, although the relation between the two has not always been the same.

In a primitive society, in which the economy is still very archaic and the individual does not enjoy any security at all outside the group, the regime is principally collective. To the extent that the economy gives increasing autonomy and freedom of movement to the individual, collective ownership decreases without, however, disappearing entirely. Even when liberalism reached its apex, collective ownership continued to play a great role and the distinction between "ours" and "theirs" was as absolute as between "mine" and "thine."

The relation and interconnection between private and collective property can take on innumerable forms, but one thing remains certain throughout, namely, that both types of ownership are "primary" and that it is erroneous to consider collective ownership as an infringement upon private ownership that is sometimes demanded by the circumstances. On the contrary, collective ownership can also be a means of insuring a greater and more just distribution of private ownership.

The Concept of "Common Good." A third point of Christian social doctrine deserves our attention—namely, the idea of "common good." Christian social doctrine insists upon the fundamental principle of political wisdom that all economic, social and political action must be governed by the common good and that it must be the decisive standard and criterion for all changes in the structure of society.

The expression "common good" (*bonum commune*) designates that maximum of general welfare that is thought to be attainable by a human society in specific circumstances.

This common welfare comprises not only economic well-being but also the intellectual, cultural, spiritual, and moral growth of the members of the community, the recognition of one another's liberties, the constant improvement of inter-human relations, the protection and promotion of the fundamental values of the person and, finally, the stability of the social order which we call "peace" and without which no vigorous society worthy of man can exist.

It is important to note, however, that it would be a mistake to conceive this "common welfare" as a static, immovable and closed reality; on the contrary, it must remain open to constant adjustment, improvement and growth. When welfare is at a standstill, it is in reality going backwards. A nation fares well only when it is directed to the future and remains eager to improve the common welfare of all.

This must be kept in mind when we take the primacy of the common welfare as our standard of economic, social and political action. For this common welfare can be conceived in two ways: either we speak of the actual situation of welfare as it has existed until now and of what is needed for its preservation, or we have in mind the welfare considered attainable in the foreseeable future and the means required for its achievement. A conservative is actually the man who rivets his attention on the welfare that has been, and who wishes perhaps some improvement of conditions, but lacks the imagination and daring to make a project of a better future and create the necessary organisms that will make this project possible. Hence the expression "that which is *necessary* for the common welfare" is rather ambiguous; it can easily be misused in favor of a conservative attitude and serve to put obstacles in the way of the free creation of a better world; for it is true that this better world is not absolutely "necessary."

Common welfare constantly develops further; consequently, there is also an evolution of the social and economic organization required by this common welfare. In other words, laws and rights are subject to development. This brings us to the fourth point: the concept of law and right and, especially of natural law.

The Concepts "Law" and "Right." The social doctrine of the Church rejects a purely positivistic concept of rights. In other words, the fact that a certain law exists does not mean that the right in question is a genuine right. A law is good, creates a genuine right only when it conforms to the natural law on the one hand, and fosters the common welfare on the other.

The idea of "natural law" is a delicate one. It is also an open and dynamic idea. Usually we understand by *natural law* the whole of fundamental, very general and inalienable rights that flow immediately from the dignity and autonomy of the human person himself and thus have to be recognized by positive legislation which respects the dignity of man. For instance, man has a natural right to life and health, to freedom of conscience and religion, to work and a form of private property, to strive for an order of society that is more in harmony with man's dignity.[17] The natural law does not indicate concretely how these fundamental rights are to be safeguarded and fostered in the course of historical contingencies; this is regulated only by the law of custom and by positive legislation. Nature demands that society be ordered, but the precise form of this order is determined by positive legislation, of which the law of custom is a part.

Positive law comprises both the law of custom and the law resulting from positive legislation. Since natural welfare is constantly developing, the task of sound statesmanship is to adjust legislation constantly to new needs and to the new possibilities that arise in accordance with the evolution of civilization. As we stated above, all legislation, to be good

---

[17]The very vague and difficult concept of "natural law" has received different interpretations in the course of history. The idea of "natural law," that is, of rights originating from man's universal nature, undoubtedly contains the idea of a norm that is universally valid always and everywhere, and transcends the historical contingencies of social systems and positive legislation. This universality however, can be conceived in two different ways, which is not surprising when one considers the ambiguity of the concept "universal nature" as applied to man. Man is "by nature" not a pure "datum of nature," but he is a cultural and ethical "project" bound up with nature. Hence the concept "universal" can be thought of in two different ways. There is the "leveled" universality of the "greatest common denominator" that is found always and everywhere; but there is also the richer universality which lies contained in the ideal of a universal recognition of man by man. For this reason there are two fundamental ways of conceiving the natural law:

1) Natural law may be conceived as a whole of abstract, ever-present rules that are found among all peoples. This "greatest common denominator" constantly decreases in content as ethnology progresses.

2) Natural law may be conceived as the standard, the ideal which positive legislation must pursue in relation to a particular development of civilization, in order that its laws may be worthy of man and just. In the first sense, right to work, right to education can hardly be considered as a part of the natural law; but they are such in the second sense of natural law.

and sound, must take into account the natural law, on the one hand, and the welfare of the whole people, on the other.

Man is a historical being. He experiences his nature as a potentiality and a never completed task rather than as something perfectly fixed. Hence new demands for rights may arise which formerly had no meaning, but which can be considered to be demands of nature when man reaches a certain level of development. In this way we arrive at the meaning that is commonly given to "right" in our modern so-called "declarations of the rights of man." By "right" here is usually understood a whole of demands or quasi-demands which, in view of the progress of civilization, must be accepted as the norm of positive legislation. For instance, it will be maintained that every child has a right to education until its fourteenth or sixteenth year, or even to a higher education if one has the necessary capacity for it. Here, of course, we are not speaking of a universal "natural right" in the sense attached to the term in the seventeenth or eighteenth centuries, that is, of a right that belongs to men of all times and all places. What it means here is that, in view of the present development of civilization, education and instruction must henceforth be considered *fundamental values of life to which every man has a right* since they have become a possibility for everyone. Therefore, the state has the duty to adjust its laws to the new possibilities in the matter of instruction and education for the purpose of securing a more equitable distribution of wealth. The same can be said of the numerous reforms of economic and social structures, such as more universal medical care, social security, and the right to work.

It is most important that we do not underestimate this new meaning of the term "right," if we do not wish to engage in endless discussions about the scope of the natural law, and especially if we want to avoid fostering conservatism through too rigid a concept of natural law.

The Concept "Social Pluralism." A last point deserves our attention but we shall consider it again in the chapter concerning *Denominational Political Parties.* I mean the problem of so-called social pluralism. The Church has always encouraged the organization of Christian social works and institutes. She sees in them a guarantee not only for the free exercise of her spiritual mission, but also a safeguard for the proper progress of temporal society. In fact, a certain type of pluralism can foster the spirit of enterprise and a wholesome competition in social life.

However, there exists at the present time, especially among intellectuals, a tendency of calling into doubt the usefulness and timeliness of this social pluralism.[18] It is feared, and not without reasons, that separate Christian organizations lead to a kind of "apartheid," an aloofness; with the result that Christian believers then live quasi-isolated from the present world, compromise the Church in temporal affairs, and prevent the unification of all progressive social forces.

Much truth is present in these apprehensions. Yet this should not be considered a sufficient motive for condemning Christian cultural and social organizations. First of all, if Christians organize themselves separately, this happens mainly because they do not feel at home in neutral organizations since the views of life and the world that often prevail in them are anything but neutral. Secondly, it is an exaggeration to maintain that the establishment of Christian works necessarily isolates the faithful from the world.

A Catholic University, for instance, which is faithful to its own mission as a university, is not foreign to university life; it is rather a contribution made by Catholics to the international world of learning. The same applies to the Christian labor movement; it does not create a separate social world

---

[18]See among others, the remarkable study of J. Vialatoux and A. Latreille, which appeared in *Esprit,* Oct. 1949, under the title, "Christianisme et laicité."

and should never consider itself such. Its task is to cooperate in the construction of a world that is more worthy of man and serves the benefit of all.

In regard to the danger that the Church may be compromised by getting involved in temporal affairs, this also should not be exaggerated. Christian social works, such as polyclinics, labor unions, cooperatives, mutual benefit societies, are not Church institutions, whose administration and responsibility should rest with ecclesiastical authorities. They are works of Christian laymen, administered by laymen who assume responsibility for them. In a democratic society, the faithful have the same right as anybody else to organize themselves freely and to strive together toward certain purposes.

This separate organization, of course, should not lead to "apartheid," to "separatism." As we have remarked, such aloofness is harmful not only for the message of faith because contact with those who think differently is then gradually lost, but also for the general welfare because a strongly organized Catholic community can easily become a state within a state. It is important, therefore, to keep constantly in mind the danger that is undeniably connected with separate organizations, and to do everything possible to eliminate it. Three points are most important in this respect.

First, the creation of separate organizations must never become an end in itself which then will go beyond all bounds; it must be done with moderation, that is, keeping in mind the welfare of the entire population and in subordination to this common welfare, for the general welfare must always remain the criterion for the separate activity of the respective population groups. For example, when Catholics establish their own schools, they must not forget the others and always keep in mind the welfare of the entire school system. Secondly, within the separate organizations themselves a spirit of openness for the preservation of a dialogue with others must exist. Thirdly, it is especially important that the Church and the temporal organization of the faithful should not be so interwoven and interconnected that they become practically indistinguishable.

A flourishing Catholic university, for example, is a blessing for the Church as well as for the world of learning, but that blessing would lose much of its significance for both the Church and the temporal society if the university world were divided into two camps: on the one side, the world of Catholic universities, where only Catholics teach and study and, on the other, a world of neutral universities which are open only to non-Catholic professors and students. The same can be said of all organizations that have secular purposes. If this is admitted, then one must draw the inevitable practical conclusion: a Catholic who does not feel at home in Catholic organizations and sincerely believes that he can serve his Church and his country better in neutral institutions—by which, of course, we mean those that are really neutral—should not be looked upon as a second-rate Catholic and be treated as such.

In short, a sociological pluralism can be healthy and sound on condition that it is a moderate and open pluralism.

PART THREE

FAITH AND POLITICS

CHAPTER TEN

RELIGION AND POLITICS

In all probability discussions about the connection or separation of politics and religion will never come to an end. This is so not because the theoretical problem is particularly difficult, but rather because this question regularly becomes a center of political conflicts, since it is so closely connected with the way in which power is exercised.

In fact, the question about the relationship of faith and politics gives rise to several problems which should be carefully distinguished, for they do not belong to the same plane. Thus, there is, first, the matter of the general *fundamental principles* that are valid always and everywhere. In this case, the question is whether, in general, religious belief has anything to do with political life. Secondly, there is the problem of *Church and politics*. Here the matter is principally one of the *competence of the Church* (in the sense of Church Authority) *in political affairs*. This question is subordinate to the previous one, for Church Authority, when it intervenes in politics, must be guided by principles just as much as the Christian laymen who is engaged in political life.

There is further the ancient problem of *Church and State*. This brings us one step closer to the praxis of political life. In this problem one is concerned with the relationship between two historically situated powers or communities: the Church as a religious community and the State as a temporal society. Finally, there exist also more particular problems, namely, those of *tolerance* and the problem of *denominational* (Christian or Catholic) *political parties*.

It is well to note that we have not arbitrarily and accidentally followed the above order of enumeration, for this sequence flows from an inner logic. We have proceeded from the more general to the more particular questions. We shall develop each point in that order, for the more particular problems are subordinate to the more general questions. One must never leave that logical sequence out of sight. Otherwise he will be unable to avoid hopeless confusion and disputes, he will put temporary historical situations on a par with immutable principles, and endow them with an absolute value. In this way he is led to fanaticism. History shows how much unhappiness has been brought into the world by fanaticism, whether that fanaticism be called clericalism or state absolutism.

Let this suffice as an introduction to our study. A first section will deal with the most general fundamental principles; a second with the relationship of the Church (in the sense of Church Authority) to politics; the third, with the relations between Church and State; in the fourth section we shall return to the principles in order to shed light on them from the standpoint of the many tensions and conflicts which regularly occur in those realms, for these conflicts are extremely instructive. Because of the importance of the problem of tolerance in our own time and the present interest in the question of the significance and opportuneness of denominational political parties, we shall consecrate two separate chapters to the latter two problems.

1. *The Fundamental Principles*

We understand here by "fundamental principles" the most general guiding principles which dominate the whole problem of the relations between faith and politics and which immediately flow from the very nature of both terms. The expression "political life" is used here in its broadest sense; it comprises any sort of contribution of the citizen to the life of the State. The proper course of political life in a modern democratic society is determined not solely by the authority or government but also by the people. This is done in two ways: 1) by the voice all citizens have through political parties, and 2) by the formation of a sound political opinion in the country, that is, a high level of sane political thinking and feeling. In other words, in the modern State, which is based on the sovereignty of the people, politics are simultaneously determined by three great powers, which are as it were the fulcrums of political life. They are: the Government, the political parties, and public opinion. We should not underestimate the significance of the third power; it happens all too often that a deformed public opinion makes difficult the work of the government and of the parties and even sometimes completely paralyzes it. Besides those three great powers, there are, of course, numerous other so-called "pressure groups," which exert influence upon political life; for instance, high finance and labor unions. However, their influence is exercised more indirectly through the channel of the three other great powers.

The question that now engages our attention can be formulated in the following words: in general, has religious faith any relation to political life? or again: Is faith one of the elements that determine the political attitude of the believer? May the religious conviction be numbered among the direct and guiding motivations of political conduct?

As is well known, this question places us before the classical dilemma of clericalism and liberal secularism. If we attribute to faith any form of competence or voice in the realm of political life, do we not inevitably fall into clericalism and all its abuses? Do we not thereby open the gate to extra-political interference? For what criterion can faith, theology or ecclesiastical authority use to estimate the value of any political measure or institution?

On the other hand, to deny all voice to faith in the realm of politics is precisely the position of "neutral" or liberal secularism, for which religion and ethics are private concerns. But is it not nonsensical to try to reduce religion and morality to man's inner private life? Is man not essentially an "existential" being, that is, a being who *expresses* himself in conduct, who *goes outside himself,* thus meets others, and willy nilly is faced with the problem of building a social life that is worthy of man? Hence the question is whether there does not exist a middle way between those two extremes. The question arises of its own accord when we compare the nature of politics with the nature of religious belief.

The Autonomy of Politics

What is meant by "politics"? What is its purpose? One fact is certain: the social, economic, and political organization, or in short, the so-called world of the "temporal," is not a datum found in nature just as we find sand, ore, water and air, but is a cultural creation of man, life, art, science and technique. By "cultural creation" we mean a creation by which man transforms crude nature into a dwelling and a workshop for mankind, into a "home" where there is room for all, so that everyone can harmoniously and with dignity unfold his life in freedom while respecting the freedom of others, with their help, but mindful of the common good. Using a term borrowed from modern philosophy, we have called this "home," the "world," or our "being-in-the-world." Man is a "world builder."

The transformation of nature into a world of culture is precisely the task of man as a *rational being*: it is the work of his *auto-nomous*[1] mind, that is, of his reason as revealing and creating order. Its functions and tasks are as varied and inexhaustible as the spheres of value of his being-in-the-

[1]"Autonomous" comes from the Greek *autos* and *nomos*. *Nomos* means law, rule, and *autos,* self, points to the independence of man in establishing law and creating order.

world. But science, technique, and art, are not enough. They cannot make our world a "home" in which there is room for all and in which reign order, peace, and prosperity. Over and above them farsighted care is required to survey the *totality* of the economy, to order and guide it toward a better future. This is the precise task of the *"political intellect,"* which aims at fostering the collective interests of the entire people, or, as it is customarily called, the *commonweal,* creates suitable *organs* and adopts the necessary *measures* to attain their purpose.

Politics, on that account, is rightly considered the highest expression of man as a creator of culture. It is also his most comprehensive expression since it has for its purpose the "common welfare." The ancients called it the "art of governing" and considered it the highest of the *"arts"* in the medieval sense of this term. Like all other "arts," it is a work of "auto-nomous" man, of man as a being who assumes responsibility for the construction and perfection of his "world."

This autonomous task of creation which belongs to man by the fact that he is man, i.e., that he is a "world builder," is confirmed by Christian faith and by theology. We find it mentioned in the first chapter of Scripture, and the Church's magisterium has never ceased to underline its importance. We read in the text of Genesis 1, 28, which has already been quoted several times, that God said to mankind when man first appeared on earth: "Increase and multiply, and fill the earth, and subdue it." These words were spoken to man when the distinction between Christians and non-Christians did not yet exist. By these words the earth was entrusted to man as his "domain," the "house" which he should rule in his own name for the welfare of all. That is why it is said of man that "God created man to his own image" (Gen. 1, 27), for just as God is the Lord and the

Master of the universe, so does man have dominion over this earth. That God has thus entrusted the administration of the goods of this world and the organization of temporal society to the free judgment and initiative of man—this is the fundamental principle of the Christian doctrine about the State and the society of Pope Leo XIII.

The Meeting of Politics and Religion by Way of Ethics

Must we conclude from this that politics is an autonomous administration of earthly goods in complete independence from all religious belief? We might at first be inclined to think that there ought to be a complete separation of the two since politics is an undertaking limited to this world and has for its purpose to provide opportunities for human life within that world, whereas faith is concerned with the transcendent mystery of God and His Will of salvation. Isn't God a reality "outside the world" and the "totally Other"? When we invoke God as "our Salvation and our Savior," we are first of all concerned with the salvation of our soul.

And yet it would be wrong to seek completely to divorce our political conduct from the religious dimension of salvation that belongs to our life. The supernatural mystery of salvation of which we have become sharers through faith, is not a pure superstructure on top of our earthly life. It encompasses and permeates our earthly life completely by the fact that it gives *ultimate meaning and significance* to this life. For this reason one may even speak of a certain "subordination" of politics to faith, on condition that this subordination be properly understood and that it does not destroy the autonomy of political life. We are thus faced with the same problem we have examined in the chapter regarding the relations of *religion and civilization*. Hence we must seek the solution of the problem in the same direction and say that politics and Christianity meet in *Christian ethics*.

We readily see that faith and politics must meet somewhere, in spite of the fact that faith is concerned with a transcendent God, whereas politics is a function within this world and our being-in-the-world. We realize that, on the one hand, no Christian life of faith is thinkable without *Christian ethics,* and that, on the other hand, authentic politics worthy of the name cannot exist without an inner *ethical dimension* which is, as it were, its soul. As John Morly expressed it very aptly: "Those who want to separate politics and morals will never understand either one or the other."

No one, not even an unbeliever, has ever denied that Christian faith, in order to be authentic, must be embodied in an ethics, that it must permeate, motivate and direct our whole life. This we have fully developed in the chapter *"Religion and Culture."* Not only St. Paul and St. John, but our Lord himself has pointed out that the whole Christian ethics is virtually contained in the great commandment of the love of our neighbor so that it is *"like* to the first commandment," according to which we "must love God above all things."

But, as we have explained, it is necessary to understand properly this evangelical "love of neighbor." It entails much more than sentimental sympathy for suffering mankind, more than charitable contributions toward the needy. It means first of all watchful understanding, and effective respect and concern for man, whoever he may be. To love one's neighbor as oneself means to show an effective interest in procuring for him all the good we wish for ourselves. This "good" encompasses not only supernatural salvation but also health, education, justice and dignity, freedom and opportunity; in short, whatever fosters a life that is worthy of man in a world worthy of man, this, as we have seen, is the aim of political activity.

On the other hand, likewise, no politics worthy of the name is conceivable without an ethical driving force, without a constant care for ethical values. Politics is more than a technique of administration that is neutral in regard to values. It is a work of man and for man, and it is born from a value judgment regarding man, that is, from a judicious concern for the dignity of the human person and for what we have called the values which free the person and constitute the person.

Hence all great politics are born of, and inspired by the appreciation of an ethical value. As Professor J. van Boxtel so clearly proves in his studies of democracy, the modern democratic regime is more than one of the innumerable possible forms of government, more than one of the conceivable methods of establishing a ruling authority. Modern democracy is born from a concern for the human person, from a special sensitivity to essential human values. It arose under the motto, "liberty, equality, fraternity," and these are not idle words. The same can be said of every progressive social politics and thus also of socialism. It is not merely a question of transforming economic and administrative structures, but, beyond those structural reforms, it is a question of a society in which the great animating force and the principle of order will no longer be the power of money but respect for man; a society, therefore, which wants to eliminate the crying inequalities between classes and peoples and desires to insure greater equality regarding the opportunities of life. In short, it seeks to introduce more truth and justice into the world.[2]

The Four Imperatives of a Politics with Christian Motivation

If, on the one hand, there can be no Christian life of faith without Christian morals and, on the other, no great politics

[2]Cf. the beautiful discourse of the late Professor H. Bouchery, during the National Study Days of the Young Socialists: *"Terug naar de toekomst."* October 31, 1956.

can exist without animating ethics, then faith and politics cannot be totally divorced. In more simple words, when a Christian enters the field of politics, he does so as a *man* and as a *Christian believer*, for he is a man like the rest, with others and among others, but he is at the same time also a man who believes in God and in the hereafter. This faith does not diminish his manhood.

The concrete consequences of this connection are fourfold. They are, as it were, the four imperatives of what could be called a "politics that is inspired and motivated by Christianity." However, even this expression, as we shall point out later, can be misunderstood.

The First Imperative. There is no true politics which does not have an historically inspired and historically situated program of welfare. In other words, true politics has a program that is concerned just as much with the universal course of civilization's history as with the actually existing economic, social and international conditions. It displays a sense of realism and courageous thought, that is to say, it harmonizes short-range aims with a long-range ideal of welfare. The Christian politician, like anyone else, must rely upon his professional competence in the formulation of such a program. The excellence of his political wisdom does not depend on his religious goodness but on his scientific capacity, his political "feeling," his creative imagination, his flexibility and determination. It depends on his human talents and statesmanship. In all this the Christian is indeed similar to other men.

The Second Imperative. Since the political organization—by this we mean the State as a whole of *objective structures,* such as law, legislation, economic and social institutions—is not an end in itself, but a cultural creation of man and for man, the Christian politician must, more than anybody else, keep *man* in mind while planning and executing his program. He must allow himself to be guided in his politics by a high concept of man, a refined sensibility for the many *material, spiritual* and *ethical values* which liberate and foster our manhood, both individually and collectively. Hence he desires to construct a society whose objective structures bear the stamp of concern for the human person and the values that constitute the person.[3] For a high-ranking *community* worthy of man is possible only where society, as a whole of *objective* structures and institutions, is the expression and echo of respect for every man and for what is best in man. In other words, we shall have such a dignified community only where the brutality of the *homo homini lupus* (man is a wolf to other men) has given way to interpersonal openness, or to use the words of St. Paul, where it has been replaced by a community of "peace, joy, and brotherliness."

The Third Imperative. In his politics the Christian believer is also concerned about his religion and his Church. History has taught him how decisive a policy can be for the unimpeded diffusion and flowering of faith. This does not mean, of course, that the Christian politician is permitted to impose his own religious convictions on the entire community by means of political pressures. However, no one can blame him for desiring a society in which are found the necessary conditions or freedom for the unimpeded proclamation of God's Word, the exercise of worship and the Church's task of spiritual education. A Church that can speak to the people only from the altar or the pulpit, is doomed to weakness, for the worship that takes place within the church building is not a point of departure but a terminus. Only those that have already grown up in the faith will be present in the Church edifice. Those who must still be introduced to the faith will be absent. If a church wishes to grow and flourish,

[3]See their description in Chapters Three and Nine.

it must be able to reach men where they grow up, work and play, live and die. The Christian politician desires this freedom of movement, this "living space" or, as it is sometimes called, this safeguard of "the essential rights and liberties of the Church," not only for his own Church but also for the other denominations, religious cults and philosophies of life, for he does not want to impose faith by violence and political pressure.

It is mainly because of the watchful concern for proper freedom for his Church that the politics of the believer differ from that of the nonbeliever. And yet, even on this point, a sincere understanding of the Christian with those who have different beliefs is not impossible, for even the unbeliever, who considers things solely from the standpoint of democratic freedoms, must cherish man's liberty of conscience and of religion as an important value for a sound social life. But there will always be a danger that this freedom will remain an empty word, unless it is guaranteed and insured by positive law. Now positive law is not a thing that drops ready-made from the sky; on the contrary, it is often won only through the struggle of the interested parties. That is why watchfulness and a readiness to fight, but not intolerance and fanaticism, will always be characteristic of the political life of the Christian believer.

The Fourth Imperative. Lastly there is a fourth motive which will guide the politics of the believer. He must never forget that he is not alone in the world, that he lives in a mixed society in which there meet many contradictory convictions about the meaning of life and religious forms of worship. It is impossible to desire to construct a home where there is room for everybody, if everybody wants the whole house for himself alone. Politics is therefore the art of mutual understanding, of moderation, of compromises. Fanaticism is neither a political nor a Christian virtue.

An intelligent "compromise" in politics has a positive value. It is sometimes expressed in the following way: "There will always be a distance between the ideal and the existing reality, between the thesis and the hypothesis." However, this expression is ambiguous and even dangerous because of the ambiguity of the words "ideal" and "thesis." For the term "ideal," which brings us into the sphere of the unreal, can be understood in two ways which should be carefully distinguished. First, there is the "unreal" that leads us away from reality toward a world of dreams, castles in the air, and acting with one's "head in the clouds," without a firm basis in reality. Secondly, there is the "unreal" that enriches our real activity because it teaches us what our conduct ought to be in these concrete finite circumstances in order to be good.

The true ideal, which can serve man as a rule and norm for his conduct is always something that is *relative;* it should never be thought of in complete isolation from reality. For instance, a lecture which is ideal for a university would no doubt be worthless for pupils in grade school. Likewise, the *ideal* of chastity for married people differs from that proper to a priest. The *ideal* relation between Church and State, that is, the relation which affords the *best* safeguards for the free activities of the Church and the proper course of state management, will be different in a homogenous Christian society, such as existed in the Middle Ages, from that in a pluralistic society like ours. In other words, what the modern Catholic politician will strive for and try to achieve as much as possible will not be a "Catholic State" based upon a medieval situation. This would even be dangerous, not only for the temporal community but even for the Church, for, instead of building a healthy modern home, he would create a "reservation" for his fellow-believers that would separate them from the rest of the world. It is unfortunate that theology when dealing with this matter, often makes use of a language that stems from the Middle Ages and as such is not adjusted to our own times. This happens, for example, when in its defense of democratic freedom, it seems to have no other argument than the famous distinction between "thesis" and "hypothesis." But we shall say more about this matter in our study of the problem of tolerance.

These, then, are the guiding principles which, in general, determine the relations of faith and politics. They are rather simple and they flow immediately from the nature of things. They can be summed up in the following text of Father E. Schillebeeckx, O.P., Professor of Theology at the University of Nijmegen: "On the one hand, the socio-economic political organization has an independent domain within the world in which both believers and non-believers are at home. On the other hand, Christian salvation is not a superstructure on top of the earthly organization. Political life stands in a supernatural order, though only by way of man's sanctification. The Christian view of life in regard to man and human society does not rest solely on the data of revelation. It is made up both of data of faith and of earthly growing and changing evaluations. Similarly, the irreligious view regarding man and society is not ruled only by earthly evaluations, but is also influenced by a non-theistic conception of man."[3a]

All this serves to show that the believer is not less free, autonomous and personally responsible in his political life than the unbeliever. Freedom, in fact, is not synonymous with willfulness, arbitrariness and want of principles, nor is autonomy synonymous with moral anarchy. This principle applies not only to believers but also to unbelievers. They too must submit to the demands of truth, law and justice in their politics. The responsibility of the believer, however, is in a certain sense greater than that of the non-believer,

---

[3a]*Geloof and Politiek,* Program of the First National Congress of the *Katholieke Staatkundige Studenten Federatie,* held at Nijmegen, December 8-11, 1960.

since he sees in human existence an eternal dimension over and above the temporal one.

2. *The Church and Politics*

At first sight, some might be inclined to say to themselves that we have neatly avoided the issue by omitting a consideration of the Church and ecclesiastical authority. The Christian's belief is an ecclesiastical belief, his Creed contains an "I believe in the Holy Church," and the Catholic recognizes within this Church an authority instituted by God. Does not this put heavy shackles on the political thinking and acting of the Catholic and considerably limit his "autonomy"? How can one speak here of autonomy if the Catholic owes obedience to ecclesiastical authority and this authority never misses an opportunity to remind the world that it has competence and a right to speak in temporal affairs? Does not the introduction of this Church element fundamentally change the relation between faith and politics which we have described above?

The answer is very simple. These relations are, at least in principle, not affected at all, for the Church's intervention in political affairs occurs solely on account of the faith and by way of the Christian moral conscience. In the strict sense of the word, the Church by virtue of her divine institution does not possess a single political mission or competence; she has only religious and ethical competence, for she has no other mission than that of announcing to the world the message of salvation as Christ commanded her: "Go and teach. . ." (Matt. 28, 18). Now, contrary to all expectations of both the Jews generally and His own disciples, who dreamt only of a national and political re-establishment of the Jewish State, Christ always maintained the purely religious and ethical meaning of His message: "My kingdom is not of this world"; "Give to Caesar the things that belong to Caesar and to God the things that belong to God." For this reason it is the explicit teaching of the Church and, e.g., the foundation of Pope Leo XIII's Christian doctrine concerning the state and property, that God has entrusted the administration of the temporal world to the free judgment and initiative of man.

This autonomy, however, as we have already seen, does not mean that politics and ethics can be entirely divorced. There is no politics worthy of man without a high standard of ethics. For the Christian, this means that there can be no true politics that is not inspired by respect for the human person and the values which liberate the person, as well as by a watchful care for the preservation of the necessary freedom of the faith and the Church.

Now it is the precise task of the Church to see to it that the believers remain faithful to the Gospel message; in other words, it is her task to watch over the soundness of their faith and morals. This explains why the Church has always considered it an inalienable right and a sacred duty to *assist* the faithful in *forming* their *conscience* even in political affairs. This is true not only in regard to her own faithful but even to all mankind. As a non-believer once told us: "The Church ought to be the conscience of all mankind in our world, in which politicians have at their disposal increasingly greater and more dangerous powers and so readily confuse democracy with demagogy. She should be the defender of the spiritual and ethical values whose voice is so little heeded in politics, the defender who unmasks the modern forms of injustice, lies and oppression, the protector of the one who is always most threatened, namely, man himself."

Precisely, because the Church's intervention in political life is for the sake of the formation of moral conscience, it can, like any intervention in matters of conscience, take on two forms: one that is more negative and refers to sin, and the other more positive, by the proclamation and diffusion of what is usually called a Christian-inspired social and political doctrine. No doubt the more "sensational" form of intervention is the negative one. It is made "because of sin," that is, when the Church considers that some particular political world view or some concrete political procedure is in conflict with the demands of the moral law, endangers the essential liberty of the Church; or, to use the words of Pius XI, "when politics touches the altar." Such an intervention takes the form of a condemnation. These condemnations, however, are rare. The best known in recent times were directed against National-Socialism and atheistic Communism.

It would be wrong, however, to reduce the Church's influence on political life to condemnations. There exists also a "social doctrine" of the Church. We have already pointed out the ambiguity of that expression. It does not mean that the Church possesses a specific concept of the State which she considers her own; nor does it mean in the least that we must ask the Church to solve the innumerable economic, social and political problems of our own time. From what we have explained it should be clear that "Christian social doctrine" means, first of all, an *ethics* concerning social and political organization of society that is illumined by faith and faith's view of man, an ethics of which we have outlined above the most important imperatives. It belongs to the Christian statesman to draw inspiration from this ethics, when, in all *freedom and autonomy,* he formulates his program for the common welfare or in any other way participates in political life.

The Church is often criticized because the great reforms in the realms of economic, social and political thought and endeavor, which are the pride of our time, have not originated with the Church, but owe their origin to thinkers and workers who belong to "the other camp." This criticism contains a dangerous play upon words. The term "Church" can mean two things: the Church as an authority instituted by God, and the Church as the living collectivity of the faithful. The task of the ecclesiastical hierarchy is to watch over the soundness of faith and morals. It is not its task to rethink the social order or to direct the progress of civilization. The latter is precisely the task of the layman. Now, if during the last two centuries, the Catholic layman has often been absent from the vanguards of cultural progress, this must be attributed primarily to the layman himself, for instance, to too passive a conception of himself as a "follower" of the Church, and to a wrong interpretation of what is called the "social doctrine of the Church." The truth is that the layman usually expects both too much and too little from the Church.

3. *The Relations Between Church and State*

We should note carefully that the question which presently draws our attention is but a partial aspect of the general problem of the relationship between faith and politics, and that it even lies on a different level from everything that we have discussed thus far. For we are now leaving the sphere of universally valid principles and are entering the realm of political practice. It is now a question of the relations between two powers and communities that are historically situated. On the one side, there is the Church as a religious-ethical community which strives to express her religious-ethical conviction in all sorts of cultural activities, such as schools and other educational establishments and hospitals. On the other side, there is the State as a temporal society. To our mind it is very important to make it clear to ourselves that we are not so much concerned here with principles as with practical problems, for otherwise we run the danger of identifying passing historical situations with unchangeable principles. This will unavoidably lead to fanaticism, whether it be the clerical or anticlerical variety. Most of the utterances of modern clericalism are rooted in a secret longing for the medieval type of relations between Church and State whose value one consciously or unconsciously attempts to make absolute by means of a theological sophism.

It is perfectly evident that the "ideal" relationship between Church and State consists in that form of mutual understanding which in a given cultural condition gives a maximum of safeguard both for the *proper course of State life* and for the *free operation of the Church.* It would be a mistake to take the medieval concept of this relationship as our standard, for we cannot determine *a priori* what the concrete form of those relations should be, for example, by deducing that form from the essence of Christianity. The medieval form is only one among many possibilities. In most civilizations we find a kind of "medieval" phase of culture which is characterized by a far-reaching compenetration of the secular and the sacred, of the temporal and the religious. "Of the three factors that were active in the construction of the Middle Ages," writes Cardinal de Jong, "[namely, the Christian, the German and the Greco-Roman], the Christian was supreme. The spirit of the Middle Ages was directed to the supernatural. A living faith animated everything and permeated both the life of the individual and the life of the community. The Middle Ages had the tendency to establish the dominion of Christ, to found a State of God, the 'City of God in its pilgrimage on earth' (St. Augustine), in which the Pope wielded the spiritual sword and the sovereign the earthly sword, in which the Pope took care of the spiritual interests, the sovereign of the temporal. The spiritual power was regarded as higher because it represented the eternal, the supernatural which surpasses the temporal, although the temporal power was free in its own domain. This ideal, however, was hardly ever or never realized. There were constant conflicts between the spiritual and the earthly powers because the earthly power sought to rule over the spiritual and the ecclesiastical authority also sometimes claimed too much power over the secular. But at the same time those who fought the spiritual power never denied the faith. *The cooperation of the Church and State* worked for the benefit of both."[4]

It is easy to understand that, during the periods of tension and conflict, medieval canonists and theologians tried to give a foundation of *divine right* to the privileged position of the Church in social life. However, this attempt has led to much confusion, for what in fact was the result of circumstances was made into something absolute. As is well known, these theologians invoked among other things the famous "theory of the two swords." According to the Gospel of St. Luke (22, 38), Our Lord, on the eve of His passion, prepared His disciples for the coming trial and these then remarked, "Lord, here are two swords," to which Our Lord replied, "It is enough." Now the medieval canonists, whose scientific accuracy in the field of exegesis was not particularly outstanding, saw in this story a confirmation of the fact that Christ had given a twofold power to His Church, one spiritual and the other earthly, the first being exercised by the Church herself and the second for the Church but through the intermediary of the sovereign.[5]

---

[4]Cardinal de Jong, *Handboek der Kerkgeschiedenis,* 1947, vol. 2, p. 3.

[5]We find an appropriate example of such a singular interpretation of Scripture in the famous Bull *"Unam Sanctam"* of Boniface VIII (1302) against Philip the Fair: "The Gospel teaches us that there are two swords in the hands of this shepherd (namely, Christ and His vicar the Pope): the spiritual and the temporal sword. For indeed, when the apostles said, 'Behold there are two swords here' (Luke 22, 38), that is, in the Church, the Lord did not reply, 'It is too much' but on the contrary, 'It is enough.' He who would dare to deny that the temporal sword is in the hands of Peter would pay little attention to the words, 'put your sword into its scabbard' (Matt. 26, 52). The two swords, the spiritual and the temporal sword, then, are in the power of the Church; the first is used by the Church, the second for the Church; the first by the priests, the second by kings and soldiers, but only for as long as the priest wills and suffers it (*ad nutum et patientiam sacerdotis*). Therefore, one of those swords must be subject to the other, the temporal power must bow before the spiritual power" (Card. J. de Jong, *op. cit.*, vol. 2, pp. 225 f).

Arguments were also often drawn from the idea of Christ's kingship. Since all power on earth had been given to Christ, some concluded: "The temporal power also comes from Christ. Through the Pope, as His Vicar, it is transferred to the earthly sovereign. The latter rules autonomously; he is not a vassal of the Pope, but could easily be deprived of his power, because of sin, for example."[6]

The attempt of the medieval canonists to justify the then existing relationship between Church and State, by trying to *derive* it from the Christian mystery of faith, has done a great deal of harm to the Church. It greatly strengthened clerical conservatism and its counterpart political anticlericalism. In a certain sense it is still causing trouble in countries with a Western European or Southern European culture. We do not mean that there are theologians who still take seriously that singularly medieval interpretation of Scripture of which we have given a few examples. But there still exists an inclination, at least in some circles to consider the medieval form of cooperation between Church and State as the ideal, to consider it as the "thesis" which, therefore, ought to be aimed at and approached as much as possible.

We have already remarked that the concept "ideal" is something relative and that it leads to useless misunderstanding when it is used in season or out of season. What may have been useful for Church and State in the Middle Ages would be a calamity for both in modern society. Moreover, one and the same juridical relationship can have various meanings according to the society in which it is adopted. Thus Catholics as well as non-Catholics in the U. S. A. consider, and not without reason, the complete separation of Church and State the best guarantee for a sound life of the State and a free Church. The same separation also exists

---

[6]Cardinal J. de Jong, *op. cit.* vol. 2, p. 227.

behind the Iron Curtain, but there it has a totally different meaning. In some countries a Concordat between the political regime and the Holy See is the most fruitful formula; in others a Concordat is useless. In Holland and in Belgium there is a rather healthy mutual understanding: the Church enjoys great freedom of action and this is due not to a Concordat but to the civil law, to the watchfulness of the Catholic Community, and to the spirit of moderation and tolerance that is rooted in the customs of the people. What should be especially avoided in this matter of the relationship between Church and State, is the upholding of rigid apriorisms and the attempt to give an absolute character to what are merely historical conditions of things.

4. *Tensions and Conflicts*

The most impressive theories regarding religion and politics and the best juridical agreements between Church and State will not prevent occasional tensions and conflicts. This should not greatly astonish or excessively disturb us. Wherever there is life there is struggle, and where there is progress values will collide. The important point is that the conflict remain humane and observe a spirit of fair play. In retrospect, moreover, quite a few conflicts, proved very advantageous for State and Church. They have often resulted in both political life and religious life emerging from the battle spiritually enriched. For instance, the long struggle between emperor and pope during the Middle Ages was beneficial not only to the Church but also to the life of the State. The absolutist concept of political power, inherited from Eastern despotism, was undermined and the way was opened for a more ethical interpretation of State authority. In other words, the Church's struggle for freedom against rulers was also of benefit to the idea of liberty in general and thereby prepared Western democracy. And in respect to the nineteenth century conflict concerning democratic freedom, the Church has been, unwillingly as it were, finally freed from the countless servitudes that afflicted her under the Old Regime, freed by the very freedom which she had first combated. We may add that even democracy has ultimately profited by it, because the inner ethical significance of political toleration has been placed in a better light. The same could be said about the struggle over the Papal States. It has undoubtedly served the Church as a point of departure for a new spiritual advance and has been for the papacy the beginning of a prestige greater than it had ever known before.

The history of the conflicts between Church and politics is very instructive and it is the task of the historian to study them with perfect objectivity and serenity, in order that the lessons of the past may not be lost. This history teaches us two things especially.

First it shows us that, with the exception of a few extreme cases, the causes of the conflict were rarely found on one side alone. The tensions between religion and politics have often been like those between faith and science. Science was not always to blame for transgressing its boundaries; theology was often unreasonable and presented, as truths of faith or connected with faith, all kind of contentions that in reality had nothing to do with the faith. We have merely to think of Galileo, the theory of evolution, the first applications of modern historical criticism to Church history and Scriptural exegesis. Many insights and ideas which are now commonly accepted were considered dangerous or contrary to orthodoxy fifty years ago.

The same has happened in the field of social doctrine. One has to recall only how moral theologians juggled with the difficult and delicate ideas of "natural law" and the "natural order," and how often they feared that Church life would be ruined when some activities of which the Church formerly had the monopoly, such as education, the care of the sick and charities, were taken over in part by the State because private initiative alone could no longer cope with the problems.

History gives us a second lesson which, to our mind, deserves a careful and scientific study. It is concerned with conflicts between Church Authority and the layman in relation to particular ecclesiastical interventions, rather than with conflicts between Church and State. These conflicts are the more painful because those involved are usually prominent, sincere Catholics, who are very earnest both in regard to their political activity and their concern for the faith and the Church. It is understandable that on such occasions the ancient theological discussions about the relationship between faith and politics, between Church and State are revived. Now, to our mind, what is characteristic of these disputes is the fact that most of the time the discussion is concerned with side issues and the heart of the matter and difficulty is not even touched. There is passionate discussion regarding the exact nature and the extent of competence of the Church in temporal affairs, whether she has that competence in virtue of her authority to teach or her power to govern, whether she has "direct" or "indirect" authority, whether she has merely "directive" or "obligating" power, or, as some express it, whether she can give an "obligating directive" etc. We do not wish to minimize the importance of those classical discussions. Yet they are largely useless when it is necessary to shed light on the intervention of the Church in concrete circumstances, because they do not touch the core of the difficulty. This core is usually located not on the level of principles but on that of facts. Most often the question is whether in these concrete circumstances a particular political action is, or is not, in harmony with the Christian conscience, whether or not the Church's intervention "because of sin" is justified. With rare exceptions (namely in cases when the political action is itself immoral), we are in the presence of what in moral theology is usually called *"actions with double effect,"* actions which simultaneously produce good and bad effects or, in ordinary language, actions with pro's and con's. The center of gravity of the problem then lies in weighing the pro's and the con's, a thing that is often difficult.

Examples of such situations are legion in the field of politics. Which course, in some definite set of circumstances, is better for the Church: that all Catholics form a Catholic party or that Catholics be divided among many parties? In a country where the regime is an enemy of the Church, for example, the first regimes after the French Revolution, the first Italian regimes after the unification of Italy, the present Marxist regimes behind the Iron Curtain, what should be the attitude of Catholics: to divorce themselves completely from politics or to try to make themselves felt? Is it permissible to close certain factories which are no longer productive and solvent, thus causing the temporary unemployment of a number of workers, if there is hope that in the long run the economy will be benefited and more work and prosperity will be offered to all? The answer to such questions is always the same: there are pro's and con's, and the alternatives must be subjected to careful examination.

It goes without saying that it is difficult, and often impossible, to solve such questions satisfactorily. It is very instructive in this respect to recall the passionate discussions of Belgian Catholics during the Dutch Regime (1815-1830). They were concerned with the advantages and disadvantages of the United Netherlands State under the central government of William I, established by the Congress of Vienna.[7] The constitution of the new kingdom, which guaranteed freedom of religion, was considered favorable by northern

[7]Cf. Cardinal J. de Jong, *Handboek der Kerkgeschiedenis,* 1949, vol. 4, pp. 109 ff.

Catholics; on the contrary, Belgian Catholics, who were accustomed to the privileged position of the Church, considered it catastrophic for religion: the Catholic South would probably not be able to hold its own against the Calvinistic North, but little thought was given to what was to happen to northern Catholics if Belgium separated from Holland.

In any case, history has shown how little substance there was to all those considerations. The Revolution of 1830 caused the division of the kingdom which had only recently been established. Since that time, the Northern Catholic community, in spite of being a minority in a predominantly Protestant country, has made constant progress both quantitatively and qualitatively. In Belgium, on the contrary, a great portion of the inhabitants of Wallonia and the large cities has become estranged from the Church, although from 1884 to 1914 the political government was homogenously Catholic.

In respect to political "actions with double effect" it is often very difficult to weigh and measure the pro's and con's. Most of the time a political stand is advantageous for one aspect of social life, and harmful for another; it is advantageous for one group, harmful for another, advantageous at short range, disadvantageous at long range. Moreover, the opposite political position likewise has its advantages and disadvantages. Hence politics is almost always a political option and a matter of statecraft; that is, it is the art of drawing the maximum advantage from a particular situation and a particular political policy. One realizes that there are disadvantages attached to his stand but *firmly intends to eliminate them as much as possible in other ways.*

It goes without saying that discussions about principles are of little use in any such case. In most of them the question is not: how far, in principle, does the Church's competence extend? but rather, how can we, in these particular situations and these particular political circumstances, obtain the maximum advantage for both the temporal and the spiritual welfare of the people?

5. *Final Consideration: Catholic Politics or Politics of Catholics?*

In connection with these problems, the question is sometimes asked whether there is any sense in speaking about "Catholic politics" and whether we ought not to speak rather of the "politics of Catholics."[8] The reply, it seems to me, should be that neither of the two expressions is perfect. "Catholic politics," in a certain sense, says too much. It could give the impression that the political wisdom of a Catholic differs from that of a non-Catholic, that it obeys other economic and social laws, is motivated by a vision of ethical value that is totally different. Now, this is not correct. A Catholic is a man like others; Christian ethics does not destroy natural ethics but gives to it a firmer foundation and integrates it into a higher purpose of existence.

On the other hand the opposite formula "politics of Catholics" does not say enough. It seems to imply that faith and politics are entirely separate, that the political thought and action of the believer are neutral in regard to value or that they are inspired by a morality which in no way differs from that of non-believers. It is perhaps preferable to speak of "a politics inspired by faith," although this expression also can be misunderstood and give rise to the idea that the believer deduces his political vision and conduct from faith "in a geometric fashion." As Professor Schillebeeckx expresses it: "The Christian's view of life in regard to man and human society is not based solely on the data of revelation. It is made up both of data of faith and of earthly, growing and

[8]There is a similar question in philosophy regarding "Christian philosophy" or a "philosophy of Christians."

changing evaluations."[9] In other words, every political program for the common welfare, whether initiated by a believer or a non-believer, must be *historically* inspired and historically situated. This, however, does not prevent a Christian from receiving additional motivation and direction for his political thought and activity from the vision faith gives him in respect to man, the appreciation of ethical values, and his desire to preserve freedom for his Church. In this sense it is permissible to speak of a politics that is inspired and motivated by faith.

---

[9] See footnote 3 of this chapter.

CHAPTER ELEVEN

THE POSITIVE MEANING OF TOLERANCE

The problem of tolerance is as old as man. Every time man realizes that he is not alone in this world and that, whether he likes it or not, he must share material and spiritual "living space" with others, he is faced with the problem of tolerance. But this problem has acquired a new content and meaning with the unification of our world.

1. *The Contemporary Problem of Tolerance*

The unification of our planet, as we have pointed out in a previous chapter, seems to be the chief event of our time. The world of modern man, in the realm of science, technology, philosophy, economics, politics, etc., is becoming more and more an international enterprise. It demands the cooperation and daily meeting of workers and thinkers of all countries, cultures, philosophical opinions and religious forms of worship. Peaceful and tolerant coexistence has become an inevitable necessity for modern society; it is henceforth a part of our *situation of life.*

But there is more at stake than a matter of sheer necessity. A situation that is at first merely "*undergone*" can always become a situation that is *understood* and *accepted,* that gradually reveals the advantages contained in it. How often has it not happened to us that being-forced to live together with someone gradually became for us a source of enrichment *thanks* to the other. And this is precisely what is now taking place. The widening of the horizon of our life has already radically changed our attitude toward others, and the necessity of living "under the same roof" with others is experienced more and more as an event full of promises. We merely have to compare our present theological reviews and missionary magazines with those of the beginning of the century, to notice how much more positive, understanding and respectful of values our judgment has become in contrast with former times. Instead of looking upon non-Christian religions as pure idolatry, moral degradation and a collection of stupidities, we have discovered in them a hidden search for God. We put greater stress upon the things that bind us with others than upon what separates us from them, and we are now convinced that all great cultures have something to teach us, without denying, however, that we have much to give them. The same can be said concerning our relations with the Christians who are separated from Rome, the Protestants and the Orthodox. Whereas we were formerly content with a forced or tolerated living-alongside-one-another, we have now gradually entered into an honest and fruitful dialogue with them.

What does all this mean except that the ancient problem of tolerance, or more exactly that of coexistence in one same community that contains different views of life and different religions, has acquired a new content and meaning? Not only has the problem itself been raised on a world-wide scale, but its meaning has changed, and this to such an extent that the term "tolerance" no longer expresses properly what it is supposed to cover.

The word "tolerance" inevitably brings to our mind a sort of negative and passive attitude in regard to evil, which one "tolerates" against one's liking, whether through necessity and civility or in order to avoid a greater evil. This we know was the only accepted meaning of the word "tolerance" before the birth of modern democracy.

We may illustrate the point by considering the concept of "tolerance" according to St. Thomas.[1] In the eyes of this great medieval theologian, who merely gives a commentary

[1] *Summa Theol.*, p. IIª IIªᵉ, q. 10 and q. 11.

of the morals of his time, heretics are common law criminals and must be treated as such. Their crime is even much greater than that of counterfeiters, for they corrupt faith itself ("It is much more grievous to corrupt the faith . . . than to falsify money.") Hence they deserve to be punished with death ("They may not only be excommunicated but may justly be killed.") It is proper, however, for the Church, to *tolerate* them for a while in view of their conversion; but when all hope of conversion is gone, they must be eliminated as one cuts out a cancerous growth ("they are to be cut out like rotten flesh, as Jerome says."); and they should be handed over to the temporal power ("he delivers the heretic to the secular judge to be exterminated from the world through death.")[2]

Recall also the Edict of Nantes, in 1598, in favor of the Huguenots of France, and the Act of Toleration of 1689, promulgated in England in favor of the Catholics. These are two typical measures of tolerance, in the sense that they somewhat softened a legislation that was based on intolerance. Let us note that what was then called "tolerance" would be considered today as the expression of systematic intolerance. In other words, "tolerance" was then almost synonymous with "moderate intolerance."

To my mind we cannot insist too much on the fact that today the term "tolerance" has a different meaning. To realize this, we have merely to think of the proclamation of "liberty of opinion, conscience and religion," in the Declaration of the Rights of Man of 1948. The purpose of this declaration was not to grant a favor to one or other class of citizens. Rather it was designed to protect the human person in general and those things which the human person rightly considers his sacred possessions, viz., his moral and religious conscience, what the ancients called the *"dictate"* or

[2]*Ibid.*, q. 11, art. 3: *Whether heretics ought to be tolerated?*

the *"voice of conscience,"* against the dictatorship of the State, i.e., the danger that a state might impose its views as a *dictate of conscience.*

In our present world, the *meaning* of tolerance is no longer a matter of tolerating a lesser evil, or a gesture of clemency toward those who break the law, but it is a *moral value that must be fostered for itself.* "We feel proud and happy," Pius XI wrote in his Encyclical *Non abbiamo bisogno,* "to fight for the freedom of conscience."

Hence the question is: May a Catholic agree with this present concept of tolerance? In other words, Is it possible for him to be a *sincere and convinced democrat,* who without hesitation accepts and praises the Declaration of the Rights of Man of 1948, as being one of the great *juridical* and *ethical* acquisitions of our time? For civic tolerance henceforth is indeed a constitutive element of the ideal of a democratic society, and this democratic ideal is now considered to be a "moral project for man and mankind."[3]

Here, then, is a question of great importance. On our attitude in regard to tolerance will depend whether or not we accept and understand our time, whether our political thought and activity are in harmony with the sensitivity to ethical

[3]Cf. J. van Boxtel, *Democratie en menselijke verhouding*: "Our times have seen a remarkable change in the meaning and appreciation of democracy. Democracy is no longer thought of as one of the possible forms of government alongside the monarchy and the aristocracy; it is no longer considered as not in itself preferable to the other two (*"wert-neutral,"* as Messner calls it). For a long time the latter was the classical conception sponsored by the social doctrine of the Roman Catholic Church, and it was supported with an appeal to Aristotle and St. Thomas Aquinas. In our own time we think differently about the meaning of democracy. It is considered more and more to be far preferable to the others, as the ideal form of government and administration. This applies not only in the realm of civil government but also in that of social, economic, pedagogical, individual-psychological . . . cultural . . . and even ecclesiastical relationships. Briefly put, democracy is now conceived as a "*moral* project for man and humanity" (p. 89, in the collection *Menselijke Verhoudingen,* Brussels, 1955).

value of our time, in other words, whether the world of today can count on us.

When we put the question in that way—and it can no longer be put in any other way—we come face to face with a strange situation. On the one hand, it cannot be denied that, in regard to democratic sentiment, modern Catholics, with few exceptions, are not lagging behind anybody else. In many countries (for example, in the world behind the Iron Curtain) it is mainly the Christian who at this time continues the ancient struggle for freedom of conscience and religion and who often does not hesitate to risk his life in a heroic policy of resistance in defense of this freedom. But on the other hand, most Catholic theologians continue to speak about this matter *in medieval terms.* Thus they give the impression that they consider civil tolerance only a lesser evil, which they accept because it is impossible not to do so, and that the ideal or the "thesis" must still be sought in the direction of the earlier formula of intolerance. Now our precise purpose in this chapter is to emphasize the positive and ethical significance of tolerance, to show that it is a value in itself and not merely a "lesser evil" to be tolerated in some circumstances. In order to avoid all ambiguity, let us first determine the meaning of the terms and see precisely what "tolerance" is and what it is not.

2. *What Tolerance is Not*

There are three principal interpretations of tolerance which we cannot accept.

Doctrinal Tolerance or Indifferentism

The *civic* tolerance, which is the subject of this study, has no relation with *doctrinal indifferentism, relativism* or *skepticism,* which maintain that all philosophical opinions, all religious and ethical doctrines regarding life are equally true and equally valuable. Such doctrinal indifferentism, which is sometimes called "doctrinal tolerance," is in conflict with the very idea of truth, for surely everything cannot be equally true and have equal value. Civil tolerance, however, does not imply any reference to a metaphysical concept of truth, it is an attitude not toward doctrine but toward persons.

For the same reason the meaning of the term "freedom," as used in "freedom of conscience," is not philosophical or theological but social and juridical. When the modern State acts as a defender of "freedom of conscience," at least when it is conscious of the true meaning of words and does not misuse its powers, it has no intention of formulating a metaphysical theory about free will for its citizens. It does not want to proclaim the anarchy of moral conscience or make a pronouncement about the value before God of the various forms of worship. The State does not have the task of taking the place of the human conscience or of playing theologian or philosopher. To guarantee freedom of conscience means no more than to create favorable *conditions of life* for the citizens, so that they can properly exercise their personal freedom.

It is in this sense that Pius XI adds to the above-quoted passage from the Encyclical *Non abbiamo bisogno* that the expression "freedom of conscience" *(libertà di coscienza)* is ambiguous; it is sometimes used improperly and given the meaning of "an absolute independence of conscience, which is absurd to the mind of every one who knows that he was created and redeemed by God." That is why he gave preference to the formula, "freedom of consciences," *(libertà delle coscienze)*.

One could even say that doctrinal, ethical and religious relativism, by the fact that it erases the distinction between the true and the false, the good and evil, is not only in conflict with the idea of truth and value but also with genuine tolerance. For, genuine tolerance considers the dialogue as the field in which truth flourishes, whereas absolute relativism excludes the dialogue and, as it were, substitutes for it a poll of opinions. Making an inventory of existing persuasions is quite different from conducting a true dialogue, which is an exchange of *receiving* and *giving,* for the purpose of arriving at a more mature and a more refined knowledge of the truth.

It should not astonish anyone that the Church has repeatedly disapproved and condemned doctrinal indifferentism. It stands to reason that in the eyes of a Christian all religions do not have the same value for the Christian, since to "believe" means for the Christian to be open to the Word of God, which has revealed itself in the course of history in Jesus Christ. Doctrinal indifferentism especially constitutes the background of the first and well-known papal documents regarding liberalism, namely the encyclical *Mirari vos* (1832) of Gregory XVI, the encyclical *Quanta cura* and the *Syllabus* (1864) of Pius IX, as well as the encyclicals *Immortale Dei* (1885) and *Libertas praestantissimum* (1888) of Leo XIII. The Popes saw in the so-called "modern freedoms" the expression on the political plane of doctrinal, ethical and religious skepticism.[4] Looked at in its historical context, this interpretation was not without foundation. For in many countries the famous Declaration of the Rights of Man made it appear as if a rationalistic and atheistic anthropology was proclaimed the official doctrine of the State and as if the democratic freedoms were primarily instruments in the service of skepticism, unbelief and even oppression of the Church. Rightly did Pope Leo XIII remark in *Libertas praestantissimum:* "It happens only too frequently that these great defenders of tolerance are in practice harsh and severe where

[4]R. Aubert, "L'Enseignement du Magistère ecclésiastique au 19e siècle sur le libéralisme," in *Tolerance et communauté humaine (Cahiers de l'Actualité religieuse),* Tournai, 1951, pp. 75-103.

Catholicism is concerned. Generous in conceding freedom to all, they often refuse to the Church the retention of her own freedom."[5] This went so far that "a French newspaper which can hardly be accused of clericalism made the following accusation against the 'liberal' regime which governed Spain in 1869: "It has granted freedom to all religions, except the one which is known to the Spaniards'."[6]

This ambiguity, which *in fact* accompanied the birth of "modern freedoms," has long weighed heavily on *liberalism,* the more so because it coincided with a second ambiguity concerning the idea of the "sovereignty of the people." Here again, when we take into account the historical circumstances which we mentioned above, the declaration that "all rights and power come from the people" easily gave the impression that this utterance was one of a godless attitude and a brutal rejection of the traditional thesis that "all power comes from God." Only gradually was it seen that these two views regarding the origin of authority, if understood properly, were not opposed to each other and mutually exclusive, since they did not move on the same level. The first (all power comes from the people) is concerned with the origin, within our world, of political authority in a democratic regime, whereas the other (all power comes from God) points to the religious dimension of human existence both for the individual and for society.

Those two views are not antagonistic but complementary. Their situation is very similar to the relationship of modern science and religion. Modern positive science is, by definition, naturalistic and a-religious; it accepts no other causal explanation than that which is proved by the facts; it is its right and even its duty to confine itself to such limitations. It is only too evident that a scientific investigation which, in

[5] *Lettres apostoliques de Léon XIII,* Paris, vol. 2, p. 207.
[6] A. Aubert, *ibid.,* p. 101.

virtue of its method, limits itself to the things that appear within this world, does not meet God or witness the radical dependence of creatures on God. But it would be wrong to conclude from that, as a certain kind of scientism is not afraid to do, that faith in God is but a mystification and deception and that, for example, the evolutionistic explanation of the universe has made useless the faith in the creation of the world by God. Scientific studies and theological studies of the universe take place on different levels of truth.

This comparison between "modern democratic freedom" and modern science enables us better to understand why the Catholic Church has been slow in recognizing the values contained in the rise of democracy. In fact, the scientific revolution, begun by Galileo and Newton, and the democratic revolution, of which the French Revolution was the principal expression, had this in common: they both signified a crisis of authority that was characterized by stripping authority of its sacred character on the one hand, and by a deliberate affirmation of the autonomy of man and human reason on the other. And this, to our mind, explains at least in part, why the theologians were so slow in recognizing that those great revolutions from which the modern world originated possessed values and forces that would contribute to the freedom of the faith.

It is really not *easy* for a believer to preserve his sensitivity to the "sacred" in a "desacralized" world; but *ease* is not synonymous with *authenticity*. Nevertheless, the fact that first science and then politics were stripped of their sacred character has in the long run been beneficial to the faith. To make the Bible the competitor of scientific investigation is to obscure the specifically religious dimension of the Word of God. The same may be said about the mixing of temporal and spiritual authority. History teaches us that any political authority that proclaims itself to be "of divine right," very quickly degenerates into uncontrolled despotism.

The "Liberal" Interpretation of Tolerance

Modern civic tolerance can be understood in a second way that is also erroneous. According to some, it is the expression on the political level of the doctrine which makes religion and morality essentially a "private affair" having no relation to public life. This was more or less the position of *liberalism* in its first period. In this view, politics is a question of economic, social and administrative techniques which, like science and technology, are by nature neutral with respect to values, i.e., they are a-moral and a-religious.

We have already shown in the preceding chapter that the complete separation of human life into two opposing sections, one of interior or private life and the other of external or public life, is unacceptable. It is just as untenable as the Cartesian dualism on which it is based. Man always lives interiorly and exteriorly simultaneously since by his very nature he expresses his manhood, reveals himself outwardly. An ethical ideal which is not aimed at improving interhuman relations and favoring the welfare of all is not worthy of the name. Now precisely this aim is the task of politics. Conversely, a politics without an ethical appreciation of man is not worthy of man. Every great and creative form of politics is always supported by a sensitivity to ethical values. The ideal of a democratic society was born of a genuine concern for the human person, just as modern social politics was born from the urge for truth and justice, equality and fraternity.

Politics and ethics cannot be completely separated. On the other hand, as we shall see later, tolerance itself is essentially a moral virtue, and like any other moral attitude, must find expression in outward deeds and objective institutions. This does not mean that tolerance consists of eliminating all the moral differences that are encountered in one and the same society, or in reducing the existing moral views to their greatest common denominator, which would then be proclaimed to be the official ethics of the State. This would be a mere caricature of tolerance. Although Christian ethics incorporates natural ethics, "natural law," it nevertheless has its own specific demands which flow from its religious concept of human destiny. Thus the religious dimension completely permeates and colors the life of the Christian and has its repercussions in the whole system of morals, such as the ethics of marriage and the family, the education of youth, the love of neighbor, worship, etc. Tolerance, properly understood, expects the statesman, whoever he may be, to show respect for those demands by creating conditions of life that will facilitate their practice. But it also expects that the Catholic statesman will not impose on unbelievers his own ethics with all the demands contained in it.

The Negative Conception of Tolerance

We must especially avoid reducing the idea of tolerance to a purely negative concept namely, that of "tolerating an evil that one has the right and the power to combat."[7]

This does not mean that the term "tolerance" can never have that meaning. In some cases society has the right and the duty to defend itself against particular forms of evil, to

[7]This definition of "tolerance" is found in the first edition of the *Katholieke Encyclopaedie,* under the word *Verdraagzaamheid.* The *American Catholic Encyclopedia,* 1912, has the following: "Theoretical dogmatic tolerance is the toleration of error as such in so far as it is in error" . . . Practical civic tolerance is the personal esteem and love which we are bound to show toward the erring person, even though we condemn or combat his error." Gregory IX (April 6, 1233) wrote: "The same benignity must be shown the Jews by the Christians which we desire to be shown to Christians in pagan lands." (*Ibid.*) Tr.

repress what endangers the community, such as movements that tend to produce anarchy, public prostitution, and the dissemination of literature that is dangerous for youth. It is understandable that society may show itself more or less lenient in regard to these expressions of evil, since there are usually two sides to any measure the government may adopt in such matters. It is sometimes better for the community to "tolerate the evil." All this stands to reason, but it would be wrong to approach the whole problem of civic tolerance from the standpoint of *this particular form* of tolerance, and thus to reduce the concept of "tolerance" to the "tolerating of an evil that one has the right and the power to combat."

It is clear that if one adopts such a negative concept, it is difficult to do justice to the true value of the modern democratic freedoms, especially freedom of opinion, of conscience and of religion. The term "tolerance" then suggests the idea of a "lesser evil" that one feels forced to accept because no other course is possible, or that of a favor granted to others through clemency, as if intolerance were the normal and ideal attitude. As we have remarked before, in such a view tolerance becomes practically synonymous with "benign intolerance." In other words, intolerance is then put forward as *thesis,* as the stand adopted, whereas tolerance is considered permissible only in the *hypothesis,* i.e., in particular circumstances. Because of the great role played by this famous distinction between "thesis" and "hypothesis" in the debate over democratic freedoms, we consider it useful to devote a special section to this subject.

3. *Thesis and Hypothesis*

This distinction may have been useful as long as it was a question of justifying one or the other rule of tolerance within the frame of the Old Regime, which was dominated by the principle *"cujus regio illius et religio,* (let the ruler's religion determine that of his subjects). The distinction made it possible, despite everything, to attribute a positive significance to a policy of tolerance, for as St. Augustine already pointed out, it is morally permissible and in certain circumstances even a positive duty to tolerate a lesser evil in order to prevent a greater evil or to achieve a greater good.

However, with respect to tolerance in the modern and positive sense of the term, such a distinction no longer has much value; it can merely serve to prolong unnecessarily the famous nineteenth century debate concerning liberalism. What is worse, it could give the impression that Christians are not honest democrats, but favor tolerance only "in the hypothesis," i.e., when they do not possess the power to practice intolerance.[8] As we shall explain later, tolerance can very well be shown to be morally justified without having recourse to the idea of "thesis-hypothesis." The traditional opposition between thesis and hypothesis merely serves to widen the gap between theological thought and modern political concepts, since *each side makes use of a wholly different terminology.*

We should not forget that if we put tolerance in the category of "hypothesis" the politician will be led to interpret it as the proclamation of the "thesis" of intolerance. Modern theologians, moreover, are well aware of this. Hence, at least the majority of them no longer give the same meaning

[8]According to Professor Aubert (*op. cit.,* p. 100) "intelligent Catholics" understood that the distinction between thesis and hypothesis in regard to the Belgian Constitution of 1831 was not very useful: "Cardinal Stercky," he writes, "always avoided using this distinction, and B. Dumortier, (the Catholic representative of Doornik) gave Cardinal Antonelli the reasons for that position by saying: 'Thesis and hypothesis, are precisely the attitude which the Church's greatest enemies want her to adopt so that they will be able to accuse her of insincerity and justify persecution. . . . Nor could anyone tell parliament: 'We want freedom for ourselves but not for you, we tolerate your worship because we are weaker than you, but if we ever become stronger we will refuse you that freedom which today we demand from you.' "

to the so-called "thesis."[9] But what do contemporary theologians mean by "thesis"? If I understand them properly, they mean that religious indifferentism or so-called "doctrinal intolerance" is unacceptable to the mind of the Christian or also that for the believer the ideal state is one in which all citizens should be Christians. Now this is undoubtedly correct, but it has no relation to the problem of *civic tolerance,* nor can one draw from it the least conclusion concerning the question which we are considering here. This question is: Is freedom of religion a *value in itself* which one must respect and guarantee by positive legislation *in all circumstances,* even when one's own party is in the majority?

We could also express it in this way: When in reference to civic tolerance we appeal to the opposition between "thesis and hypothesis," we should avoid making the term "thesis" refer to *"doctrinal intolerance"* or rejection of religious indifferentism, and "hypothesis" refer to *civic tolerance.* No one should speak that way unless he wants to violate the most elementary rules of logic which demand that "contraries be found in the same genus"; in other words, the two opposed terms must belong to the same order of realities. When one says that political tolerance is permitted only "hypothetically," that is, in certain concrete circumstances, he implies that intolerance ought to be practiced in other political circumstances. That the Christian believer dreams of a world in which everyone is a Christian is his perfect right; that he strives with all his might to spread the Gospel message is even his duty. But he is not permitted to use this right and duty as a justification for violence and social oppression; he must accomplish this duty by the means Christ has pointed

[9] We say on purpose "at least the majority of them," for there are still theologians who continue to consider the system of intolerance of the Old Regime as the ideal. However, their number is constantly growing smaller.

out, that is, by the powerful influence of a living faith and by the peaceful proclamation of the Word.[10]

Of course, the Christian who is involved in politics can always ask himself, whether, by guaranteeing and fostering democratic liberties, he does not foster unbelief and heresy, or to use the language of moralists, whether he does not *cooperate,* even if only indirectly, in what he *as a believer* considers to be the evil of unbelief or of heresy. This is the classical and well-known question of tolerating or permitting some evil that results from "an act with double effect."

To solve it we must have recourse to the equally classical and well-known principles of the "act with the double effect," instead of having recourse to the device of thesis and hypothesis. Those principles teach us that an action with a double effect is fully justified if the action itself is good (and this is certainly the case here, since to guarantee conditions of existence that favor the exercise of freedom and the safeguard of conscience is an excellent thing); and if, on the other hand, the so-called "evil" effect is not willed, but merely permitted (and this also applies to our case, since the democratic freedoms can favor unbelief solely by the use which the unbeliever himself will make of them).

What then ought we to conclude? That we should at any cost avoid approaching the modern problem of tolerance with its modern meaning by using a concept of tolerance that originated in the Old Regime. Unfortunately this is precisely what has happened most of the time with the result that the term "tolerance" has such an unfavorable reputation in the West and always makes people think of concealed intolerance and a lack of sincerity. If concealed intolerance were the only meaning of "tolerance," then we should admit that the term has become unbearable, delete it from the

[10]Sometimes the "thesis" is defended by the argument that "error has no rights." But this is a mere play on words. *Man* alone is the subject, the bearer of any rights. Even an erring man has rights.

vocabulary of modern man, and replace it with more positive expressions such as "respect for the human person" or "peaceful coexistence."

Many writers are in favor of this deletion. They are not wrong but I do not believe that it will be easy to eliminate the word from the language of man, for the simple reason that a negative factor is present in every human community, even when it is based on respect and kindness. For respect and kindness do not take away from the fact that the other always remains "other" for me, that he is sometimes a burden and even a possible danger. For this reason "tolerance" plays a role even in the most peaceful and most charitable forms of co-existence with our fellow-men. Without tolerance it is impossible that many live together in peace and have fruitful contact with one another in the same world. This assertion applies not only to tolerance on the level of private life (so-called "private tolerance"), but also on the level of organized and political society, (so-called "civic tolerance" or "freedom of opinion and of religion").

4. *The Ethical Significance of Tolerance*

The idea of tolerance introduces us to the world of "living-together-with-our-fellow-men." We must therefore see what the essence of this "togetherness" is, if we wish to get a better insight into the nature of tolerance and shed light on its various expressions.

The "being" of man, says Heidegger, is a "having to be," a cultural and ethical project or task. This also is true, *a fortiori,* of our "being-together." We must shape this being-together-with-others into a society that is worthy of man and that fosters our manhood. This "humanization" of "our-being-together" is not an easy task, for the introduction of "the other" into our own life and in our world presents a trinity of meanings which at first seem hard to reconcile.

First of all, the other is a burden to me, a competitor, an intruder; he cuts off a part of my world and puts obstacles in the way of my free movement. Whether we want it or not, we have to divide one world among ourselves. Moreover, the other can become a danger for me, an enemy, for we must constantly take into account the possible wickedness of man. "The other is the enemy," Sartre has said, and it is but a modern translation of an old saying, "man is a wolf to man" (*homo homini lupus*).

Secondly, the other is not only a burden and a danger for me; he is also a *companion* and a *fellow-traveler* on my journey through life. I need the other if I want to preserve and develop my life. The best things I own, I owe to others.[11]

Thirdly, the other has still another meaning for me. He comes into my life as someone for whom I can work, someone who is worthy of my care and my love, not merely because I may need him but because he is someone to whom I can give something. If I were all alone upon earth, there would be no longer anything for me *to do,* and life would lose its meaning. Above the satisfaction of receiving a gift, there is the joy of disinterested giving: "It is more blessed to give than to receive" (Acts, 20, 35).

These three meanings of "the other" may not be separated. They evoke one another and are interwoven. By love and care the burden which the other is for me becomes in a sense even heavier, for love strives to establish the other in his "otherness."

Whereas the philosophy of society formerly put the accent mainly on the second meaning of the "other-for-me" (I need the other in order to live), today there exists a tendency, especially in Christian centers, to give preference to the third

[11]Cf. our analysis of the concept of solidarity, Chapter Five.

meaning and to consider the problems of social human life from the standpoint of man's characteristic eagerness for love. This tendency can easily lead to a new kind of idealism. Human society is not a community of angels, in which there is nothing but love and no need of laws. Since the "other" is always also a burden and a danger for me, every co-existence worthy of man contains an element of tolerance. The simplest solution would be to get rid of the other, to get that burden that the other is, out of the way, but this would not be worthy of man, it would be sinful. I must "tolerate" him, or, as the Chinese proverb expresses it, I must "learn to forgive him his-being-other." Moreover, I have to protect myself against the danger that he might become for me and my liberty, but this also must be done in a manner that is humane, that is worthy of man. The means to accomplish this is the creation of a system of laws.

The meaning and purpose of all law is to delimit and safeguard for the future the sphere of "mine" and "thine," of what belongs "to us" in contrast with what "belongs to the others." The law accomplishes this not merely by protecting the sphere of my free activity against possible intruders but also by making me respect the sphere of the other's freedom. When laws are made, even when this is done by those who have authority as representatives of the community and its protectors, there is a kind of mutual pledge: I give my word to the other, and he gives his to me. In this sense the phenomenon of law belongs to the order of a pledge, of a "given word."

When we learned from our parents how to call things by their names, there was as it were a silent agreement between father, mother and ourselves in regard to our conduct concerning each individual thing. So it is when things are called "mine" and "thine." Just as speech, law is a work *of* intersubjectivity, and *for* intersubjectivity, a way of developing our "being-with" others in a manner that is worthy of man and full of respect for the other's freedom. The fact that a sanction is often attached to a legal enactment in order to give it more power, does not change the matter.

This lofty meaning of law in general, is valid not only in regard to the right of ownership in the ordinary sense of the term, but applies just as well to the more spiritual and subtle forms of property. These latter are usually called democratic freedoms or civic tolerance and aim at safeguarding the highest possessions of man, those which more than anything else make him an autonomous person; namely, freedom of conscience in his moral and religious life, an unrestricted search for truth and, finally, free and sincere encounter of others in dialogue.

In that sense, both "private" and "civic" tolerance are first of all an *ethical* task—it is an aspect or quality of every co-existence worthy of man. Hence tolerance is essentially and basically a moral virtue, that is, a project and a dynamic quality of our will in regard to the "humanizing" of our "being-with" others. It is an ethical task of justice. Accordingly, it is not by mere chance that the term "tolerance" in modern language has been replaced by that of the "rights of man."

But the fact that "tolerance" is a moral attitude does not mean that it is purely and simply spiritual. "Good-will" alone is not sufficient to make us really "will the good." Tolerance, to be effective and valuable, must *express* itself outwardly. This will be done in private life in my way of acting toward others, by being patient toward them, "bearing with one another" (Col. 3, 13) ; and in public life, by the creation of a system of positive law, that is, by creating a social and juridical system which establishes and safeguards the indispensable conditions of life in order to protect the liberty of others. To recognize the others' freedom of conscience and of religious belief, while refusing them the objective conditions of life that are necessary for effective freedom, is not tolerance but only a caricature of tolerance. Pope Leo XIII wrote elegantly about this positive and ethical meaning of modern freedom of conscience and religion. In the encyclical *Libertas praestantissimum,* after indicating that the idea of freedom is frequently misunderstood, as though it meant that henceforth man's conscience no longer had to acknowledge a transcendent law, he remarks that freedom can also *admit* of an exact and high interpretation: "It can be understood," he wrote, "in the sense that the citizen in whatever State he may live, always has the right to follow the dictates of his conscience, to recognize and accomplish God's will, and to fulfill his obligations, without being hindered in this by anyone or anything. This genuine freedom, the only one that is worthy of a child of God, is the best safeguard of the dignity proper to the human person. This freedom stands above all violence and pressure."

It is certain that we must interpret in the same sense the famous expression "freedom of thought, conscience and religion," contained in the *Declaration of the Rights of Man* of 1948. This declaration is on record in the history of mankind as the solemn and official confirmation of that for which the free world fought and suffered during four years, namely, the dignity of the human person and the inalienable rights of personal conscience against the State. When modern governments, in accord with this *Declaration of the Rights of Man* of 1948, introduce freedom of conscience and of religion into their legislation, they cannot intend to dispense man from obedience to the voice of his conscience, or from his obligations toward God. If, nonetheless, this were their intention, it would flagrantly contradict that *Declaration,* for the State then would once more claim to replace the conscience of the individual man. This precisely is the most horrible of all dictatorships.

The State does not have the task of taking the place of conscience, but of safeguarding the necessary room and freedom for the exercise of personal conscience. Properly understood, civic tolerance or freedom of conscience has undoubtedly a positive and ethical meaning. In the framework of modern society, in which the government constantly takes on more responsibility, tolerance is the only way to confirm, not merely by words but in reality, that *the human person precedes the State and stands above the State in dignity and destiny, since the State is for man and man is not for the State.*

5. *Obstacles*

If tolerance is in the first place a moral project, it is also a *difficult* task. It is a task that is never finished and that must constantly be defended against its enemy, namely, the tendency to intolerance. This intolerance itself is the result of several factors.

Man's Innate Tendency to Intolerance. First of all, our innate desire for freedom contains a tendency to intolerance inasmuch as we experience others as being for us a burden and a danger. This we have already mentioned.

A Monolythic Concept of Truth. Secondly, this intolerance is greatly fostered by a monolithic concept of truth, of the world of values and law. Man is easily inclined to imagine truth as a gigantic monolith, a strong and compact system that can be deduced "in geometrical fashion" from a handful of *supreme* truths. Such are the truths of faith for the believer, and a few positive axioms for the positivistic unbeliever. In both cases we are dealing with a kind of dogmatism, i.e., the dictatorship of one truth which suffers no other worlds of truth besides itself or denies to them their necessary autonomy. History reveals how often this naive conception of the truth has been and still is a nursery of intolerance.

This is why we have so often insisted in the previous chapters that, in view of our spiritually divided world, the relations between "Christianity and civilization," "religion and life," must be carefully reexamined. What relation has faith with the order of the "temporal" and the "secular"? And again: What does it mean that the Church has a "social doctrine"? We have said that the ordering of society is a creation of man's culture; it is not *deduced* "in a geometrical fashion" from the faith, but faith and its view of man shed light upon this cultural creation.

Moreover, we must not forget that the terms "Christian social doctrine" and "Christian order of society" are ambiguous expressions. If they are not treated with care, they easily lead to sophistical reasoning. Do they refer to the medieval order of law? Or to a society that accepts no other ethics in its legislation than the Christian ethics and endeavors to impose Christian ethics on all citizens to the greatest possible extent? Or do they mean that a Catholic politician, in view of his Christian concept of his calling (and not merely because he is not supported by a majority) and in all sincerity endeavors to construct a society where there will be equal place and opportunity of life for all, whether they be Catholics or not, a society characterized by a peaceful and fruitful co-existence based upon positive tolerance? Is not such a co-existence contained in the very idea of the "common good," of "what is good for all"? Rightly, therefore, did the Belgian Christian Popular Party declare in its program of March, 1958: "The Christian Popular Party in no way proposes the construction of a Christian State that is composed of Christians, but rather an ideologically neutral State which guarantees ideological freedom, as well as equality of rights to the citizens whatever philosophy they may adhere to."[12]

[12]*Tijdschrift voor Politiek,* March, 1958, p. 389.

A monolithic conception of the truth is often fostered by the sociological structure of the political society. A society in which the *political structure coincides with the existing religious divisions,* will easily lapse into intolerance and fanaticism because political oppositions, which after all have but a relative meaning, are readily made something absolute. For this reason, to "deconfessionalize" political life is of great importance for the development of a spirit and a regime of tolerance. However, this will be the subject of the following chapter.

Tension Between Ethical Intentionality and Objective Structures. There is a third factor which makes tolerance a task that is both difficult and never finished. I mean the inevitable tension between the *inner* and the *outward* which belongs to the very nature of tolerance. Tolerance is an ethical "work" ("*oeuvre*"). Like any human "work" it is the fruit of a dialectic relation between two "moments": an interior, ethical intentionality and its exteriorization or expression in objective structures, such as the social and juridical statute of the democratic freedoms and the freedom of political association. These two moments are inseparably united and need each other. Sincere tolerance will express itself in a regime of freedom, but this objective regime of freedom, in turn, needs a spirit of tolerance, lest it degenerate into a caricature and endanger tolerance.

Even the best regime of freedom can foster the greed for power of those who rule; they can use the regime both for and against *tolerance.* It can also—and this happens frequently—lead to fossilization. Instead of fostering encounter and dialogue, the recognition of one another's freedom becomes the road to "apartheid," to the formation of isolated sociological groups that live *alongside* each other. A "living together" that is worthy of man, however, is not a "living-alongside-one-another," but is a fruitful exchange of receiving and giving, of listening and speaking.

We should never forget that tolerance is but a phase of our "being-with" the others; it is a necessary condition for encountering them and conversing with them.

In this conversation, speech becomes eloquent for man. This is true of every word, but also of the word that is spoken to bear witness to the faith and that is *God's word,* in the twofold sense of the term: as a word that comes from God and as a word that speaks of God to man. Only in free and sincere conversation does the word attain its full value, does it *reveal* and *make free.* Where no one listens, there is no conversation, and speech degenerates into a hollow sound that touches no one and accomplishes nothing. The same thing happens where violence and oppression takes the place of free speech. In such an atmosphere, automatisms can be created, and habits of thought too, but no true thinking is had and the liberating power of the word is lost.

CHAPTER TWELVE

DENOMINATIONAL PARTY SYSTEM[1]

1. *Statement of the Problem*

Vigorous debates have always raged around the question: Is it a good thing both for political life and for the Church and the spreading of the faith, to have in a democratic state political organizations which are formed primarily along the lines of world views or religious beliefs? This is easy to understand since the so-called "confessional" or denominational formula, like any other formula, has its good and its bad points. In most cases it is difficult to determine whether the advantages outweigh the disadvantages, the more so because in some circumstances the denominational formula may be useful for a short period but disadvantageous over a long time, and vice versa.

Whatever one may think about it, this much is certain: at present, or more exactly, since the Second World War, the problem of the denominational party system has entered a new stage of its history as a result of a fundamental change in social life, both on the national and the international levels. Three factors are especially noteworthy in this respect.

First of all, there is the very important phenomenon of the growing *complexity* of the economic, financial, social and organizational problems that have to be tackled by modern politics. These problems are mostly so involved from the technical standpoint, that they demand great competence on

[1]Much of what the author says in this chapter is not directly applicable to the United States and English-speaking countries in general. However, as Professor Dondeyne points out, our world is rapidly becoming more and more unified. For the United States especially with its world-encompassing role, it is important that the public be well-informed about the background and problems of the European scene. For this reason we have retained this chapter in the American edition of this book. (Ed.)

the part of the government and the administration. One's philosophy of life has little relation to those problems. Hence there results an increasing tendency to give government a strictly scientific and technical foundation free from philosophical considerations.

The second factor is that the idea of *religious tolerance* has progressed greatly in the Western countries. Here again, the Second World War has exercised considerable influence. Fighting together for several years in a common war against a common enemy in the name of freedom, brought together many people of different world views and different philosophies of life. This common task made them realize the great value which more political freedom of conscience and religion had for society. Thus many came to the conclusion that nineteenth century anticlericalism is just as foolish and as antiquated as dogmatizing clericalism.

The final factor is again the *unification* of the world. This unification has placed all great problems on the international level. It forces individuals and peoples, regardless of their philosophies of life, constantly to cooperate with one another.

Understandably these three factors have contributed much to making a more clear-cut distinction between politics and religion and permitting this distinction to find better expression in political structures. Not only have several "Catholic" or "Christian" parties disappeared from the political scene since 1945, but where they are still existing, their members do almost the impossible to take away their strictly denominational character. They rightly insist that an organization that is inspired by Christian principles is not on that account a "confessional" or denominational party.

Moreover, while the former denominational parties tend to drop their denominational label, many neutral groups make efforts to shed ancient anticlerical habits and to adopt an "open neutrality," which leaves room for every metaphysical and religious philosophy of life within its group. No doubt, this is most strikingly exemplified in the Labor Party of Holland. This party not merely tolerates but actively promotes a diversity of "work groups" based on the diversity of philosophies of life.

There is also the fact that, generally, post-war socialism, after its break with communism, has shown a greater independence from dogmatizing Marxism, and has moved in the direction of ideological neutrality. The declaration of policy and progress of the Conference of Frankfurt (July 3, 1951) is not without interest in this respect. It said that "Socialism is an international movement which does not demand any rigid or uniform views of life. . . . Whether their action finds the ultimate source of its inspiration in religion or humanitarianism, the aim of the socialists remains the same; to bring about a system of social justice, greater welfare, freedom and peace." What "socialist society" desires is the establishment of a "higher form of democracy" which is the synthesis of "political, economic, social and international democracy." The Conference explicitly recognized that the sovereignty of the people and "political freedom, such as freedom of thought, of faith, of a system of education, of association and the right to strike" belong to the essence of political democracy and therefore have to be guaranteed.

The present problem of "denominational parties" must be situated in the perspective of all those events, which undoubtedly have profoundly modified the political climate of Western Europe.

To my mind, however, it is of the utmost importance to note, if we do not wish to get entangled in endless and useless debates, that the problem of so-called denominational parties contains in reality *two* problems. They must be carefully distinguished, although they are closely related. There is on the one hand, the question of the *meaning* and *justi-*

fication of the denominational formula and on the other, the question of the *"deconfessionalization" of political life,* i.e., of removing its denominational aspect. This second question is much broader than the first; it arises wherever man engages in politics, but is especially very urgent where no denominational or religion-inspired political parties as yet exist.

2. *Meaning and Justification of a Denominational Party System*

The question is: What is a denominational party and how can its existence be justified? It stands to reason that the second part of this question, the justification of such a party system, depends on the first part, the nature and the meaning of a denominational party. Now one can conceive several forms of denominationalism.

The expression "denominational" or "confessional" party is very ambiguous. Etymologically it points to a relation between a political group and a religious confession of faith. This connection, however, can be more or less close. There are several possibilities but to avoid unnecessary complexities, we will reduce them to four kinds.

Profession of Faith. The most *extreme form* would be a party which demands an explicit profession of faith from its members. We do not know whether that kind of party has ever existed. We hope that not a single denominational party has ever thought of binding religion to politics in such a brutal and irresponsible fashion. Hence we can think of it only as a possible extreme.

Christian State. Secondly, we can imagine a party—here we are already getting closer to historical reality—which calls itself Christian or Catholic because it has for its *purpose* to establish a *Christian State,* a social order which proclaims the Christian religion as the State religion, takes Christian ethics for the sole standard of its laws and, by that fact, imposes this ethics on all citizens through legislation. In other words, such a denominational party is a political organization which wants to realize the so-called "thesis" so far as it will be possible. As we have shown, it is obvious that such a position can hardly be reconciled with true democracy and democratic freedom.

We may ask ourselves here whether this kind of party has actually existed. Only a careful historical investigation can give the answer. History would probably reveal three things. First, that this concept of "denominationalism" was most widespread when the first of the denominational political organizations were started in France, Italy and Spain. Secondly, many still speak about political denominationalism in this sense and do not realize that what they really mean is something else. The reason is that they do not pay attention to the fact that expressions such as the "Christian social order" are ambiguous and need to be clarified.[2] Thirdly, at the present time not only are more and more people abandoning the former idea of denominationalism but the language used makes more careful distinctions. For example, the Belgian Christian People's Party most emphatically emphasizes that it "does not intend to construct a Christian State, composed of Christian people, but rather *an ideologically neutral State, which guarantees ideological freedom as well as complete equality of right to the citizens,* whatever philosophy they may adhere to."[3]

General Party of Christian Inspiration. There exists a third possibility which is undoubtedly the most widespread at the present time, and exemplified by the Belgian Christian People's Party. The party appeals to all citizens, earnestly

[2]Cf. above p. 287.

[3]*Tijdschrift voor politiek,* March 1958, p. 389.

strives to build a true democracy, but calls itself *Christian* for two reasons:

1) It takes its inspiration from the great social principles of Christian ethics whose explicit personalistic tendency is a powerful factor in building a society worthy of man.

2) It does not limit itself to affirm in a general way freedom of conscience and of religion, but gives to this freedom a *concrete, programmatic form.* For liberty of religion remains a vain word, if the various denominations do not enjoy the freedom of movement and living space which they consider concretely necessary to fulfill their religious mission. It is difficult to determine concretely what this "living space" comprises, but the more "living space" there is, the more life can unfold itself. In any case this "living space" is unthinkable without a whole system of juridically guaranteed conditions of existence, such as a minimum of material means, the possibility of instruction and education on a religious basis, the possibility of cultural and charitable activity.

Here now we are faced with a very important question. In the case we have just described, a certain connection exists between a political organization and a religious denomination or confession. But is this sufficient to permit our speaking of "denominational party" in the strict sense of the term? Professor Georges Phillips rightly remarked that this expression is not very appropriate in such a case, for the question is then one of a "party inspired and guided in a Christian way" which "explicitly places itself on the civic and political plane and elaborates a positive program for the common temporal welfare."[4]

Moreover, Professor Philips adds, it is wrong, though it is often done, to consider such a party simply and *a*

---

[4]G. Philips, in *De Maand,* January 1959, p. 57.

priori as a "necessary evil." For, as we have shown in detail, politics is a human "work," a creation by and for man. To be worthy of man and foster man's liberation, a policy must start from a value judgment concerning man, both individually and collectively. Now Christianity affirms a value judgment regarding man which is certainly not inferior to any other view of life. Hence to seek in the Christian view of value regarding man and society a source of inspiration for political activity can hardly be considered an "evil."

These considerations at the same time show us how the existence of Christian-inspired party organizations, in the sense in which we use this term here, can be justified. Christians who live in a democratic society which guarantees freedom of association, have the right to choose the kind of formula of organization that they consider the best, i.e., the one which in particular circumstances seems to offer the best guarantees both for the welfare of the people and for the freedom of religion. When there is danger that antichristian organizations will abuse their political power to put their own stamp on the entire community and to impede the free proclamation of the religious word, it can easily happen that the Christian believers have no other resource than to form their own independent party. A glance at the history of the denominational parties that have arisen in Europe since the French Revolution suffices to realize that the vast majority of the Christian parties owe their origin to such dangerous situations and that, in general as, e.g., in Belgium and Holland, they have actually served to secure equal rights for the religious groups which they specially represent.

Sociological Meaning. The term "denominational" can have a fourth meaning, which may be called "sociological." By this we mean that as a result of historical oppositions, and in spite of antidenominational declarations of policy, a Christian-inspired party organization can in fact perfectly and permanently coincide with a definite group of believers. We once more illustrate this possibility with the same example. In itself, that is in virtue of its own purpose and programs, the Belgian Christian People's Party is not a denominational party, in the strict sense of the term, as we have already shown. However, considered in the concrete *sociological* circumstances in which it has to function, it is a denominational party, since there is a general opinion in Belgium that a Catholic is not in his right place if he is found in the ranks of non-Christian parties.

This conviction is rooted in one hundred years of political history. On the one hand, it was fostered by the more or less explicit anticlericalism of most non-Christian organizations, and on the other hand, it was regularly strengthened by the interventions of ecclesiastical authorities on the occasion of elections. As long as this sociological condition continues to dominate Belgian politics, the Christian People's Party will preserve its character of a "denominational party," in spite of its best intentions and sincere efforts. However, a similar line of thought applies also to the other parties. The mingling of politics and religion then becomes an inevitable *sociological reality* which affects both the Christian and the neutral organizations. This brings us to our second problem, that of the "deconfessionalization" of political life.

3. *"Deconfessionalization" of Political Life*

The Disadvantages of Mixing Religion and Politics. The many disadvantages of the intertwining of political life and religious faith, or disbelief, are well-known.

First of all, the danger exists that the Church will become too much involved in temporal affairs. This certainly is not a desirable situation for either the purity of the Gospel message or for her power of expansion, especially in a world so spiritually divided as is ours.

A danger of fanaticism also exists by the fact that political contrasts, which after all have but a relative importance, tend almost inevitably to become absolute.

The mingling of politics and religion also obscures political thought and action since this thought and action are constantly subjected to a non-political criterion.

But there is still another danger that often is not sufficiently stressed, namely, the danger that freedom of political choice is often eliminated. The freedom of economic and political choice is in itself a very important value, it is as high and noble as the freedom of choice in the field of medical care, education, cultural creation and work. For this reason it is regrettable that, e.g., the Catholic in Belgium, at least practically, lacks that freedom of choice in political affairs. A Belgian Catholic who sincerely believes that a more socialized economy alone would produce a greater equality of opportunities of life for all, is not able to express his cherished view in an effective political choice, as is possible for Catholics in England, Germany, Austria, France, the Netherlands and the United States.

The Pastoral Letter of the Dutch Bishops in 1954, which was none too gentle toward the Labor Party, purposely did not forbid Catholics to belong to the *political* structures of that party. It did this precisely because it did not want to shackle the freedom of political choice. True, this freedom of choice is certainly not an absolute value and in exceptional circumstances it may have to give way to higher values. Nevertheless, this does not mean that it is not a very precious value. It is the duty of everybody to watch over it with care and to do all that is possible lest freedom of political choice become an empty word. Catholic sociologists and moral theologians, because of their personalistic concept of human society, ought to be the first to establish this freedom of choice as a value and to underline its great importance in their social ethics. Unfortunately, to my mind, they fail to do so sufficiently in Belgium.

"Deconfessionalization." These dangers lead us to the problem of the "deconfessionalization" of politics. The elimination of the denominational aspect from politics has always been important both for a sound political life and for religious belief, but it is more important now than ever because of the enormous influence of politics on the life of the ordinary man. As a result of the intimate connection of today's political problems with economic and social question, wherever political organizations of parties have been formed according to distinct philosophies of life, the whole of society has gradually become divided along the same lines. In most West-European countries, political parties are more than exponents of a particular political program of welfare. They are centers of crystallization around each of which autonomous and closed worlds of culture are organized. These worlds have a hold on a man from his earliest years to his death, by way of youth organizations, clubs for sports and cultural activities, workers' unions, cooperatives, clinics, the press and publicity.

Concretely speaking, this means that, e.g., in Belgium, a large part of the population, thousands of young workers, young couples, old people, the sick and the dying, never enjoy the unimpeded freedom in religious matters to which they have a right, because access to the Church, to the priest, to the wealth of Christianity is not as easy for them as it is for others. They feel handicapped for no other reason than that they have entrusted their temporal interests—as they have a right to—to this representative, this senator or minister, rather than that one who belongs to the denominational party. In our opinion, considering the "apartheid" pattern which characterizes the sociological structures of "our" society, the problem of political "deconfessionalization" is much more important and fundamental than one might at first imagine.

To our mind, from the standpoint of the Church, "deconfessionalization" is a fundamental condition for the renewal of the apostolate, and from the standpoint of social life, it is an indispensable element in the establishment of true democracy and the guaranteeing of man's rights. If freedom of conscience and religion is not to remain an empty word, it is not enough that no one is forced to accept or renounce a particular religion. This is only a negative condition. This freedom requires that positively everyone have free access to religious values, without any handicaps whatsoever.

How can such a "deconfessionalization" of political life be attained, gradually of course, since a sociological situation of "apartheid" is not softened and modified in one day?

One might at first be inclined to say, "by abandoning the denominational formula." For many this means, "by abolishing the Christian parties." However, first of all, as we have pointed out before, parties that are inspired by Christian thought are not on that account "denominational" parties in the strict sense of the term. Secondly, political parties are no more inclined to suicide than are individuals. In other words, political parties do not dissolve themselves, but only under the pressure of extraordinary circumstances, such as wars and profound political crises, do they disintegrate. This is why we said at the beginning of our discussion that the two questions, that of the meaning and justification of a Christian party, and that of the "deconfessionalization" of political life, should be carefully distinguished, lest we waste time in idle speculation and useless debates.

The question, for example, that faces the Catholics of Belgium and the Netherlands is not, as is often said, one of *opportuneness* of the Belgian Christian People's Party and the Dutch Catholic People's Party. This, from the political standpoint, is a useless and wrongly stated question, for it gives the impression that we are in the presence of a dilemma, namely, that of the perpetuation or dissolution of these parties. Now, that dilemma from the political standpoint makes no sense. True, it is possible to conceive such alternatives as theoretical and logical possibilities. However, politics is not concerned with logical entities but with concrete political possibilities and aims. A party, which like the Belgian Christian People's Party, can rightly boast that it is the greatest political organization of the country, that its welfare program is inferior to no other, which, moreover, has repeatedly shown its capability for governing the country and its readiness to fight, if necessary, for the threatened religious freedoms—such a party will not bring about its own voluntary dissolution.

Moreover, such a thing would not be good for political life. No one, not even its socialist and liberal opponents, would want to ask for it. The only thing that is asked is that Belgian politics be less intertwined with religion, so that freedom of choice in political affairs can become a reality for the Catholic as for any other citizen. Differently expressed, no one should be considered a second-rate Catholic because he belongs to a party other than the Catholic People's Party.

In other words, the crucial point is not the matter of the right and the opportuneness of having a Christian party, but the *"deconfessionalization" of politics.* This purification, however, cannot be achieved by the Christian party alone but is an ethical task for the entire society. No doubt, the conclusion of the school-pact was a step in the right direction and could ring in a new period if it is applied honestly. In any case if we want to attain the desired "deconfessionalization" of political life in Belgium other types will be necessary. A few of these are the following:

1. On the part of Catholics, moral theologians ought to subject the concrete problem of the relations of politics and religion in Belgium to a new and thorough examination, while taking into account the changed and still changing circumstances. This, to my mind has not yet been done. When we consult the literature on the subject we get the impression that things are still dealt with as they were thirty years ago when we were students.

2. On the part of neutral party organizations, some deeply rooted anticlerical habits of thought ought to be abandoned and greater openness should be shown toward effective freedom of religion. Proclamations of policy, however sincere, are not sufficient. As we have already shown, not only the House of Representatives and the Senate have to breathe a new atmosphere but the same purification should reach also and more especially the closed worlds of culture which form the background of political life. Notably the press is one of the principal factors that need to be purified.

3. Finally, everybody should attune himself to the future rather than to the past. The problem of the "deconfessionalization" of politics is primarily a practical and ethnical problem, a problem which belongs to the world of political practice and political ethics. Account must also be taken of historical facts and possibilities. But to take account of history does not mean to look constantly backwards and to transfer the inertia of the past to the present. The past, precisely because it is past and escapes from our grasp, is inert: what

is done cannot be undone. But from this we must not conclude, as many people like to do, that everything must go on as before and that nothing must be done with an eye on the future. It is one thing to write history, describe the past and explain the present by means of the past, but another to "make history," that is, to prepare the future from the present and use the potentialities it contains for a better world.

CONCLUSION

IS CHRISTIANITY STILL OF TIMELY INTEREST?

We have come to the end of our confrontation of faith and the world. Many a reader may ask himself the question which we mentioned but did not develop in our first chapter, and which is one of the most disturbing among the many that bother the Christian mind. This question is: Is Christianity still of actual interest? What "chances," if any, does it have in the times that are to come?

That Christianity has played an unsurpassed role in the spiritual humanization of mankind cannot be denied nor is it denied by non-believing historians. We can repeat here the famous words of Christopher Dawson in *The Making of Europe* that Christianity to a great extent has "made" the West. And through the West, it still continues to put its seal on the spiritual, ethical and social unification of our world. But we are justified in asking ourselves whether Christianity has not been overtaken by history, whether its greatness belongs to the past rather than to the present and the future. In other words, will there still be room and opportunity for Christianity in the world of tomorrow?

This question, however, contains a dangerous ambiguity. For it can be interpreted in two different ways depending on the point of view from which one considers it.

1. *"Christendom is Dead"*

Firstly, there is the standpoint of objective history which looks back to the past and sees Christianity as one of the most powerful history-shaping factors of the Western world. In this way, the question about the chances of Christianity in tomorrow's world comes down to something like this: "Will Christianity remain an historical force in the life of peoples, in the social history of mankind? Will Christianity retain the influence which it once had in Western culture and in the

European community of nations?"[1] If the question is asked in this way, we view the future of Christianity from the standpoint of the past and as a prolongation of the past or rather of what used to be called "Christendom," the Christian world. Now, as is clear from our analysis, this "Christendom" definitely belongs to the past. We all remember the word of Emmanuel Mounier: "Christendom is dead" (*Feu la chrétienté*).[2]

By "Christendom" as opposed to "Christianity" we now usually mean the particular form or way the Christian faith and the Catholic Church appeared in cultural history during the Middle Ages. Medieval society was characterized by the fact that it was marked by the Christian religion and the visible Church organization in all its members and structures. Christianity was the unifying and guiding factor of the entire civilization, and the Church was the highest cultural and social power. She had the monopoly of instruction, education and charitable works; even the political power of princes was subordinated to the spiritual authority of the Pope. Hence, from the standpoint of the philosophy of life and socio-politics, the medieval world was one world and this unity had its origin in Christianity and the Church. Secular history and Church history fully coincided.[3] All this was the result of the fact that shortly after the proclamation of peace by Constantine, Christianity was raised to the position of State religion in both the Eastern and the Western Empire.

---

[1]Karl Rahner, *Christendom en Kerk in onze tijd,* 1955, p. 22. German title: *Gefahren im heutigen Katholizismus,* Einsiedeln, 1950.

[2]E. Mounier, *Feu la chrétienté,* Paris, 1950; also *L'affrontement chrétien,* Neuchatel, 1945.

[3]"Until the Renaissance," writes Henri Pirenne, "the intellectual history of Europe was but a chapter of the history of the Church. So little lay thought existed that even those who fought against the Church were totally dominated by her and thought only of transforming her." *Histoire de l'Europe des invasions au XVIe Siècle,* p. 393.

The breakdown of medieval Christendom did not take place at once; it resulted from a long process of "desacralization." Three great events played a decisive role in that process. We have already met them in the course of our study. Firstly, the Renaissance, during which scientific and philosophical thought began to establish their independence from theology. Secondly, the French Revolution sounded the end of the theocratic regimes because political life became secularized and the former relations between Church and State were replaced by a regime of freedom of conscience and of religion. Thirdly, the contemporary unification of our world which, for the first time in history, gathers all mankind into an effective historical unity, beyond all differences in religion and philosophies of life.

It is remarkable, however, that this breakdown of Christendom has not harmed the vitality of Christianity. Rather the contrary is true. The Galileo case benefited theology, by the fact that the earlier subordination of secular sciences to "sacred doctrine" could be replaced by a fruitful dialogue, on the basis of a mutual recognition of each one's autonomy. In the Middle Ages, *Physica* was a subdivision of philosophy and the latter the handmaid of theology. There is no doubt that philosophy rendered great services to theology, but on the other hand, we must not forget that the "handmaid" was not always an example of obedience and that she sometimes exchanged her role of servant for that of mistress of the house with the result that faith itself became rationalized.

The secularization of politics has likewise been a priceless blessing for the Church. Numberless restrictions that oppressed the Church under the Old Regime have disappeared one after another. Among these, we may name the constant interference of civil authorities in the administration of dioceses and monasteries, and the forced participation of the Holy See in the political life of Europe due to the temporal power of the Popes over the Papal States. Never has the spiritual and moral prestige of the papacy been so great and world-wide as in our own day. In regard to the unification of the world, no one knows what the future will bring, but there is basis for hope. As Karl Rahner remarks, "Christianity has held its own throughout the centuries and among many peoples and has thus proved its universality as a world-embracing religion. Everything seems to indicate that it will become even more universal in the concrete physiognomy of our world."[4]

Whatever the truth may be, one fact is certain and is of the utmost importance for us who live in the present world: the breakdown of medieval Christendom has put Christianity in a *new situation* with respect to the world, a situation that can best be compared with the situation of the Diaspora of the Jews after their exile. We no longer live in a closed and homogeneous society, but in a spiritually mixed and open world in which believers and non-believers meet one another every day and must work together to build a better world. The medieval Christian world has disintegrated and the Christian believers have thereby become aware that they constitute only a minority of the world's population. In reality they have always been a minority, but as long as they remained shut up in themselves and were master and lord in their own house, they did not realize it. We may add that the Middle Ages did not know the extensiveness in time and space of our world.

It goes without saying that the Diaspora situation both causes new difficulties for the faith and offers new possibilities and opportunities. It especially gives greater opportunity for a faith that is more personal, more daring, more relying on God Himself, and that has a more apostolic orientation.

---

[4]K. Rahner, *op. cit.*, p. 46.

Even in this respect does the comparison with the Diaspora situation of Israel offer a lesson. Israel also had its Middle Ages, when it introduced a kingly rule against the wishes of Yahweh, and thus let it be known that Palestine belonged to it forever. The promised land did no longer appear to Jewish consciousness as the symbol of God's promise: "I am with you," but took on the appearance of an established kingdom. This precisely was the beginning of decadence for Israel. It began to live as an established nation amidst other nations, full of self-confidence and self-reliance. The daring faith of Abraham and Moses gradually belonged only to the past and it was less alive in actual life than in the singing of the Psalms. In fact, Israel's downfall was soon to come, at least its downfall as an established kingdom, and very soon it would once again become a wandering race. It was driven into exile, but the Israel of the Diaspora increased greatly in numbers and was more fruitful than the Israel of Palestine. When Christ appeared, it was not the Jewish community of Jerusalem that became the principal bearer of the message and that took over the service of the chosen people, but the Jewry of the Diaspora, i.e., Paul, the convert Jews and Greeks of Thessalonica, Corinth, Ephesus and Rome.

Because everything shows that "Christendom" is definitely something of the past, there is for the present Church no more dangerous a temptation than that of homesickness for the past. I mean the inclination to consider the medieval form of Christianity and of the Church as the ideal—or rather as the "thesis"—and the criterion for modern action. This will only foster "apartheid" and render more difficult the dialogue of the Church with the present world. Yet this dialogue with the world belongs to the essential mission of the Church, since the Christianity for which the Church is responsible is a joyful message and whoever speaks of message means conversation, witnessing, effective presence.

Moreover, Christianity is a divine and religious message which speaks to man in his religious, that is, in his most profound and most universal, dimension of existence. Now it is clear that this religious and absolutely universal significance of the Christian message can be diffused and proclaimed only with difficulty if the Church appears to modern man as a world that is closed and lives apart. This will happen when, for instance, she appears too Western or gives the impression of being more interested in her own social and cultural organizations than in the sighs and needs of today's humanity. Let this not be misunderstood. We are not saying that there is no longer any room in our time for a cultural and social mission of Christianity. The religion of Jesus Christ, as we have seen, is no world-hating mysticism, but an ethics of love for the whole of mankind. Wherever men live, labor and suffer, wherever they strive for truth and justice, there the Christian believer must be present and there the Church has a mission to fulfill.

However, this earthly mission of the Church will assume another form than it had in the Middle Ages. Rightly does Karl Rahner say in the study already quoted: "The influential position of the Church in public life and her significance in history, as they existed in the West from around the years 1000 to 1500, and by which we almost spontaneously measure her success, was not only the concrete embodiment of what is and must remain the message of the Church in virtue of her supernatural life and her supernatural mission, but it was also the result of an accidental and temporary concurrence of historical circumstances. For this reason it is quite possible that the Church will be a factor in public life in another way and that her historical significance will become quite different, when those circumstances disappear."[5]

---

[5]K. Rahner, *op. cit.*, p. 31.

Where and when and in what manner this will happen, and in general, how the diffusion and development of Christianity will be accomplished in the future, no man can foretell. In other words, the question of the *actual future* of Christianity is one that cannot be solved. Moreover, the question is a dangerous one, for it easily leads to thinking or dreaming about the future as a prolongation of the Christendom of the past.

2. *The Timeliness of the Christian Message*

The question whether Christianity is still timely and whether there will still be room and a role for it in the world of tomorrow, can be understood in another way. It can be understood, not from the standpoint of the historian who goes out of bounds and plays the part of a prophet, but from the standpoint of what Christianity is in its inner essence, as *a message on the part of God.* The meaning of the question is then as follows: Does the Christian message still have to fulfill a role in the world, does it still have something to say that is of actual interest for the world? And, on the other hand, does it have a chance of finding in the world of tomorrow the openness and room it needs to fulfill its task fruitfully and not be lost like a voice in the wilderness?

Taking the second part of that question first, let us for the last time stress the idea which is perhaps the *leitmotiv* of this whole book: Christianity is no mechanical or magical reality, but a *message*, that is, a living witnessing in the service of the supreme liberating realities. In short, it belongs to the order of the *logos*, the word. Now it belongs to the very nature of every authentic word that it, as it were, *creates its own room or space*, that it *opens* the hearts for the message which it brings, and *paves* itself *the way* that gives entrance to the reality of which it speaks.

The immediate and easy success of the work of a poet, artist or philosopher is not yet a sign of authenticity, but rather the fact that their work stands the test of time and slowly but surely awakens in mankind a *new "space" and openness,* namely to those mysterious worlds of truth and value in which the poet, the artist, the philosopher live, and into which they endeavor to introduce their fellow-men by means of the revealing power of their word.

All this is true *a fortiori* of Christianity, which is the message that reveals God. Where Christianity is truly and faithfully proclaimed and made present, there God's Word appeals to and touches men, there is growth and openness for the mystery of God and His liberating love, there room is made in the human heart, thus liberating the soul for God and his work of salvation. When Christianity first appeared on earth, there was little or no room for it, and the Christian message faced a closed, distrustful and hostile world. But the living witnessing of the first Christians, their fidelity to the movement of God's Word and God's Spirit unto martyrdom, awakened the dormant sense of God in a great part of the world and *created room* for God's work of salvation.

Will there still be room for Christianity in the world of tomorrow? Surely, not in the sense that such "room" is given once and for all and is guaranteed for ever, for, both in the individual and in mankind as a whole, this "room" must constantly be remade, just as light must constantly be reconquered from darkness. But the possibility of *creating room* will continue to exist in the world of tomorrow, at least as long as Christians will remain true to their Christianity and as long as man will remain man. That is, as long as man remains a being who in his hunger for truth and justice, openness, love and freedom, finds no rest and peace on earth. In short, as long as man continues to ask the question about his salvation.

This reply gives at the same time an answer to the first part of our question: Is there still a task for Christianity in the present world? Has the Christian message still something to say that has timely value for contemporary man?

When we look at it from the standpoint of faith, the Christian message preserves its permanent timeliness in virtue of its divine and supratemporal character. As long as God continues His work of salvation in the world through His Word and His Spirit, Christianity will remain timely. This is as true of the world of tomorrow as it was of the world of yesterday. The words of the Lord, "Go and teach all nations" cannot be changed by man's history of civilization nor can they be undone.

But the problem of Christianity's timeliness can also be shown to be meaningful from the standpoint of the history of civilization, a standpoint that can be taken by both believer and unbeliever. For, once again, Christianity is not a "mysticism" that is hostile to the world, but a message of truth and justice, of respect and concern for man, without distinction of persons. Now in view of all that we have discussed above, we come to realize that, when things are also considered from that standpoint, Christianity appears to preserve its timeliness, and that it is even more *timely than ever,* in view of the geographic, social, and international unification of our world.

We have constantly pointed to the extraordinary significance of the Christian message for our time. We were able to conclude from every analysis, that the solidarity of the Christian believer with the world of today is not only an absolute necessity for the proclamation of the message, but that it is an important guarantee for the great process of renewal at present going on in the world. For this reason we were able to confront the words of Cardinal Suhard: "The greatest fault of the Christians of the twentieth century would be to let the world make and unify itself without them," with the famous passage from the last chapter of Bergson's *The Two Sources of Religion and Morality,* in which the great French philosopher indicates that the mankind of tomorrow will be in need of a "supplement of soul," if it does not want to be crushed under the weight of technology and anonymous bureaucracy. It is perfectly evident that Christianity in no small measure can and ought to contribute toward this "supplement of soul."

There is perhaps no better way of feeling and realizing the exceptional value of Christianity as a "supplement of soul," for our world-in-the-making, than to meditate, and let us say, pray, the exquisite medieval prayer attributed to St. Francis of Assisi, the *Poverello.* With this prayer we want to end our long conversation with the world of today:

> Lord, make me an instrument for your peace!
> Where hate is at work, I want to bring love.
> Where there has been insult, I want to bring forgiveness.
> Where disunity reigns, I want to bring unity.
> Where there is gnawing doubt, I want to bring faith.
> Where error spreads, I want to bring truth.
> Where there is despair, I want to bring hope.
> Where sadness oppresses, I want to bring joy.
> Where darkness reigns, I want to bring light.
> O Lord, make me seek not so much:
> to be consoled as to console,
> to be understood as to understand,
> to be loved as to love.

In our century of technological and economic progress, of social and political emancipation, that Franciscan prayer, which contains the whole of Christianity in a capsule, preserves all its timeliness and perhaps it is more timely than ever. No social legislation, even one that is most progressive, will ever be able to prevent man from being a danger to his fellow-man in some particular circumstances, it will not prevent envy and hatred, doubt and despair, the suffering and the sorrow on account of the death of a beloved and the ensuing loneliness. Man is undoubtedly a "world builder," a being whose task it is to fashion the world of matter into a worthy dwelling for man, where there will be room for everybody. But even the most beautiful and comfortable dwelling is only a *condition* of life. Man can indeed create better conditions of life for mankind by means of objective civilization and culture, especially by the progress of technology, of the economy, social legislation, instruction and education, but all this can be done only within definite limits which he is unable to transcend and which modern philosophy calls "limit situations." Medicine can reduce suffering and lengthen man's span of life, but the power of death remains undefeated. Death is a "limit situation" for man, and the same can be said about suffering, sorrow, doubt and loneliness and even about the experience of the "otherness" of other men.

That is why, after the work of objective civilization and creation of culture, there will always be room in the world for ethical attitudes and especially for Christianity's ethics of love, for an ethics which, while caring for law and justice, pays close attention to the mystery of the individual man in his uniqueness and solitariness, which raises respect for all mankind to the sublime heights of evangelical charity and "seeks more to console than to be consoled, to understand than to be understood, to love than to be loved."

INDEX OF NAMES

INDEX OF SUBJECT MATTER